Dictionary of JEWISH WORDS

Dedicated by the R.A.B. Food Group, LLC
(formerly the B. Manischewitz Company)

In honor of
our many dedicated employees

past and present

who helped create the definition of
quality kosher products in America
since 1888

Dictionary of JEWISH WORDS

Joyce Eisenberg | Ellen Scolnic

Updated and Expanded

2006 • 5766
The Jewish Publication Society
Philadelphia

The Jewish Publication Society
2100 Arch Street, 2nd Floor
Philadelphia, PA 19103
www.jewishpub.org

Design and composition by Sandy Freeman
Manufactured in the United States of America

06 07 08 09 10 11 12   10 9 8 7 6 5 4 3 2 1

Library of Congress Cataloging-in-Publication Data

Eisenberg, Joyce.
    [Dictionary of Jewish words]
    JPS dictionary of Jewish words / by Joyce Eisenberg and Ellen Scolnic.
        p.   c.m.
    Over 1000 entries for Jewish holidays and life-cycle events, culture,
history, the Bible and other sacred texts, and worship. Each entry has a
pronunciation guide and is cross-referenced to related terms.
    Includes bibliographical references and index.
    ISBN 0-8276-0832-2
    1. Judaism—Terminology.   2. Hebrew language—Terms and phrases.
I. J.P.S. dictionary of Jewish words.   II. Title: Jewish Publication Society
dictionary of Jewish words.   III. Title: Dictionary of Jewish words.
IV. Scolnic, Ellen.   V. Jewish Publication Society.   VI. Title.

BM50 .E47 2001
296'.03—dc21

2001029218

To my parents, Jean and Stanley Spitzer, who unfailingly support and encourage all my projects; to our own Jewish children, Michael, Jessica, and Andrew, from whom we "*shep nachas*" every day; and most of all for David, my first—and best—editor of everything I do.

—E. S.

To my "support staff": my son, Ben, whose keen interest in the world stimulates my mind; my daughter, Samantha, whose wisdom soothes my soul; and my husband, Ted, for 30 years of humor, *menschlikhkeit,* and unconditional love.

— J. E.

Contents

Acknowledgments

When we set out to write a dictionary of Jewish words, we focused on those words with which we were most familiar—particularly those related to Jewish holiday foods, Hebrew school homework, and Bar and Bat Mitzvah planning. But as we compiled our lists, we realized we had to define everything from *agunah* to *zemirot,* and when it came to distinguishing a *piyyut* from a *pupik,* we needed some help.

Several people took considerable time reading our rough draft, contributing words to our list, and offering valuable criticism and encouragement. We wish to thank:

David Scolnic, smartest all-around guy and most supportive Hebrew- and Torah-literate spouse, who could answer any question about Torah and prayer and retained all the knowledge he learned as a child, when he won a Bible contest.

Pearl Kouzi, who put her years of Hebrew day school teaching experience and her fluency with Hebrew to work on our text.

Mitzi Eisenberg, a loving *bubbe,* who can define any Yiddish word with all the color it deserves.

Ben Eisenberg, who contributed many words to this book and brought home resources each week from Hebrew school.

Jean E. Spitzer, English teacher, grammarian, and grandmom extraordinaire.

Mitchell Schwartzman, for his love of the Yiddish language and his calendar.

Rabbi Samuel and Judy Scolnic, wonderful and knowledgeable *machetunim.*

Rabbi Max Hausen, religious leader emeritus of Main Line Reform Temple in Wynnewood, Pennsylvania.

The members of the Playpen Writers Group, for their encouragement and support.

Carol Hupping, COO and publishing director of The Jewish Publication Society, for her steadfast support and calm guidance through the editorial process.

Bryna Fischer, Helaine Denenberg, and Rabbi Jill Hammer, who expertly assisted in the preparation of our manuscript.

Janet Liss, managing editor of The Jewish Publication Society, Janet Greenstein Potter, and Rabbi Yitzchok Gurevitz, who contributed their considerable knowledge to our second edition.

Ellen Frankel, CEO and editor-in-chief of The Jewish Publication Society, who gave us her vote of confidence to create this dictionary and was in favor of the project from the start.

The authors of all the books in our bibliography, for their insight and scholarship, from which we benefited as we prepared this book.

Introduction

Back in high school, a gentile friend of the family was invited for Sunday brunch. The table was set, as any good Jewish Sunday breakfast table would be, with bagels, cream cheese, and—a treat for us—a fish platter from the deli. "Help yourself to some bagels and lox," the guest was instructed, to which she replied, "I've never had it before. Can I try just one lock?"

That's a true story. And it's stories like this one that made us realize how many familiar Jewish words are not as well-known to mainstream America.

Likewise, even though we consider ourselves practicing Jews—Jewish mothers who put a chicken in the oven for every holiday—we encountered Hebrew and Yiddish words that left us puzzled. We didn't want to drag out the *Encyclopaedia Judaica* every time Hebrew school homework was due. There had to be an easier way.

We set out to draft a practical, easy-to-understand reference—a dictionary of Jewish words—not just for practicing Jews and intermarried families, but also for non-Jewish writers, businesspeople, and others who encounter a Jewish word and don't know where to look up its meaning.

We hope that our dictionary will be a user-friendly reference for everyday life—one where a Jew can find out the meaning of *hakhnasat orchim* when he comes across the phrase in his synagogue bulletin; where an intermarried couple planning their child's Bar Mitzvah can find out what to do when they're asked to "make a list of everyone who gets *aliyot*"; and where a gentile friend can read about what to expect when making a shivah call.

Our A-to-Z guide is not a book of Jewish law. It's not even a definitive dictionary. But it does include the definitions and pronunciations of many common Hebrew and Yiddish words; cite the "whys" behind some Jewish customs, practices, and rituals; and offer further resources for the reader who is interested in a more comprehensive explanation.

What We Included

We set out to identify all of the words—Yiddish, Hebrew, Aramaic, and English—that you might come across in daily life in the United States. This includes, for example, categories like Jewish foods, holidays, and life-cycle events, as well as words pertaining to historical events, sacred texts, and the various movements within Judaism.

To compose our list, we began by scrutinizing the indexes of dozens of books—from scholarly tomes on Jewish law to etiquette guides on how to plan a Jewish wedding, from books extolling the joys of Yiddish to those disclosing the secrets of Kabbalah. Then we listened in to the sounds of our Jewish lives. Our children brought home words from weekly Hebrew school classes. We heard unfamiliar phrases in the rabbi's announcements at the end of services. We carefully reviewed the menu at the deli. Jewish magazines, newspapers, and catalogs gave us more possibilities.

Our parents, grandparents, and in-laws reminded us of the favorite Yiddish phrases we grew up with. Some of those Yiddish phrases are well-known; others more mysterious, such as "*Rednik* for the *kinder*" (not in front of the children).

Some words we rejected at first as being too obscure or too old-fashioned, but as our research progressed, we decided they needed to be included on our list. We also added English words that have special meaning in Jewish life, such as "candlelighting," "naming," and "bitter herbs."

We limited the dictionary's "people" entries because we could have created a whole dictionary of Jewish personalities alone. We included those who are directly related to a Jewish holiday, such as Haman of Purim infamy and Judah Maccabee of Hanukkah glory. The patriarchs, matriarchs, and various tribes of Israel are included because they are mentioned in many of the prayers that are recited on Shabbat and holidays. In addition, we included several great Jewish scholars—among them Akiva, Hillel, Rashi, and Maimonides—because any understanding of Jewish texts and laws would be incomplete without them.

But Hillel and the other early Jewish scholars didn't write in "Jewish." Indeed, there is no language called Jewish. Jews speak the language of the country in which they live. Parisian Jews speak French, while Jews in Florence speak Italian and American Jews speak English. However, since ancient times, Jews around the world have been connected by the Hebrew language because Judaism's sacred texts and prayers are largely written, read, and sung in Hebrew.

Until the 2nd century B.C.E., Hebrew was the everyday language of the Jewish people. Then Aramaic, another ancient Semitic language, also written with Hebrew characters, took its place. With the birth of the State of Israel, Hebrew was reborn as the daily, spoken tongue of a new nation. Modern Israeli Hebrew is a growing, changing language, with many words appropriated from English (like *telefone* for telephone and *compootair* for computer), and other words invented for modern life, such as *seret* (movie) and *ofnayim* (bicycle).

Yiddish is the language many people think of when they say that a word or expression "sounds Jewish." In fact, the word Yiddish actually means "Jewish." Yiddish was first spoken about 1,000 years ago by French Jews who emigrated to towns along the Rhine. To their vernacular, which was a combination of Hebrew and Old French, they added German dialects. In fact, nearly one-fourth of Yiddish words come almost unchanged from Hebrew.

This new language allowed the Jews to converse freely among themselves without fear of reprisals from non-Jewish neighbors. As Jews were expelled from Western Europe, they moved to Eastern Europe, carrying Yiddish with them and picking up new words from the local languages, including Russian, Polish, and Ukrainian. Throughout the years, Yiddish transformed from old to medieval to modern versions.

But unlike many languages, Yiddish never had a country of its own. Yiddish lived where the Jews of the 18th and 19th centuries lived. For the Jews of the shtetl, Yiddish was the language of daily life. It is sprinkled with colorful expressions, idioms, and curses—we found more than two dozen words to describe a "no goodnik." It is lovingly nicknamed the *mama loshen,* the mother tongue. In the years after World War I, more than 11 million people in Eastern Europe, Russia, and elsewhere spoke Yiddish. After the Nazis destroyed those Jewish communities, Yiddish in Eastern Europe died, too.

In the late 1800s, when Jewish immigrants shlepped across the Atlantic Ocean, Yiddish came with them. This was the height of Yiddish culture in America: *The Forward* was launched as a daily Yiddish language newspaper, Isaac Bashevis Singer wrote short stories in Yiddish, and the comedic opera *Kuni Lemel* played in the Yiddish theater. But as the years passed, the children of these new immigrants were eager to learn English and become Americans. They no longer wanted their language to keep them apart from mainstream America.

Today, although Yiddish is enjoying a quiet revival on college campuses and in communal conversational groups, fluent Yiddish speakers are rare. Yiddish is no longer the shared daily language of the Jewish people. Jews speak the language of the country where they live. An exception are some Hasidic Jews in Brooklyn, who continue to speak Yiddish as their daily language to set themselves apart from their secular neighbors.

Another "Jewish" language, Judeo-Spanish, or Judezmo, (often referred to as Ladino), was born in the Middle Ages when the Sephardic Jews of Spain and Portugal melded their Old Spanish tongue with Hebrew. Today, Judeo-Spanish is lesser known than Yiddish, but it survives in Mediterranean Jewish poetry, songs, and other expressions of Sephardic cultural and ethnic heritage.

How to Use This Book

Many reference books choose to organize material by subject, in chronological order, or by topic or source. We chose an A-to-Z dictionary format so that you can look up a word alphabetically without knowing anything of its meaning. Consider the word *"bimah,"* for example. You'd begin by looking it up under "b" and finding out that it is "a raised platform or stage in a synagogue from which the Torah is read and services are led." If you want more information about a *bimah,* you could:

1. look up all the words within the definition that are in boldface **(synagogue, Torah, Sephardic, Askenazic ark,** *ner tamid,* and **menorah).**

2. look for the word *"bimah"* in the category lists in the back of the book and find it in the "objects in the synagogue" category, along with words like *Aron Kodesh, mappah,* and *parochet.* Looking up these related words would provide you with additional information and background material.

SPELLING

Before you look up a word, you have to know how to spell it. That's no easy feat, especially when you're trying to spell the words in this dictionary. Indeed, choosing a spelling for our "Jewish" words was one of our most challenging tasks. Hebrew, Yiddish, Aramaic, and Judeo-Spanish are all written with Hebrew characters; we had to select English letters to represent those characters—a process called transliteration. Since transliteration is based on how a word sounds, there is no "correct" spelling, and variations in transliteration can be found in every prayer book.

We aimed to be consistent within the arbitrary set of rules that we adopted:

1. If the word can be found in *Merriam-Webster's Collegiate Dictionary,* 11th edition, the preferred style of The Jewish Publication Society is to follow the dictionary's lead and stick with that choice of spelling. We tried to follow this rule. For example, this means that the Festival of Lights is listed under Hanukkah rather than Hannukkah, Chanukah, or Hanukah. Of course, there are exceptions. For example, for the flat cracker we spell matzah, *Merriam-Webster's* provides three alternative spellings, with "matzo" listed first. Because the English pronunciation is closer to "ah" and there is no Hebrew character similar to "o" in the word, we prefer to eat matzah.

2. If a word appears in that dictionary, it is treated like any other "English" word and set in roman type; words that are not in *Merriam-Webster's* are treated as "foreign" words and set in italic type in the entry.

3. If the Hebrew word begins with the letter *hay,* we spell the English transliteration with an "h," as in the word "haggadah," for example. This is similar to the clear "h" sound of the English word "home."

4. In many cases, if the Hebrew word begins with the letter *het,* we also spell the English transliteration with a "h," as in the word "*haver.*" Technically, this is a gutteral "kh" sound, but since most people pronounce it with the clear "h" sound of the English word "home," we've indicated it as such in the pronunciation guide.

There are a few times when we picked the more common spelling instead of following this rule, most notably for the words *"chai"* and "challah."

5. When there is a *het* or *haf* in the middle of a word, it is sometimes spelled with a "ch," as in Simchat Torah. In the pronunciation guide, we've indicated that as "sim-KHAT toe-RAH" to give you a clue that it's a gutteral "kh," not "ch" as in "cheese."

Because there are so many spelling variations—and because some spellings are more familiar (and seem more correct) than others to some people—we've cross-referenced many of these words. So if you want to spell *huppah* as *chupah,* you will find your favorite spelling under "ch," where we'll invite you to come with us under the *huppah.*

The spelling of Yiddish words was equally complicated. You'll often see Yiddish words spelled with "sch"—indeed, *schlump* seems to have more oomph than *shlump.* But we took a cue from Gene Bluestein's book *Anglish/Yinglish: Yiddish in American Life and Literature,* in which he points out that the "sch" sound (like in "schmo" or "schtik") is a basically German approach. In Yiddish, the "sch" sound is made by the letter *shin,* which means that the "sh" spelling is technically more correct than is the "sch" version. Since we admit that words like shnook look a little funny without the "c," we've listed them both ways so you can be sure to find your *schmo* or *schmendrick.*

Just as there are multiple spellings for a single word, so too are there multiple words for a single item. Many texts, rituals, and objects in Jewish life have both Hebrew and English names—and both of these names are often used. We've listed everything with a multiple name in two places and put the full definition under the more commonly used term. So, for example, if you look up Shemot, the Hebrew name for the second book of the Torah, you are redirected to the entry for Exodus, where you will find the definition. Likewise, Shavuot can be called the Feast of Weeks. But because virtually no one refers to this holiday as the Feast of Weeks, the definition is entered under Shavuot. The Feast of Weeks entry will direct you there. The definitions for all Jewish holidays can be found under the Hebrew word; for example, the Passover story is told under Pesach.

It's also common for a "Jewish" word to have both a Hebrew and Yiddish spelling and pronunciation. Because so many American Jews come from Central and Eastern European Ashkenazic backgrounds, the Yiddish versions are very familiar to us. In fact, it's what many of us over the age of 35 grew up hearing and speaking. We'd wear a tallis to shul on *Shabbos;* we'd clean out the *chumetz* for Passover. Today, we've been retrained to wear our tallit on Shabbat and clean out the *hametz* for Pesach. That's because the Sephardic spellings and pronunciations, which replace many of the "s" endings with a "t," are standard in modern Israel and have been adopted as such in the United States.

In this book, we've given the Sephardic version priority, but if a word is commonly pronounced in the Yiddish or Ashkenazic system, we've listed it both ways. So, for example, the word for blessing can be found as *bracha* (the Hebrew) and *brucha* (the Yiddish). The *brucha* entry refers you to *bracha* for the definition.

READING AN ENTRY

> **aggadah** n. Hebrew (ah-gah-DAH); pl. **aggadot** (ah-gah-DOTE) Literally, "narrative." *Aggadot* are Jewish stories that are presented in the **Talmud,** along with *halakhah,* the body of Jewish law. Unlike *halakhah,* these legends, historical stories, jokes, ethical tales, and sermons are not legally binding; their purpose is to explain and elaborate on Jewish laws and customs.

Parts of Speech

After the entry in boldface each word is assigned a part of speech. The abbreviations for the traditional parts of speech we've included are n. for noun, pl. n. for plural noun, v. for verb, adj. for adjective, and int. for interjection. If a word has more than one definition, the appropriate label precedes each definition. Different and distinct meanings are numbered as such.

Masculine and Feminine

For words that can be used to describe either a man or a woman, we've included both the masculine (masc.) and feminine (fem.) forms. An example is *baal teshuvah*, a term for a man who returns to more stringent religious practices, and *baalat teshuvah,* his female counterpart. As is the case with English, people often simply use the masculine word, no matter what the gender, even though it may be technically incorrect.

Language of Origin

For each entry, we've noted a language of origin. For some words, it is hard to distinguish if the word is Hebrew or Yiddish, because many Yiddish words have their roots in Hebrew. Often, pronunciation is the only difference. Consider "meshugge," for example. It's a Hebrew word meaning "nuts." In Hebrew, it's pronounced "meh-shoo-GAH." But the word is firmly a part of the Yiddish language, where it is pronounced "meh-SHOO-gah." There are also variations of the same root word that change the gender—meaning a "crazy woman" or "crazy man."

Pronunciation

Word pronunciation appears in parentheses. In order to make our pronunciation guide user-friendly, we spelled out words phonetically. Thus, the pronuciation of the word "milchig" (which refers to dairy foods) is presented as "MILL-khick"; the stressed syllable appears in capital letters. To indicate syllables that have the distinctive, guttural "ch" sound of both Yiddish and Hebrew, we've generally used a "kh" in the pronunciation guide. This is a clue that the word should be pronounced with a guttural "kh" sound, which has no equivalent in English. Using "kh" also differentiates it from the hard "ch" sound, as in the English word "cheese."

We've included a pronunciation guide for every word, except in the case of familiar English words whose pronunciations should already be familiar to you or which can be looked up in any English dictionary.

Plurals

We've included plurals for many of the objects that you might encounter more than one of, such as matzah. We've listed the correct Hebrew plural, which is the form often seen in print. In daily speech, it's not unusual for English speakers to simply add an "s" to the Hebrew singular form, even though this is technically incorrect. Consider, for example, the singular word "mezuzah": You are much more likely to hear someone ask "Did they get any mezuzahs for their new house?" rather than the technically correct "Did they get any mezuzot?"

Definitions

Almost every aspect of Judaism is open to interpretation and explanation—from how much, how often, and even how certain holidays are celebrated to who is considered a Jew and by whose standards. A definition can vary greatly, depending on how you were raised—what you learned as a child; what your family believed, worshiped, and celebrated—and with which movement of Judaism you most identify. For example, an American Jew whose parents emigrated from Israel might consider *sufganiyot* an integral part of his family's Hanukkah celebration, while most American Jews whose grandparents came from Eastern Europe have never heard of these Israeli jelly donuts. Their Hanukkah delicacy is the potato latke.

We define many words from our own particular perspectives—that is, modern, American, liberal, matriarchal, and from Conservative and Reform backgrounds. We assume, therefore, that women are participating equally in many of the rituals and customs we discuss. We made a careful, conscious decision to give this dictionary that slant. For example, we chose to define the word "minyan" as "a gathering of 10 people, the minimum necessary for a communal religious service according to Jewish law." Further on, the entry adds, "for traditional Jews, a minyan is composed only of men."

When referring to the most strict and stringent interpretation of Jewish law, often related to Orthodox practice, we use the adjective "traditional." When referring to more modern interpretations of Jewish law, we use the words "liberal," "modern," and "progressive." We choose not to use the words "religious" or "observant" to describe the practices of particular Jewish movements because we don't believe that any one movement should lay claim to being the "observant" or "religious" one.

Old-fashioned Usage

Some entries, particularly Yiddish ones, conclude with the notation "old-fashioned usage." This tells the reader that the word is seldom heard and rarely used anymore. As the generation of Jewish immigrants who spoke Yiddish as their daily language dies out, some of these Yiddish expressions are vanishing, too. Yiddish is no longer the common tongue of Jews in the Diaspora. Happily for those of us with Yiddish-speaking grandparents, these words may be familiar.

Other Yiddish words live on, having made their way into mainstream English slang. Words like "shlep" and "maven" can be found in English dictionaries, with just a note of their Yiddish pedigree.

CATEGORY LISTS

The category lists are organized alphabetically into major subjects, grouping words that are related to each other, including for example, Jewish foods, holidays, and ritual objects. Thus, the word "matzah" can be found in the categories "food" and "Pesach."

BIBLIOGRAPHY

Our bibliography includes all of our reference material, from the books whose indexes we consulted to collect our words to those we read thoroughly to gain an understanding of each word. Out of all the resources we used, we found the following four books to be the most well written and easily understood; they are well worth a careful look.

Jewish Literacy by Rabbi Joseph Telushkin is a thorough, comprehensive volume that covers the Jewish religion, ethics, holidays, life-cycle events, Jewish history, and more. The book starts off by summarizing the highlights of the sacred Jewish texts—from reviewing the "most important" moments in the Torah to pointing out the "best sections" of the Talmud—and ends by defining the practices and histories of many common Jewish rituals and life-cycle customs. Although he writes from a semi-scholarly perspective, Rabbi Telushkin uses humor, anecdotes, and plain language to make the most difficult concepts, laws, and histories accessible to everyone.

Anita Diamant and Howard Cooper's *Living a Jewish Life* truly celebrates what being Jewish today is all about. It is a wonderful and easy read for those looking to learn more about Jewish customs, enlarge their own repertoire of holiday traditions, or even create some new family rituals. With explanations of common customs and traditions, as well as points of departure for further discussion, this book is useful for anyone interested in living a Jewish life in the 21st century.

Leo Rosten's classic, *The Joys of Yiddish,* has been in print and in demand since 1968. Each alphabetical listing includes a pronunciation guide, definition, background information, and anecdotes and jokes. His appendixes elucidate topics ranging from how to name a Jewish child to the names for God, from the history of India's Jews to an account of the first cantors. But what distinguishes this book most of all is Rosten's tangible love for the *mama loshen.* His enthusiasm alone might be enough to keep the Yiddish language alive.

Every Person's Guide to Judaism by Stephen J. Einstein and Lydia Kukoff is a straightforward introduction to Judaism. Using Jewish holidays and life-cycle events as their template, the authors discuss the rituals and explore their underlying Jewish philosophies. In the chapter on Simchat Torah, for example, they write about the customs of the holiday as well as the meaning of the Torah itself. In the chapter on marriage, they discuss sex in the Jewish tradition.

For the complete bibliography, turn to the back of the book.

We hope, dear reader, that when your mother-in-law asks if she can start planning a *simchat bat,* or the rabbi talks about *ushpizin* in the sukkah, or you want to know who Moses Maimonides was, you'll turn to this book as a helpful resource.

What We've Learned

In the years since our dictionary was first published, we've traveled around the country talking about "Jewish" words with members of sisterhoods and men's clubs, seniors and communal groups. We've shared what we've learned about Jewish traditions, celebrations, religious life, and foods—and the words that describe them.

Our audiences have shared with us their family memories, their favorite recipes, the rituals that connect them to Judaism, and, most of all, their love of Yiddish. Without a doubt, Yiddish words are the source of the craziest stories, funniest reminiscences, and unintended insults our audiences have shared with us. Today, reporters, sportscasters, and regular folks are peppering their conversations with spicy Yiddishisms—used correctly and incorrectly. There's the movie about the friendly green ogre (*Shrek,* literally "terrible" in Yiddish), a newspaper article about a restaurateur who went to Thailand to buy *tchotchkes,* and a decision handed down by Italian-American Supreme Court Justice Antonin Scalia, who said that the National Endowment for the Arts had a lot of *chutzpah.*

We were told a true story about a salesgirl in a ritzy women's boutique who was standing on a chair, trying to reach an item.

"*Oy,*" she said. "*Oy, gevult.* I can't reach it."

"What is that word you're saying?" the customer asked.

"I don't know. I've heard people say it. I think it's French," the salesgirl replied.

Many Yiddish words have a flavor (to use a Yiddishism, a *"ta'am"*) that goes beyond a stodgy dictionary definition. When a friend warns you, "Don't be a *shmeggegge* and get stuck on that committee," you know what he means. All of his unspoken advice for you and his pity for those who didn't heed his warning are conveyed in that one single word.

While many seniors in our audiences can still speak Yiddish, the baby boomers generally know only a few words, because their parents and grandparents spoke Yiddish when they didn't want the *kinder* to understand what they were saying. They enjoy our stories, which remind them of time spent with their *bubbes* and *zaydes.*

Although bagels are sold in almost every supermarket, it doesn't mean that matzah, Shabbat candles, and Pesach are familiar to everyone. In fact, Judaism—and the words that define it—remains unfamiliar to many people in mainstream America. We have heard from audience members in Houston who wanted a Shabbat brisket, only to be handed a Texas beef barbecue sandwich. A woman from Tennessee who still remembers the day in kindergarten when her teacher scolded her for making up a "fake word" that started with the letter "K." Her word was knish. A man in suburban Philadelphia who asked a supermarket clerk for matzah. The clerk was puzzled, so the man described it as a square box of flat crackers, to which the clerk replied, "Oh, yeah. Jewish wafers. Aisle 8."

We've discovered that the ways in which people celebrate being Jewish, the customs and traditions they identify with, the beloved foods they cook, and even the rituals they practice have a great deal to do with how their families did it, how their parents taught it to them, and where they grew up.

Haroset, the mixture that plays a supporting role on the seder table, is a striking example of this. Haroset is a ritual food—you could even call it a sacred food. But what exactly goes into the recipe varies from person to person, place to place, and even within families. While there are many instructions and stories in the haggadah, there is no recipe for haroset. Because Jews were a wandering people, they adapted their diets to the local fare. So Sephardic Jews include the fruits and spices of the Mediterranean region—like dates, figs, or cardamom—in their haroset. We've heard that Jews in the exotic land of Georgia use pecans.

At a sukkah-building workshop in suburban Philadelphia, we met a California woman who had recently moved to the East Coast. "What do you use for the *skakh,* the branches on the roof, if you don't have a palm tree growing in your yard?" she asked. We told her that on the East Coast, evergreen branches usually provide the most colorful coverage. Yes, there are certain *halakhic* requirements for building a sukkah, such as it should have three temporary walls and you should be able to see the stars through the *skakh*. But should you use palm or evergreen branches? Should the decorations be from a florist or crayoned posters made by your children?

That's part of what makes being a modern Jew so interesting. Judaism is a continually evolving religion; there are various ways to celebrate and new traditions to consider, such as placing a Miriam's Cup on the seder table, using a hand-sewn *atarah* for a Bat Mitzvah tallit, or lighting a preschooler's mosaic *hannukiah* along with the others.

We look forward to sharing our love of "Jewish words" with many more *haimish* audiences. We will continue to collect stories of yangled Yiddish malapropisms, Hebrew heroics, and zany *zaydes*. We welcome yours.

Aaron   Older brother of **Moses.** Aaron was a leading figure in the **Passover** story and the **Exodus** from Egypt. He is generally thought to be the first high priest of the ancient **Hebrews.**

abba   n. Hebrew (AH-bah)   Literally, "father." Some Jewish children are taught to use the word Abba instead of "Daddy" when referring to their father. "I'm done with my homework, Abba. Can we go to the playground now?"

Abraham   One of the three **patriarchs** of the Jewish people, Abraham is known for his belief in one God. In **Genesis,** God commands Abraham to "go forth from his native land, to a new land that I will show you and I will make you the father of a great nation." Abraham and his wife, **Sarah,** had a son, **Isaac.** Later, God tested Abraham's loyalty by telling him to sacrifice his beloved son. (See *Akedah.*) Abraham proved his obedience to God by preparing for the sacrifice, but God sent an angel to stop him and Isaac was saved. The 12 **tribes of Israel** are descended from Isaac's son **Jacob.** Abraham and his wife's servant, **Hagar,** had a son, **Ishmael,** who is considered by Muslims to be the patriarch of the Arab people.

acharonim   pl. n. Hebrew (ack-row-NEEM)   **acharon** sing. n. (ack-hah-RON)   From the Hebrew word for "later." A term for rabbis and scholars from the 16th century (after the *rishonim*) to the present. **Isaac Luria** is one of the well-known *acharonim.*

Adam   The first man. In Genesis God creates Adam "from the dust of earth. He blew into his nostrils the breath of life" on the sixth day of Creation. Adam and the first woman, **Eve,** lived in paradise, the Garden of Eden, and God provided for all their needs until they ate the forbidden fruit of the Tree of Knowledge of Good and Evil. God punished them and banished them from Eden. God told Adam that he must make his way in the world by the sweat of his brow. Adam was the father of Cain and Abel. See *Gan Eden.*

Adar   n. Hebrew (ah-DAR)   The twelfth month in the **Jewish calendar,** it falls around February or March. In leap years, when a second Adar is added, the first is called Adar I.

Adar II n. Hebrew (ah-DAR TWO) Seven times in every 19 years, an extra month is inserted in the **Jewish calendar,** creating a leap year. Adar II comes after the month of **Adar,** in March or April.

Adonai n. Hebrew (ah-doe-NYE) Literally, "my Lord." Another name for God, and the one used most often in prayers. Because God's name is so sacred, it is not spoken as it is written. The Hebrew letters *(yud, hay, vav,* and *hay)* that spell the name are read only as *Adonai.* See also *Adoshem, ha-Shem,* and **Tetragrammaton.**

Adon Olam n. Hebrew (ah-DOAN oh-LAM) Literally, "Lord of the world" or "eternal Lord." One of the songs traditionally sung to end **Shabbat** and holiday morning services. Sung by the entire congregation together in Hebrew, the words to "Adon Olam" date from the Middle Ages. The hymn praises eternal God, "who rules everything and will exist long after the world." There are many different melodies for the song, some ancient, some modern.

Adoshem n. Hebrew (ah-doe-SHEM) A contraction of two of the Hebrew words for God: *Adonai* and *ha-Shem. Adonai* is the word most often used in prayers; traditional Jews use the term *ha-Shem* when referring to God.

afikoman n. Hebrew (ah-fee-KO-men) From a Greek word meaning "dessert," a piece of **matzah** that is hidden during the **Passover seder.** On the seder table are three symbolic *matzot* covered with a cloth. Following the text of the **haggadah,** the leader breaks the middle matzah in half and hides one half—the *afikoman*—somewhere in the house. Toward the end of the seder, it is traditional for the children to look for the *afikoman.* They are rewarded for its return with a small toy or money. In some families, the children hide the *afikoman* and then demand a prize for its safe return. Finally, the *afikoman* is divided and everyone gets a piece as "dessert"; this marks the end of the meal, although the seder itself continues.

aggadah n. Hebrew (ah-gah-DAH); pl. **aggadot** (ah-gah-DOTE) Literally, "narrative." *Aggadot* are Jewish stories that are presented in the **Talmud** along with *halakhah,* the body of Jewish law. Unlike *halakhah,* these legends, historical stories, jokes, ethical tales, and sermons are not legally binding; their purpose is to explain and elaborate on Jewish laws and customs.

agunah n. Hebrew (ah-goo-NAH) Literally, "anchored." A woman whose husband has deserted her or simply disappeared. Without either a *get,* the Jewish divorce decree that a Jewish man must grant to his wife, or proof of his death, she cannot remarry, according to Jewish law. While **Orthodox** and **Conservative** rabbis generally require a *get,* **Reform** and **Reconstructionist** rabbis do not.

Ahasuerus, King (ah-HOSH-vair-oash) The ruler of ancient Persia (486–465 B.C.E.) during the time of the **Purim** story. According to the Purim **megillah,** Ahasuerus was a foolish king who allowed his adviser, **Haman,** to hatch a plot against the Jews. Ahasuerus was first married to Queen **Vashti.** He later took a Jewish girl, **Esther,** as his bride.

Ahavat Olam n. Hebrew (ah-hah-VAHT oh-LAHM) Literally, "Eternal Love." **1.** The initial words of the prayer that precedes the *Shema* in the evening service. It expresses God's eternal love for the people of Israel. **2. ahavat olam** Generally expressed as "love of the world." A term to describe the motivation behind giving *tzedakah* or doing a **mitzvah** "just for *ahavat olam.*"

ahavat Yisra'el n. Hebrew (ah-hah-VAHT yis-rah-ALE) Literally, "love of the Jewish people." The phrase is most often used to describe relationships between Jews. "That play had anti-Semitic overtones; the characters were such stereotypes. For a Jewish writer, he certainly has no *ahavat Yisra'el.*"

Aish HaTorah n. Hebrew (AYSH HAH-toe-RAH) Literally, "fire of the Torah." Jewish outreach organization founded in Jerusalem in 1974 by Rabbi Noah Weinberg to stem Jewish assimilation and help Jews rediscover the relevance of Judaism in contemporary life. The international network now has 25 Jewish educational centers and provides creative programming in over 80 cities. Programs might include Torah study, introduction to **Kabbalah,** a spiritual fitness class, and Hebrew 101.

Akdamut n. Hebrew (ahk-dah-MOOT) Literally, "introduction." A hymn in praise of God, written in **Aramaic,** that is sung responsively in **synagogue** on **Shavuot.**

Akedah n. Hebrew (ah-kay-DAH) Literally, "binding." Specifically, the incident in **Genesis** when God tells **Abraham** to bind (tie up) his son **Isaac** and prepare to sacrifice the boy. At the last moment, God stops Abraham from going through with the deed. Explanations of the *Akedah* include that God was testing Abraham's obedience; that it shows God never would allow human sacrifice; and that God is benevolent, understanding, and respectful of a parent's love for his or her child. The word is also symbolic, in a larger sense, of a Jew's willingness to "sacrifice" for his beliefs. Also called *Akedat Yitzchak* (the Binding of Isaac).

Akiva ben Joseph (50–135 C.E.) A **rabbi** and **talmudic** scholar who was considered one of the greatest teachers of Judaism. According to legend, he was a shepherd who began his Jewish education late, at the age of 40, but his determination and love of learning proved him a natural scholar. He collected and arranged the whole **Oral Law** according to subjects, which laid the foundation for the editing of the **Mishnah.** Many of his wise sayings and teachings about learning and Jewish law are contained in *Pirke Avot.* When Roman conquerors forbid the study of **Torah,** Akiva continued teaching. He then supported Shimon bar Kokhba in his messianic revolt against the Romans. This fatal mistake led to Rabbi Akiva's death. His martyrdom is legendary. As he was tortured to death, he continued to recite the words to the *Shema.* Akiva died for *kiddush ha-Shem,* the sanctification of God's name.

alav ha-shalom masc. int. (ah-LAHV hah-shah-LOME); **alehah ha-shalom** fem. int. Hebrew (ah-LEH-hah hah-shah-LOME) This expression is similar to "rest in peace." This phrase is customarily said immediately after mentioning the name of someone who has died.

Alef Bet n. Hebrew (AH-lef BET) A name for the **Hebrew** alphabet, formed from its first two letters: *alef* and *bet.* Using the term "Alef Bet" is comparable to calling the English alphabet the "ABCs." The alphabet consists of 22 consonants and five final letters. The 10 vowels in Hebrew, which are indicated by seven vowel signs, were added to the alphabet in the 7th century C.E. Because the **Torah** precedes this change, Torah scrolls are written without vowel signs. Each Hebrew letter has a numerical value, which plays a role in a mystical mathematical system called *gematria.* Besides Hebrew, the **Aramaic, Judeo-Spanish, Ladino,** and **Yiddish** languages also use Hebrew characters.

Aleichem, Sholom (SHOH-lum ah-LEH-khem) Pseudonym of Solomon Rabinowitz (1859–1916), perhaps the best-known **Yiddish** humorist, dramatist, and short-story author. His stories of Jewish **shtetl** life in Russia—complete with descriptions of eccentric characters, Jewish holiday celebrations, and religious persecution—became known worldwide. Stories featuring one of his most famous characters, Tevye the Dairyman, were the basis for the musical *Fiddler on the Roof.* Sholom Aleichem fled Russian persecution in 1905 and lived the rest of his life in New York City.

Aleinu n. Hebrew (ah-LAY-noo) Literally, "it is upon us." A prayer in praise of God, *Aleinu* acknowledges the unique relationship between God and the Jewish people. It is sung toward the end of **synagogue** services while the congregation stands. Originally from the **High Holy Day** liturgy, the *Aleinu* is now part of all services. It's customary for worshipers to bow slightly during the part of the prayer that reads, "We bend the knee and bow before the Holy One, blessed be He, who stretched out the heavens and established the earth."

alevai See *halevai.*

Al Het   n. Hebrew (ahl HATE)   A **Yom Kippur** prayer that asks forgiveness for a multitude of sins committed during the previous year. The congregation says the *Al Het* aloud as well as silently because Jews are responsible not only for themselves but also for their entire community. It is customary for a Jew to tap over the heart with the right hand while enumerating each sin.

aliyah   n. Hebrew (ah-LEE-yah); pl. **aliyot** (ah-lee-YOTE)   Literally, "to go up." **1.** The honor of being called up to the *bimah* to recite the blessings before and after the **Torah** reading. The term is often also used for any of the other rituals associated with reading the Torah, including *hagbah* and *gelilah*. During a synagogue service, those receiving an *aliyah* are called to the *bimah* by their Hebrew name. Traditionally the first *aliyah* is given to a **Kohen,** the second to a **Levite,** and the remaining ones to the **Israelites.** The number of *aliyot* at a religious service varies from three to seven, depending on the occasion. During a **Bar Mitzvah** or **Bat Mitzvah** service, *aliyot* are often given to family members and friends. **2.** (ah-lee-YAH)   The act of immigrating to Israel. Almost always used with the verb "make," as in "Did Lisa and her husband make *aliyah?* I heard they wanted to live in Tel Aviv."

alter-kacker   n. Yiddish (AHL-ter COCK-er)   A vulgar expression, literally meaning "old shitter"; equivalent to the English expression "old fart." Used to describe a fussy, crotchety old man, or sometimes a dirty old man. Sometimes abbreviated as "A.K." Old-fashioned usage.

amen   int. Hebrew (ah-MEN)   Literally, "so be it." The word said in unison by a congregation in response to a prayer to signify solemn agreement. According to the **Talmud,** "amen" is an acrostic of the three Hebrew words *El Melekh Ne'eman* (The Lord is a trustworthy King). It is sometimes pronounced awe-MAIN.

American Israel Public Affairs Committee (AIPAC)   n. English   A registered political action committee since the 1940s, AIPAC lobbies the United States government on behalf of the **State of Israel.** AIPAC's goal is to protect Israel's interests on issues such as foreign aid, sales of military items, treaties, and such.

American Jewish Committee (AJC)   n. English   Established in 1906 in response to hundreds of **pogroms** in Russia, the American Jewish Committee works to fight **anti-Semitism,** safeguard principles of democracy, and nurture pluralism and cooperative relationships among diverse ethnic and religious groups. The AJC also publishes *Commentary,* a journal of political thought.

American Jewish Congress (AJC)   n. English   A national volunteer organization, the American Jewish Congress protects fundamental constitutional freedoms by promoting legislation to preserve religious freedom and the separation of church and state. It also litigates cases with significant civil rights or First Amendment issues.

American Jewish Joint Distribution Committee (the Joint)   n. English   Created in 1914 by the merger of several war relief organizations, the Joint's original purpose was to raise funds for war victims and refugees. Today, the Joint sponsors programs of relief, rescue, and reconstruction in the **State of Israel** and around the world. Many of its efforts focus on restoring educational and cultural institutions and helping the remaining elderly Jews in the vanished communities of Eastern Europe.

am ha-eretz   n. Hebrew (am hah-ARE-etz)   Literally "people of the land." A derogatory term, which originated during the time of the **Second Temple,** for the common people who were neither learned in **Torah** nor religiously pious. The opposite of *haver.*

Amidah   n. Hebrew (ah-MEE-dah)   Literally, "standing." A silent or whispered prayer said while standing. The *Amidah,* considered the centerpiece of the **synagogue** service, is a plea to God to fulfill spiritual and physical needs, as well as those of the Land of Israel. It is said three times a day in synagogue, and in an abbreviated version during **Shabbat** and holiday services. The *Amidah* usually includes time for personal meditation. Also known as the *Tefilah* and *Shemoneh Esrei.*

amoraim   pl. n. Aramaic (ah-MOE-rah-eem)   Literally, "explainers." The ancient rabbis who are quoted in the **Gemara,** the legal and ethical commentaries on the **Mishnah.** *Amoraim* are contrasted with the *tannaim,* ancient rabbis who are quoted in the Mishnah. The Mishnah and Gemara compose the two sections of Jewish law known as the **Talmud.**

am Yisra'el   n. Hebrew (AHM yis-rah-ALE)   Literally, "people Israel." A general expression for the worldwide Jewish community. A popular Hebrew song, "Am Yisra'el Chai" (The People Israel Live) uses this phrase.

Ani Ma'amin   n. Hebrew (ah-NEE mah-ah-MEEN)   Literally, "I believe." These are the first words of **Maimonides'** *Thirteen Principles of Faith,* the 12th of which says, I believe with complete faith in the coming of the **Messiah.** Even though he may tarry I will wait for him on any day that he may come." These words have been set to music as a prayerful song of faith that is said to have been sung by victims of the **Holocaust** as they went to their deaths. Today, it is often sung at the **Pesach seder** and at **Yom ha-Shoah** services.

An'im Zemirot   n. Hebrew (ah-NEEM zeh-meer-OTE)   A hymn composed of an alphabetic acrostic of 31 lines, generally sung in front of the open ark at the conclusion of the **Musaf** service on **Shabbat** and festivals. A child often leads the congregation's singing of *An'im Zemirot*. It is also known as *Shir ha-Kavod*, "the Hymn of Glory."

aninut   n. Hebrew (ah-nee-NOOT)   The period of time from the moment of death until burial. Since it is traditional for Jews to be buried within a few days of death, this period lasts for only a few days at most. Because the family's focus is on caring for the deceased and preparing for the burial, condolence visits, or **shivah** calls, are generally not made during this time.

Anti-Defamation League of B'nai B'rith (ADL)   n. English Established in 1913, this division of **B'nai B'rith** works to combat hate, racism, and **anti-Semitism**. The ADL fights instances of discrimination against Jews and defends the civil, religious, and educational rights of all citizens. The ADL also works to expose hate groups and racist organizations, such as the Ku Klux Klan, white supremacists, and religious right extremists. The organization produces numerous resource materials for teaching understanding and tolerance.

Antiochus IV, King   (an-TIE-ah-cuss)   A Syrian king who ruled **Judea** and ancient Israel from 175 to 163 B.C.E. In his efforts to wipe out Judaism, Antiochus demanded intense Hellenization and forbade many Jewish practices, including **circumcision** and **Sabbath** observance. He desecrated the **Temple** in Jerusalem with animal sacrifices and statues of Greek gods. The **Maccabees'** rebellion against Antiochus and rededication of the Temple is the story of **Hanukkah.**

anti-Semitism   n. English   Prejudice or discrimination against Jews and the Jewish people. This term dates from the 19th century, although anti-Semitism can be traced back to ancient times.   adj. **anti-Semitic.**

anusim   pl. n. Hebrew (ah-noo-SEEM)   Literally, "compelled ones." The historical term for Jews who were forced to convert to another religion. The *anusim* often tried secretly to preserve their Jewish customs and teach them to their children. Perhaps the most famous *anusim* are the Spanish and Portuguese Jews who were compelled to convert to Christianity during the Spanish Inquisition. See also **Marrano** and **Converso.**

apikoros   n. Yiddish (ah-peh-KAY-riss)   A religious heretic or skeptic; one who doesn't believe. The term was first used in the **Mishnah** to refer to a Jew who renounced the Torah. *Apikoros* is a Yiddish variation of Epicurus, the Greek philosopher who championed the pursuit of sensual pleasures.

Apocrypha   n. Greek (ah-POCK-rih-fah)   A group of 14 religious books that were originally included in the **Septuagint,** the oldest Greek version of the **Old Testament.** The writings are thought to have been translated by Jewish scholars at the request of Ptolemy II. These books, which the ancient rabbis referred to as *sefarim hizonim* (extraneous books), are not included in the **TANAKH.**

apostate   n. English (ah-POS-tate)   A Jew who rejects **Judaism** for another faith. Jews distinguish apostates from those who were forced to convert. See *anusim.* Old-fashioned usage.

Aramaic   n. Aramaic (ar-ah-MAY-ick)   An ancient Semitic family of languages with distinct dialects, some of which are still spoken today. Aramaic is written with Hebrew characters. It was the everyday language spoken in ancient times in Palestine, Mesopotamia, and Syria, and by Jews who returned to Palestine after the Babylonian exile (536 B.C.E.) until the end of the talmudic period. It is the language of the **Talmud;** Jewish documents, such as the *ketubbah* and the *get,* as well as some important prayers, including the *Kaddish* and *Kol Nidrei,* are written in Aramaic.

aravah   n. Hebrew (ah-rah-VAH)   pl. n. **aravot** (ah-rah-VOTE)   **1.** Willow tree; the branches of the willow that are part of the *lulav* used on **Sukkot.** See *arba minim.*   **2.** The dry lowland area of the eastern **Negev,** often called the Aravah Valley.

arba kanfot   pl. n. Hebrew (ar-BAH can-FOTE)   Literally, "four corners." See *tallit katan.*

arba kosot   n. Hebrew (ar-BAH co-SOTE)   Literally, "four cups." It is traditional to drink four cups of wine during the **seder** on **Pesach.** The four cups of wine mirror the four ways that God delivered the Israelites from slavery in Egypt, as written in Exodus 6:6-7: "I will free you from the labors of the Egyptians and [I will] deliver you from their bondage. I will redeem you with an outstretched arm…. And I will take you to be My people, and I will be your God."

arba minim   pl. n. Hebrew (ar-BAH mee-NEEM)   Literally, "four species." The name for the three parts of the *lulav* and the *etrog,* which are used to fulfill the commandments to "rejoice before the Lord" during **Sukkot.** On Sukkot, both in **synagogue** and in the **sukkah,** it is traditional to hold the *lulav* in the right hand and the *etrog* in the left, and then to shake the *lulav* while reciting a blessing. The *lulav* is composed of three kinds of plants: the *lulav* (palm), the *hadas* (myrtle) and the *aravot* (willow). They are said to correspond to the human body: the long, strong palm is the backbone; myrtle leaves are round like eyes; willow leaves are oval like a mouth, and the *etrog* symbolizes the heart. When Jews wave the *lulav* and hold the *etrog*, they are praying with all parts of their body, with all of their senses.

ark   n. English   **1.** Shorthand for Holy Ark *(Aron Kodesh),* the cabinet at the front of an **Askenazic synagogue** that houses the **Torah scrolls.** It is usually set into or against a wall that faces east toward **Jerusalem.** The ark is sometimes large and ornate, sometimes small and plain. A depiction of the tablets of the **Ten Commandments,** or portions of their words in Hebrew, is often part of the decoration. During synagogue services, being asked to open the ark or assist in any way with the Torah is considered a high honor.   **2.** Shorthand for Noah's ark, the boat Noah built at God's command (in **Genesis**) before the Great Flood. See *tik.*

Ark of the Covenant   n. English   According to **Exodus,** the ancient chest built by **Moses** at God's command to house the stone tablets inscribed with the **Ten Commandments.** According to legend, it was a gold box with two large angels on it. After King **Solomon** built the **Temple** in **Jerusalem,** the Ark of the Covenant was kept in the **Holy of Holies.** It was lost during the destruction of the **Second Temple** in 70 C.E.

Aron Kodesh   n. Hebrew (ah-ROAN CO-desh)   Literally, "Holy Ark." See **ark.**

Asarah be-Tevet   n. Hebrew (ah-sah-RAH bih-teh-VET)   A minor **fast day** that falls on the 10th of **Tevet.** It commemorates the start of the siege of **Jerusalem** by King Nebuchadnezzar of Babylonia in 586 B.C.E., which is considered the beginning of the destruction of the **First Temple.** On minor fast days, fasting begins at dawn and ends when stars appear in the sky.

Ashamnu   n. Hebrew (ah-SHAHM-noo)   Literally, "we have sinned." A prayer recited on **Yom Kippur.** It is customary to tap over the heart with the right hand during the prayer. The *Ashamnu* is in the form of an acrostic, with a sin listed for each letter of the alphabet. For example, "we abuse, we betray, we are cruel." See *Al Het.*

Asher   The eighth son of **Jacob** and the second son of Zilpah, who was Jacob's concubine and **Leah's** handmaid. Asher is also the name of one of the 12 **tribes of Israel,** whose members were said to be descended from him. The tribe occupied the northwestern part of **Canaan.**

Ashkenazim   pl. n. Hebrew (osh-keh-NAH-zeem)   The name given to the group of Jews who were originally from Germany and France (and their descendants). The word *Ashkenaz* is the Hebrew name for Germany. The Ashkenazim migrated to Central and Eastern Europe during times of oppression. In pre–World War II Europe, Ashkenazim comprised 90 percent of world Jewry. Although millions were killed in the **Holocaust,** the Ashkenazim still greatly outnumber the **Sephardim,** the other large group of **diaspora** Jews. The majority of American Jews are Ashkenazim. The holiday customs, liturgy, pronunciation of Hebrew, and cuisine of the Ashkenazim distinguish them from the Sephardim. For example, Ashkenazim spoke **Yiddish** as their everyday language, while Sephardim spoke **Judeo–Spanish.** Ashkenazim generally don't eat rice and legumes on **Pesach**, while Sephardim do. While Ashkenazim name their children in memory of a deceased relative, Sephardim name their children in honor of a living relative. adj. **Ashkenazic.**

Ashrei n. Hebrew (OSH-ray)   Literally, "happy are they." A responsive prayer recited during daily and **Shabbat** services. It includes language from three psalms; its theme is God's concern for humankind. The prayer is an acrostic; each line begins with the next letter of the **Hebrew** alphabet except for the letter *nun*.

asiyah n. Hebrew (ah-see-YAH)   The world of action; the physical world in which we live. According to **kabbalistic** teachings, *asiyah* is the lowest of the four worlds of existence, which emerge from the *Ein Sof's* infinite light and culminate in the physical universe.

atarah n. Hebrew (ah-tah-RAH)   The decorative neckband sewn to the top of a **tallit**. It indicates the way a tallit should be draped over the shoulders. The *atarah* may be elaborately embroidered and may include the Hebrew blessing that is recited when putting on a tallit. When a man is buried in his tallit, the *atarah* is removed.

atzei chayim pl. n. Hebrew (ah-TSAY khigh-YEEM)   Literally, "trees of life." The poles to which a **Torah** scroll is attached. The ends of the poles, which are generally made of wood or ivory, protrude to serve as handles for lifting and carrying the Torah and rolling it to the next section of text.

atzilut n. Hebrew (ah-tse-LOOT)   The world of Divine emanations. According to **kabbalistic** theory, *atzilut* is the first and highest of the four worlds of existence, which emerge from the *Ein Sof's* infinite light and culminate in the physical universe. On this level, the light of the *Ein Sof* radiates and is still united with its source.

aufruf n. Yiddish (AUF-ruff)   Literally, "calling up." A congregation's public acknowledgment and blessing of a marriage. In many congregations, both the bride and groom are called up to the *bimah* either to read from the **Torah** or to recite the blessings before and after the reading. In **Orthodox** congregations, only the groom is called up to the *bimah;* if the couple is observing the custom of not seeing each other for the week before the wedding, the bride will not be present. After the reading, it is customary for congregants to throw small, wrapped candies, called *peklach,* at the groom or the couple as a token of sweet wishes and a sweet future. After the service, it is common for members of the community to offer their congratulations to the couple and their families. In **Ashkenazic** custom, the *aufruf* takes place on the **Shabbat** immediately preceding the wedding; **Sephardim** have theirs after the wedding.

Av n. Hebrew (AV)   The fifth month in the **Jewish calendar,** it usually corresponds to July or August.

aveilut n. Hebrew (ah-vay-LOOT)   The year of mourning, which Jewish law mandates only for the death of a parent; it is considered an extension of the **mitzvah** to "honor your mother and your father." Traditionally, children of the deceased attend services daily to recite the **Kaddish.** During this time, mourners are not supposed to visit the grave. The **unveiling** takes place at the end of this period.

Avinu Malkeinu n. Hebrew (ah-VEE-noo mal-KAY-noo)   Literally, "our Father, our King." A **High Holy Day** prayer in which God is asked to "be gracious to us and answer us, even though we have not done all the good that we might have." The words *Avinu Malkeinu* are repeated at the beginning of each line of the prayer. The melody is one of the most beloved of the High Holy Days.

avodah n. Hebrew (ah-voh-DAH)   Literally, "Divine service." In the *Pirke Avot,* it is written that the world stands on three pillars: **Torah;** *gemilut hasadim,* acts of kindness toward our fellow man; and *avodah,* service and worship of God. **2. Avodah**   A unique part of the *Musaf* service on **Yom Kippur,** the *Avodah* prayers describe the sacrificial ritual in the **Temple** in ancient Jerusalem on the Day of Atonement.

azoy int. Yiddish (ah-ZOI)   A definitive declaration that means "thus," "like so," or "that's how it is." When *azoy* is used as a question, it conveys doubt, such as "Really?" or "Is that so?"

baal korei masc. n. (BAHL co-RAY); **baalat korei** fem. n. Hebrew (bah-ah-LAT co-RAY)   Literally, "master (or mistress) of the reading." A **cantor** or other **Torah** reader who has mastered both the words and the **trope.** The *baal korei* reads the weekly *sidrah* to the congregation in **synagogue.** In ancient times, a *baal korei* was needed because people weren't knowledgeable enough to read their own Torah portion. Today, the reader might be the cantor or a member of the congregation who is trained to read the Torah. At many synagogues, even teens are offered this honor.

Baal Shem Tov   n. Hebrew (BAHL SHEM TOV)   Literally, "master of the good name." The name given to Israel ben Eliezer (1698–1760), the Ukrainian-born rabbi, mystic, scholar, and teacher who founded the **Hasidic** movement in Eastern Europe. Many Hasidic legends are based on his life and deeds.

baal tefilah   n. Hebrew (BAHL teh-fee-LAH)   Literally, "master of the prayers." A member of the congregation, other than the **rabbi** or **cantor,** who can lead a prayer service. "Do you think we can ask one of the Hebrew school teachers to be *baal tefilah* for the children's service?"

baal tekiah   n. Hebrew masc. (BAHL teh-kee-YAH); fem. **baalat tekiah** (bah-ah-LAT teh-kee-YAH)   The title for the person who blows the **shofar** on **Rosh Hashanah** and **Yom Kippur.**

baal teshuvah   n. Hebrew masc. (BAHL teh-shoo-VAH); fem. **baalat teshuvah** (bah-ah-LAT teh-shoo-VAH)   Literally, "returnee." A Jewish person who has become more observant and returned to more stringent religious practices. "Now that he's a *baal teshuvah,* it's only a matter of time before he goes to study in a yeshivah in Israel."

babka   n. Yiddish (BOB-kah)   A loaf-type coffee cake swirled with nuts, cinnamon, sugar, and sometimes chocolate or rum. Babkas are a traditional **Ashkenazic** Jewish delicacy, brought to America by Jews who emigrated from Russia and Poland.

Babylonian Talmud   See **Talmud.**

badchen n. Hebrew (BOHD-khen) Literally, "joker." A professional entertainer who for centuries performed at Eastern European Jewish weddings and other festivities. At a wedding, the *badchen* would sing songs and recite poems specially written for the bride and groom, as well as make toasts, dance, and tell tales from the **Midrash.** Today, the term is occasionally used for the master of ceremonies, usually the bandleader, at a wedding reception. Old-fashioned usage.

bagel n. Yiddish (BAY-gull) A leavened, firm, donut-shaped roll. Bagel dough is simmered in hot water for two minutes before it is baked and glazed with egg white. The first printed mention of the bagel comes from 1610 Poland. In those days, black bread was the daily fare; bagels made with white flour were a delicacy. Bagels are traditionally served at home after a funeral because their roundness is symbolic of the continuing circle of life. The eating of bagels with smoked fish and cream cheese is an American Jewish tradition.

balabusta n. Yiddish (bah-leh-BOOS-teh) Literally, "mistress of the house." A complimentary term for a woman who can manage everything involved in running a household, including cooking, baking, and cleaning. "A full-time job, no help in the house, and still she's baking a cake and making treat bags for the birthday party. She's a real *balabusta.*"

Balfour Declaration n. English A statement, issued by the British government in 1917, that declared Great Britain's support for the establishment of a national homeland for Jews in **Palestine.** It was named for British foreign secretary Lord Arthur Balfour, who wrote the document declaring England's support for **Zionism** as a letter to the president of the British Zionist Federation. Legend has it that English chemist **Chaim Weizmann** was instrumental in the declaration.

Banot Mitzvah fem. pl. n. Hebrew (bah-NOTE MITS-vah) The plural of **Bat Mitzvah.** See **B'nai Mitzvah.**

baraita n. Aramaic (bar-ee-TAH) pl. **baraitot** (bar-ee-TOTE) Literally "outside." Teachings and explanations that are not included in the **Mishnah,** which was kept short so that it would be practical to copy. Thus, many additional discussions and clarifications of **Torah** were omitted. These were compiled as *baraitot* of a particular scholar.

Barchu n. Hebrew (bar-KHOO) The prayer that introduces the main part of **synagogue** services, the *Barchu* is recited at every morning and evening service. It is also known as the "Call to Worship." The prayer takes its name from the Hebrew word for "knee." It is traditional for worshipers to bend slightly and bow their heads when reciting the *Barchu.*

bar Kokhba, Simon   A charismatic Jewish military leader who led a revolt against the Romans in 132 C.E. Rabbi **Akiva** was convinced that Bar Kokhba was the long-awaited Jewish Messiah, and he urged thousands of his followers to join the Jewish rebellion. The revolt was successful for a few years until Emperor Hadrian sent 35,000 reinforcements. By the time the bloody rebellion was crushed, **Judea** was a wasteland, and nearly 50 percent of the Jewish population was dead. When the Romans crushed the revolt, they sentenced Rabbi Akiva to death. Bar Kokhba was killed in battle.

Bar Mitzvah   n. Hebrew (BAR MITS-vah) pl. **B'nai Mitzvah** (buh–NAY MITS-vah)   Literally, "son of the commandment." When a Jewish boy becomes 13, he is bound "by the commandment"; in other words, he now is responsible for fulfilling Jewish law. The phrase also refers to the boy himself. A Bar Mitzvah is fully accountable for performing the **mitzvot** of Jewish life, including participating in a **minyan,** reading from the **Torah,** wearing a **tallit,** and fasting on **Yom Kippur.** He will gain this responsibility whether or not he has a ceremony to mark the event. Although not mandated by Jewish law, the Bar Mitzvah ceremony had become an established custom by the 14th century. At a Bar Mitzvah ceremony, which usually takes place at **Shabbat** morning services, the young man will generally have his first *aliyah,* read from the Torah and the **haftarah,** and give a speech to explain his **parashah.** During the Torah reading, family members and friends are honored with *aliyot.* The ceremony is usually followed by a joyous party in the afternoon or evening that includes a meal, music, and **candlelighting.**

Baruch ata Adonai   int. Hebrew (bah–RUKH ah–TAH ah–doe–NYE) The three Hebrew words that begin many Jewish blessings or *brachot,* such as the blessing recited before eating a meal or the blessing over wine. *Baruch ata Adonai* is most often translated as "Blessed are you, *Adonai.*" After these opening words, the blessing names the mitzvah, action, or item (bread, wine, long life, etc.) for which one is thanking and praising God.

Baruch ha-Shem   int. Hebrew (bah–RUKH hah–SHEM)   Literally, "blessed be the name." An expression meaning "Thank God!" It is often used when reporting good news, for example, "*Baruch ha-Shem,* she's home from the hospital."

bashert   adj. Yiddish (bah–SHAIRT)   Predestined, fated. Used when talking about two people who seem "made for each other," it is similar to the expression "a match made in heaven." *Bashert* can also refer to things other than marriage that are a happy coincidence or seem fated. For example: "I can't believe you happened to drive this route home, and on the very day my car died. I think it's *bashert* that you showed up to offer me a ride."

Bat Mitzvah   n. Hebrew (BAHT MITS-vah)   pl. **B'not Mitzvah** (buh-NOTE MITS-vah)   Literally, "daughter of the commandment." When a Jewish girl becomes a Bat Mitzvah, she is bound "by the commandment"; in other words, she now is responsible for fulfilling Jewish law. Although this coming of age can take place when she is 12, it usually happens when she is 13. The phrase also refers to the girl herself. A Bat Mitzvah is fully accountable for performing the **mitzvot** of daily Jewish life. It was a radical idea when it was introduced by the **Reconstructionist movement** in 1922; the first ones were held on Friday nights. The Bat Mitzvah today is routinely marked by **Reform,** Reconstructionist, and **Conservative** Jews in a ceremony that is identical to the **Bar Mitzvah.** At a Bat Mitzvah ceremony, the teen will generally have her first *aliyah,* read from the **Torah** and the **haftarah,** and give a speech to explain her **parashah.** During the Torah reading, family members and friends are honored with *aliyot.* The ceremony is usually followed by a joyous party in the afternoon or evening that includes a meal, music, and **candlelighting.** In many **Orthodox** communities, a girl at age 12 is honored with a Bat Mitzvah, but her participation is very different than that of a Bar Mitzvah. She may instead deliver a *devar Torah,* often at a Saturday night celebration rather than in **synagogue;** read Torah or haftarah at a women's study gathering; or learn a section of **Talmud.**

B.C.E.   n. English   The abbreviation for "Before the Common Era." When writing the date, Jews often use the religiously neutral B.C.E. in place of B.C. (Before Christ). This is because Jews don't believe that Jesus Christ is the Messiah, although they do measure time according to the year of his birth. For example, a Jew might write, "The destruction of the First Temple was in 586 B.C.E." 586 B.C.E. is identical to 586 B.C.

bedeken   n. Yiddish (beh-DECK-in)   Literally, "to cover." The final ritual prior to the marriage ceremony, in which the groom lifts the veil from the bride's face while the rabbi recites a blessing. The custom is said to have been inspired by the story of **Jacob,** who married the veiled **Leah** by mistake instead of **Rachel,** the woman he loved; the *bedeken* gives all grooms since Jacob's time the opportunity to make sure they don't make the same mistake. The custom, practiced at traditional weddings, usually takes place in the rabbi's study or the bride's room and is attended only by the immediate family and the wedding party.

bedikat hametz   v. Hebrew (beh-dee-KAHT hah-MAYTS)   The ceremony immediately before **Pesach** in which family members conduct a ritual search of the home for *hametz,* pieces of bread or leavened food that are forbidden on Passover. It is traditional to save a few pieces of bread or cookies and place them around the house so that those conducting the search will be sure to find some *hametz.* Families customarily search for *hametz* by candlelight and use a feather to brush the bread crumbs into a paper bag or napkin that can be burned or thrown away. Special prayers are also recited during the search for *hametz*.

Begin, Menachem   (1913–1992) Statesman, military commander, and prime minister of the **State of Israel** (1977–1983). In 1941, Begin deserted the Polish Army while stationed in British-controlled **Palestine.** He joined the Irgun, an underground military group that bombed and harassed the British forces in Palestine in order to hasten the establishment of the State of Israel. A lifelong politician, Begin opposed the dominant Labor party in the **Knesset** and formed the Likud Party. In 1978, United States President Jimmy Carter negotiated the Camp David Accords between Begin and Egyptian President Anwar Sadat. Under the terms of the treaty, Israel gave back the **Sinai** Peninsula to Egypt in exchange for peaceful relations between the countries. Begin and Sadat shared the 1978 Nobel Peace Prize.

beit din   n. Hebrew (BAYT DEEN)   A Jewish court of law. In ancient days, the *beit din* was made up of three rabbis who arbitrated disputes between Jews. Today, a *beit din* is most often called upon to rule on religious matters, such as the granting of a *get* or decisions regarding conversion.

beit knesset   n. Hebrew (BAYT kuh-NESS-et)   Literally, "house of assembly." The phrase is used to refer to a **synagogue.** See also **Knesset.**

beit midrash   n. Hebrew (BAYT mid-RASH)   Literally, "house of study." A religious school or **synagogue Hebrew school.**

beit sefer   n. Hebrew (BAYT SAY-fair)   Literally, "house of (the) book." It usually refers to a religious school.

beitzah   n. Hebrew (bay-TSAH)   The roasted egg placed on the **seder plate** during the **Pesach seder.** The egg is symbolic of several things, including the sacrifices in the ancient **Temple** in **Jerusalem,** rebirth in spring, and the **Israelites'** new lives in freedom after the **Exodus** from Egypt.

Be-midbar   n. Hebrew (be-MID-bar)   The Hebrew name for the Book of **Numbers,** the fourth book of the **Torah.**

ben Eliezer, Israel   See **Baal Shem Tov.**

Ben Gurion, David (1886–1973)   First prime minister of the **State of Israel.** Born in Poland, he became an ardent **Zionist** and moved to Palestine in 1906. In the years after World War I, he was a leader of the Labor Zionist movement, which worked to establish the State of Israel. In January 1949, Ben Gurion became both prime minister and defense minister of the new country and led Israel in its **War of Independence.** As prime minister, he championed the National Water Carrier (canal) project, the establishment of new cities, such as Dimona and Beersheva, and development and farming in the desert of the **Negev.** He retired from politics in 1970 to live on his kibbutz, Sde Boker, in the Negev.

Benjamin   The 12th and youngest son of **Jacob** and second son of **Rachel**, who died during his birth. He was the brother of **Joseph.** Benjamin is also the name of one of the 12 **tribes of Israel,** whose members were said to be descended from him. When the Israelite kingdom divided after the death of King **Solomon** in 930 B.C.E., the two southern tribes, **Judah** and Benjamin, remained loyal to King David and his descendants.

bentsch   v. Yiddish (BENCH)   To recite a blessing. It usually refers to *Birkat ha-Mazon,* the Grace after Meals. This is a colloquial expression used by traditional **Ashkenazic** Jews: "We're all done eating. Who's going to start the *bentsching?*" The word can also refer to the reciting of any blessing; for example, the expression *bentsch licht* means to light **Shabbat** candles.

bentscher   n. Yiddish (BEN–cher)   The small booklet containing *Birkat ha-Mazon,* or the Grace after Meals, and other songs and prayers associated with a meal. Often, at a wedding or other *simcha, bentschers* are personalized with the names and date of the celebration and given out to guests as favors after the festive meal. This reciting of blessings after a meal in unison, often with gusto and quite quickly, is referred to colloquially by traditional **Ashkenazic** Jews as *bentsching. Bentschers* also contain the words to traditional songs, or *zemirot,* in addition to prayers. Thus they are often used on **Shabbat** by those singing *zemirot.*

bentsch licht   v. Yiddish (BENCH licked)   Literally, "blessing the lights." To recite the blessing over the candles that are lit to welcome **Shabbat** and other Jewish holidays. See **candlelighting.**

Ben-Yehuda, Eliezer (1858–1922)   **Hebrew** writer and lexicographer responsible for the revival of Hebrew as a modern spoken language rather than a liturgical language. Born in Lithuania, Ben-Yehuda published articles encouraging emigration to **Palestine.** In 1881, he emigrated to **Jerusalem,** where he founded and headed the Hebrew Language Committee, an institution that later established the Hebrew Language Academy, which is still in existence. He predicted the need for a common modern language for everyday communication among the many diverse peoples making *aliyah* to the new State of Israel. He also wrote one of the first comprehensive dictionaries of ancient and modern Hebrew.

ben zachar   n. Hebrew (BEN za-KHAR)   See *shalom zachar.*

Bereshit   n. Hebrew (buh-ray-SHEET)   The Hebrew name for the Book of **Genesis,** the first book of the **Torah.** Bereshit is the first word of the entire Torah. It is translated as "When [God] began" or "In the beginning."

beriah   n. Hebrew (beh-ree-AH)   The world of creation; the place of the heavens, the throne room of God and the archangels. According to **kabbalistic** theory, *beriah* is the second of the four worlds of existence, which emerge from the *Ein Sof's* infinite light and culminate in the physical universe. It exists between *atzilut* and *yetzirah.*

berrieh   n. Yiddish (BER-yeh)   Complimentary term for a talented, competent, energetic woman, especially one who gets a lot done—and does it well—around the house. Synonym for *balabusta.* Old-fashioned usage.

besamim   pl. n. Hebrew (beh-sah-MEEM)   **1.** Literally, "spices." It almost always refers to the spices in the **spice box** used for the *Havdalah* ceremony. **2.** Modern Israeli slang for illegal drugs.

bevakashah   int. Hebrew (beh-VAH-kah-SHAH)   Literally, "please." It can be used in various ways, including "please go ahead" and at the end of a sentence as "you're welcome."

bialy   n. from Russian (bee-AH-lee)   A round, crusty, chewy bread roll with an indented center well, the bialy is usually topped with toasted onions and—at its most authentic—with poppy seeds. The bialy, an alternative to the **bagel,** originated in the town of Bialystok, Poland.

Bible   n. English, from the Greek *biblia* (books)   When Jews refer to the Bible, they are referring to the **TANAKH.**

bikur holim   n. Hebrew (bee-CORE hoe-LEEM)   Literally, "visiting the sick." It refers to doing **mitzvot,** or good deeds, for someone who is ill. Acts of *bikur holim* include taking a meal to a sick person's home, visiting a friend in the hospital, or sending a get-well card. In Judaism, performing the mitzvah of *bikur holim* is considered an important obligation for everyone.

bimah   n. Hebrew (BEE-mah)   A raised platform or stage in a **synagogue** from which the **Torah** is read and services are led. In **Sephardic** and traditional **Ashkenazic** synagogues, the *bimah* is often in the center of the room, and the Torah is carried to and from the **ark.** In modern synagogues, the *bimah* is at the front of the sanctuary, where the ark sits. On the *bimah* are one or two pulpits; the *ner tamid,* or eternal light; and a variety of other decorative and functional objects, such as a **menorah** and Israeli and American flags. See *teba.*

binah   n. Hebrew (bee-NAH)   Literally "understanding." The third of the 10 *sefirot,* or aspects of God's creative nature. According to **kabbalistic** teachings, *binah* represents intuition, understanding, and the analytic aspect of the *Ein Sof.* It is one of three *sefirot,* along with *keter* and *hokhmah,* in the category of the intellect. Each *sefirah* is associated with a part of the body; *binah* corresponds to the ears.

Birkat ha-Kohanim   n. Hebrew (beer-KAHT hah-co-hah-NEEM)   The Priestly Benediction. In ancient times, the *Kohanim* (the Temple priests) would bless the people each day from a platform in front of the **Holy Ark.** In this ceremony, known as *dukhening,* the **Kohen** stands with his hands and arms outstretched and his fingers forming a V while he recites a blessing from the Book of **Numbers.** In Jerusalem synagogues, *Birkat ha-Kohanim* is recited each morning. Outside of Israel, it is commonly said on the Sabbath, on major Jewish holidays, and at weddings, baby **namings,** and **B'nai Mitzvah.**

Birkat ha-Mazon   n. Hebrew (beer-KAHT hah-mah-ZONE)   The Grace after Meals. This lengthy prayer, which consists of four benedictions, is often sung quickly and with gusto by those familiar with the Hebrew words and the tune. Among traditional Jews, it is customary at an occasion like a wedding to give out a small prayer book *(bentscher)* containing *Birkat ha-Mazon,* other blessings, and songs. The *bentcshers* are often personalized with the names of the celebrants, and guests are invited to take them home as a memento of the occasion. The act of reciting *Birkat ha-Mazon* is often referred to as *bentsching.*

Birkat ha-Shachar   n. Hebrew (beer-KAHT hah-sha-KAR)   The first section of the morning prayers, which contains several individual blessings.

bissel   n. Yiddish (BISS-el)   A little bit of something, a tiny piece. It is also used in cooking; for example, a cook might say she adds "a *bissel* of salt" to everything. Old-fashioned usage.

bitter herbs   See *maror.*

blech   n. Yiddish (BLEKH)   A sheet of metal that can be placed over the burners on a stove to retain heat, so that precooked food and water can be kept warm during the Sabbath. It is used by Jews who observe the **Shabbat** restrictions on cooking.

blintz n. Yiddish (BLINTZ); pl. **blintzes** (BLIN-tsez) A folded pancake, similar to a crepe, that is filled with fruit or sweet cheese. Blintzes are usually served with sour cream or a fruit topping, like cherries, for brunch or lunch. It is also traditional to eat blintzes and other dairy foods on **Shavuot.**

Blood Libel n. English An accusation that a particular group kills people as a form of human sacrifice and uses the blood in religious rituals. This lie, which first appeared in the 12th century, alleged that Jews kill Christian children and used their blood in **matzah.** This virulent form of **anti-Semitism** reappeared in Russia in the 20th century, and the **Anti-Defamation League of B'nai B'rith** is currently battling Blood Libel propaganda in the radical Arab media, which accuses Jews of using Arab blood for their rituals.

B'nai B'rith Organization n. Hebrew (buh-NAY BRITH) Founded in New York in 1843 by German Jewish immigrants, B'nai B'rith is the oldest Jewish charitable organization in the United States. It is also the largest Jewish fraternal organization in the country. In addition to social, intellectual, and fraternal activities, B'nai B'rith supports the activities of its **Anti-Defamation League.** It also sponsors a speakers bureau on topics of Jewish interest.

B'nai Mitzvah n. Hebrew (buh-NAY MITS-vah) Literally, "children of the commandment." The plural form of **Bar Mitzvah.** Today, the term may be used to refer to teens who "share" their Bar Mitzvah date by reading **Torah** at the same **Shabbat** service. In the late 20th century, U.S. Jews often symbolically shared a B'nai Mitzvah with Soviet Jewish children who were unable to celebrate; this was known as twinning. If both children are girls, the plural would be B'not Mitzvah.

Book of Life n. English A "book" in which God inscribes the names of the righteous. The **Talmud** explains that on **Rosh Hashanah,** this book is opened for the righteous, while the Book of Death is opened for the wicked. The fate of all others is on hold until **Yom Kippur;** during the 10 days of self-examination between the two **High Holy Days,** Jews can influence their fate with prayer and repentance. The greeting *"le-shanah tovah tikatevu,"* used during the **High Holy Days,** means "May you be inscribed [in the Book of Life] for a good year." The Hebrew term is *Sefer Chayim.*

boreka n. from the Turkish word, *borek,* "pastry" (boor-ECK-ah) A filled pastry turnover served warm, it is the **Sephardic** version of a **knish.** Like knishes, borekas can be savory, filled with potato, onion, mushrooms or other vegetables, or sweet, filled with cinnamon, sugar, and sweet cheese. In Israel, borekas are popular as a snack food and appetizer.

borscht n. Yiddish (BOARSHT) An Eastern European soup traditionally made with beets. Borscht can also be made with potatoes or cabbage and served hot or cold. True beet borscht is pink, served cold, and topped with a swirl of sour cream.

Borscht Belt n. English A term for the resort hotels in the Catskill Mountains of New York that catered primarily to Jews. These resorts were known for their bountiful **kosher** cuisine (hence the "borscht") and for nightclub entertainment featuring big-name comedians and singers. These resorts were in their heyday in the 1950s and 1960s.

boychik n. Yiddish (BOY-chick) A young boy. Used as an affectionate way to address a man or boy; the equivalent of the American expression "buddy" or "kiddo." Old-fashioned usage.

bracha n. Hebrew (brah-KHAH); pl. **brachot** (brah-KHOTE) Literally, "blessing." The many different prayers that thank God for specific things. Almost all *brachot* begin with the phrase *Baruch ata Adonai* (Blessed are You, *Adonai*). For example: "Blessed are You, *Adonai,* who brings forth the fruit of the vine" is the translation of the blessing recited before drinking wine. In Jewish life, there are blessings for almost any and every event—including seeing a rainbow and having a successful harvest. One of the most widely used is the *Shehecheyanu,* which thanks God for sustaining us and allowing us to live long enough to be here for this (particular) happy event.

breaking the glass v. English The custom at the end of a Jewish wedding ceremony in which the groom smashes a glass under his foot. It is common for the guests to respond with a hearty *"mazel tov."* There are many interpretations of this ancient practice; some popular ones include that the breaking of the glass is a reminder of the destruction of the **Temple** in **Jerusalem** and that it is a symbol of how fragile relationships are. Often, the broken glass is saved and incorporated in a piece of **Judaica,** like the stem of a *Kiddush Cup* or the frame of the couple's *ketubbah.*

bris n. Yiddish (BRISS) **Circumcision** ceremony. The **Ashkenazic** pronunciation and abbreviated name for a *brit milah,* the covenant of circumcision.

brisket n. English An economical, grainy cut of beef that is prepared similar to a pot roast, slow-cooked at a low temperature. This makes it an ideal choice for **Shabbat** meals because a cook can leave it to simmer for hours without breaking the laws of *melakhah.* Along with roasted chicken, beef brisket is a traditional choice for Shabbat and Jewish holidays meals.

brit   n. Hebrew (BREET)   A covenant, specifically one between man and God. This type of covenant is mentioned several times in the **Torah.** For example, to reward Noah's obedience in building the ark and gathering the animals, God made a covenant with him, promising never to destroy the earth again by flood. God also made a covenant with **Abraham,** promising that he and his descendants would become a great nation. As a sign of this promise, God commanded that every Jewish male be circumcised at the age of eight days. See **brit milah.**

brit bat   n. Hebrew (BREET BAHT)   Literally, "daughter of the covenant." A name for the celebration to welcome the birth of a daughter. See **naming.**

brit chayim   n. Hebrew (BREET khigh-YEEM)   Literally, "covenant of life." Another name for the celebration welcoming the birth of a daughter. See **naming.**

brit milah   n. Hebrew (BREET mee-LAH)   Literally, "covenant of **circumcision.**" The ceremony of circumcision, the removal of the foreskin of the penis. Circumcision is the oldest ritual in Judaism, dating back 5,000 years to the patriarch **Abraham** and his **covenant** with God. The Book of **Genesis** (17:12) commands: "Throughout the generations, every male among you shall be circumcised at the age of eight days." Today, ritual circumcision is done by a *mohel,* usually in the family's home, on the eighth day, even if that falls on **Shabbat.** The ceremony may be postponed if the baby is ill or premature, if he must remain in the hospital, or if he is adopted and arrives after eight days of age. During the *bris,* the godparents (if any), parents, grandparents, and special friends of the newborn are recognized and recite prayers, including the *Shehecheyanu.* Sometimes, a grandfather or friend is given the honor of *sandek* and asked to hold the child during the ceremony. The Hebrew name of the baby and for whom he is named is announced publicly for the first time. Blessings often include a wish that the child will "grow to enjoy a life of *huppah,* **Torah,** and *ma'asim tovim.*" This joyous occasion includes a celebratory meal, gifts, and congratulations for the new baby.

brucha   n. Yiddish (BRAW-khuh)   Blessing. The Yiddish pronunciation of *bracha.*

b'tayavon   int. Hebrew (buh-tay-ah-VONE)   Literally "with appetite." The Hebrew equivalent of *bon appetit.* A waiter might say it to his customers as he places their dinner on the table; it's also often printed on paper napkins in Israel.

bubbe   n. Yiddish (BUH-bee)   A name given to a grandmother; the Yiddish version of Grandma, Nana, or Mom-Mom. It is sometimes also used as an affectionate, old-fashioned term for any grandmotherly older woman.

bubbeleh   n. Yiddish (BUH-beh-leh)   Literally, "little grandmother." A term of endearment for a woman of any age, similar to "darling" or "honey."

bubbe meise   n. Yiddish (BUH-beh MYE-suh)   Literally, "grandmother's story." **1.** A superstitious story; an old wives' tale. "My mother used to tell me not to go outside with wet hair because I'd catch a cold. What a *bubbe meise*." **2.** Something of little importance, an inconsequential thing or minor happening. "Stop complaining about how much trouble it was to return that sweater. What a *bubbe meise*."

bubkes   int. Yiddish (BUP-kiss)   Literally, "beans." Indicates something worthless or something that falls far short of expectations. Used as a mild expletive. "I thought he would pay me for doing that job, but I got *bubkes!*"

BuJew   n. English (BOO-joo)   A contraction of "Buddhist" and "Jewish." A derogatory slang term for a Jewish person who embraces the philosophies and traditions of Buddhism, such as the search for sacred moments in everyday life. Sometimes it is used as an insult to describe a Jew who merely has an interest in spiritual matters such as meditation, yoga, or feng shui.

bulvan   n. Yiddish (BULL-vahn)   An ox or oaf; someone who is thick-skinned and thick-headed. A bulvan is physically strong, but also coarse, boorish, and unrefined.

burtshen   v. Yiddish (BORT-chin)   To gripe or complain; to mutter to oneself. Distinct from **kvetch,** which is to complain to others. Old-fashioned usage.

Canaan   n. English (KAY-nan)   The ancient region between the Jordan River, the Dead Sea and the Mediterranean Sea, also called **Palestine.** It was the land that God promised to **Abraham** in the Book of **Genesis.** After the **Exodus** from Egypt, **Moses** appointed a delegation to go ahead and see what the land of Canaan and the people who lived there were like. The scouts returned, reporting on a bountiful, beautiful land "flowing with milk and honey"—a phrase still used today to describe **Israel.** Canaan is often referred to as "the **Promised Land.**"

canary   n. English   Slang contraction of *kine-ahora,* the **Yiddish** expression for warding off bad luck or the evil eye, which might be listening in when things are too good. It is used in response to a compliment so that the opposite does not occur. "Mitzi, did you get your hair done? It looks so thick and gorgeous." "Did you have to say that? Don't give me a canary."

candlelighting   n. English   **1.** The custom of lighting candles to welcome **Shabbat** and other Jewish holidays. Candlelighting is one of the most universally practiced Jewish customs. Traditionally, the woman of the house lights two Shabbat candles and says the blessing over them; often the whole family joins in. In some households, a candle is lit for each family member. A single braided candle is lit for *Havdalah,* a service that ushers out Shabbat. Some **Reform** congregations light candles in the synagogue at the beginning of the Friday evening service.   **2.** A modern custom, part of a **Bar Mitzvah** or **Bat Mitzvah** reception, during which 13 candles are placed in a birthday cake. Relatives and friends of the family are honored with poems and fond words as they light the candles.

cantor   n. English   The official at a **synagogue** who leads the congregation in prayer and song. The cantor, who stands on the *bimah* with the **rabbi,** sings and chants the prayers, solo or with the worshipers. He or she often teaches and helps children prepare for their approaching **Bar Mitzvah** and **Bat Mitzvah** ceremonies. Called *hazzan* in Hebrew.

carpas   See *karpas.*

C.E.   n. English   The abbreviation for "Common Era." When writing the date, Jews often use the religiously neutral C.E. in place of A.D. (Anno Domini), which means "Year of Our Lord." This is because Jews don't believe that Jesus is the Lord, although they do mark time according to the year of his birth. For example, a Jew might write, "Columbus sailed to America in 1492 C.E." 1492 C.E. is identical to 1492 A.D.

Central Conference of American Rabbis (CCAR)   n. English   The international association of Reform rabbis, founded in 1889. The CCAR publishes prayerbooks and a quarterly journal and issues responsa on questions of Jewish law and platforms on social issues such as capital punishment.

Chabad Lubavitch   n. Hebrew/Yiddish (khah-BAHD)   See **Lubavitch movement.**

Chad Gadya   See **Had Gadya.**

chag sameach   See *hag sameach.*

chai   n. Hebrew (KHIGH)   Literally, "life." The two Hebrew letters (*het* and *yud*) that make up the word *chai* have come to symbolize long life. The word is often engraved on jewelry and **Judaica.** *Het* and *yud* together have a numerical value, according to *gematria,* equal to 18; for this reason, charitable donations and wedding and **Bar** or **Bat Mitzvah** gifts are often given in multiples of 18 as an implied wish for long life.

challah   n. Hebrew (hah-LAH); pl. **challot**   (hah-LOTE)   The braided egg bread that traditionally is eaten on almost every Jewish holiday and **Shabbat.** On Shabbat, some Jews put out two loaves of challah, reminiscent of the double portion of **manna** the ancient **Israelites** received each Friday when wandering in the desert. On **Rosh Hashanah,** *challot* are made round, rather than shaped like a loaf, to celebrate the fullness of the New Year and the circular nature of the calendar. Some *challot* have raisins in the dough; others are topped with sesame seeds or poppy seeds.

chaloshes   n. Yiddish (khah-LUH-shess)   A disgusting, horrible thing; in bad taste. Can refer to anything from an ugly dress to a vile meal.

chalutz   See *halutz.*

chametz   See *hametz.*

chametzdik   See *hametzdik.*

chamsa   See *hamsa.*

Chanukah   See **Hanukkah.**

chanukat ha-bayit   See *hanukkat ha-bayit.*

chanukiah   See *hanukkiah.*

charoset   See *haroset.*

Chasidism   See **Hasidism.**

chatan   See *hatan.*

chaver   See *haver.*

chazak u baruch   int. Hebrew (KHAH-zak oo bah-RUKH)   Literally, "be strong and be blessed." A term of congratulations and good wishes that is said when one completes an **aliyah** or performs another **mitzvah**. It's the **Sephardic** equivalent of the Yiddish *"yasher koach."*

chazer   n. Yiddish (KHAH-zer)   Pig, glutton. Derogatory term for someone who overeats or is greedy, not necessarily relating to food. "You're a grown man. Don't be such a *chazer,* grabbing all the free keychains and notepads at the auto show."

chazerai   n. Yiddish (khah-zeh-RYE)   Anything of little value; cheap, worthless trinkets; junk. "He came back from the **Purim** carnival with his pockets filled with *chazerai.*"

chazzan   See *hazzan.*

cheder   See *heder.*

chesed   n. Hebrew (HEH-said)   Literally "kindness." The fourth of the 10 *sefirot,* or aspects of God's creative nature. According to **kabbalistic** teachings, *chesed* represents the generous and compassionate aspect of the **Ein Sof.** It is one of three *sefirot,* along with **gevurah** and **tiferet,** in the category of the heart or emotions. Each *sefirah* is associated with a part of the body; *chesed* corresponds to the right arm.

cheshbon ha-nefesh   n. Hebrew (HESH-bone hah-NEH-fesh)   Literally, "inventory of the soul." Soul searching, spiritual introspection, self-examination. *Cheshbon ha-nefesh* and **teshuvah** are the central themes of the **High Holy Days.**

Cheshvan   See **Heshvan.**

chevrah kadishah   See *hevrah kadishah.*

chief rabbi   n. English/Hebrew   The name for the head of the rabbinical authority in many **Orthodox** communities. Many times, he serves as a member or leader of the *beit din,* the Jewish legal court. In the **State of Israel,** there is both a **Sephardic** and an **Ashkenazic** chief rabbi.

chiloni   See *hiloni.*

cholent   n. Yiddish (CHO-lent)   A slow-cooked stew made of beef, beans, potatoes, and other vegetables. *Cholent* is a common Sabbath dish because it can be prepared the day before and cooked overnight on a low flame that is lit before **Shabbat;** thus the prohibition against kindling a light on the Sabbath is honored. See also *blech.*

chol ha-moed   See *hol ha-moed.*

chopped liver   n. English   A mixture of chopped chicken livers, sautéed onions, and hard-boiled eggs traditionally made with **shmaltz.** Chopped liver is served chilled and usually eaten on crackers or **matzah;** it used to be a popular appetizer for **Shabbat** dinner before the days of cholesterol concerns. Today it often shows up on the table at holidays and *simchot.*

Chosen People   n. English   The belief that as descendants of **Abraham,** the Jewish people have been chosen by God. It comes from a phrase in **Deuteronomy** (7:7) that reads, in part, "It is not because you are numerous that God chooses you." Many scholars believe that the phrase refers to the Jews' task of spreading monotheism—the belief in one God—to the world. Others believe Jews were chosen to inhabit the Land of **Israel,** as God promised Abraham. The phrase has been used against Jews by **anti-Semites.**

chossen   n. Yiddish (KHUSS-in)   The groom.

chossen's tish   n. Yiddish (KHUSS-ins TISH)   Literally, "groom's table." The gathering of the groom and certain male guests prior to the wedding ceremony, at which time the *tenaim* and *ketubbah* are signed. The celebration, which is observed at traditional weddings, can include wine and cake, singing, and dancing. The groom is supposed to give a speech about the week's **Torah** portion while the guests try to disrupt him. During this same time, the bride and her guests are gathered for the *hakhnasat kallah.* These ceremonies precede the **bedeken.** In some non-Orthodox communities both groom and bride have a *tish.*

chotchke   See *tchotchke.*

chozer   See *chazer.*

chozerai   See *chazerai.*

chremslach   n. Yiddish (KREMS-lock)   A fried fritter or **latke,** made of **matzah meal** and eggs, that may be stuffed with ground meat, nuts, or fruit. An old-fashioned **Pesach** recipe.

Chumash   See *Humash.*

chumetz   n. Yiddish (KHUM-etz)   See *hametz.*

chumetzdich   adj. Yiddish (KHUM-etz-dick)   See *hametzdik.*

chupah   See *huppah.*

chutzpah   n. Yiddish (KHUTZ-pah)   From the Hebrew word for "audacity." Nerve, gall. Gutsy, sometimes arrogant, behavior that is outrageous but at the same time admirable.

circumcision   n. English   A surgical procedure to remove the foreskin of the penis. In Jewish tradition, circumcision is performed as a religious ritual called a **brit milah** or **bris.**

cockamamy   adj. French (cock-ah-MAY-mee)   Absurd, ridiculous, foolish. Often thought to be a Yiddish word, cockamamy is a misspelling of the French *decalcomania,* a removable tattoo. "You want to go to Times Square on New Year's Eve? What a cockamamy idea."

Cohan   See **Kohen.**

Cohen   See **Kohen.**

concentration camps   pl. n. English A general term for the labor or extermination camps established by the Nazis during the **Holocaust.** These camps, operated by Henrich Himmler's SS troops, were a major element in the **Final Solution.** Concentration camps, such as Dachau and Belsen, were located mostly in Germany and intended for the forced labor of Jews, homosexuals and political prisoners. Death usually resulted from starvation or disease; people were shot when they were no longer able to work. The Nazis also established six extermination or death camps, including Sobibor, Treblinka, Auschwitz–Birkenau and Belzec. Prisoners were killed in gas chambers, sealed rooms into which poison gas was released, or in mass shootings. The bodies were usually destroyed in crematoria. It is estimated that almost 10 million people died in these Nazi camps. Auschwitz, the largest concentration camp, has come to symbolize the horrors of the Holocaust.

Confirmation   n. English   A group ceremony, held on **Shavuot,** that recognizes students (ages 15 to 16) who are completing the religious school curriculum. The ceremony may include reading from the **Torah** (particularly the **Ten Commandments**), speeches by the teens, and blessings by the **rabbi.** The service may be followed by a party. Confirmation was introduced by the **Reform movement** at the end of the 19th century to replace the **Bar Mitzvah** celebration; today it has been widely adopted by the various branches of Judaism as an addition to the Bar or Bat Mitzvah. During the Confirmation ceremony, students affirm their intention to live their lives as Jews. Some **synagogues** publish a list of the confirmands' names in the local newspaper, congratulating them on their achievement.

Consecration   n. English   A modern ceremony that marks the formal beginning of religious instruction for Jewish children. Celebrated by most **Conservative, Reform,** and **Reconstructionist** congregations, Consecration is sometimes held on **Sukkot,** a holiday near the beginning of the school year, or on **Simchat Torah,** to make the connection between study and celebrating the **Torah.** The ceremony may be held when the child is in an early grade, or *alef* class. There is no formal liturgy for the occasion, but it is customary to say a prayer for the child's successful Jewish education and to present the child with an object of **Judaica** or a book of Jewish content.

Conservative movement   n. English   One of the four movements with which North American Jews identify themselves, the Conservative movement is the major Jewish denomination today, with more than one million affiliated Jews. It was founded in Germany in the mid-19th century by those who considered the **Reform movement** too liberal. In 1913, its cause was forwarded by **Solomon Schechter,** who founded the **United Synagogue of Conservative Judaism.** The Conservative movement, which takes the middle ground between **Orthodox** and Reform, holds that Jewish law is binding and divinely inspired. It upholds standards of **Shabbat** observance and **kashrut.** The **rabbi** of each Conservative congregation serves as the interpreter of *ha-*

lakhah for his or her congregation, applying Jewish law in consultation with the congregation. At **synagogue** services, most prayers are in Hebrew. **Rosh Hashanah** is observed for two days. Girls are given the same education as boys in Conservative schools. Policies on counting women in a **minyan** and calling women to the **Torah** vary from one congregation to another. Female rabbis were first ordained in 1983.

The movement is committed to supporting the **State of Israel** and Jews around the world, and is involved in social action and interreligious programs in local communities. The Jewish Theological Seminary in New York and the University of Judaism in Los Angeles are the Conservative movement's rabbinical schools; **The Rabbinical Assembly** is its rabbinical association. Conservative congregations generally belong to **United Synagogue of Conservative Judaism.**

Converso   n. Ladino (con-VUR-so)   From the root word for "convert." The term for those Jews who were forced to convert to Christianity in the late Middle Ages during the Spanish Inquisition. Jews were often forced to publicly convert to avoid torture or death (which usually meant being burned at the stake in a ceremony known as the auto-da-fé), but they continued to practice aspects of Judaism in secret. Through the centuries, these families became assimilated into Spanish society. Today, some Catholics in these countries still practice rituals that echo of Judaism, like not eating pork. Converso is a more accurate, less disparaging term than the more frequently used **Marrano,** which comes from the Spanish word for "swine."

covenant   n. English   The word used to describe the agreements made between God and the Jewish people. Tradition says that God made several covenants. The **Torah** tells of the covenant God makes with **Abraham,** promising him that he will be the patriarch of a great nation. In return, Abraham agrees that every male will be circumcised as a sign of this covenant. This ancient rite is still practiced today; Jewish males are circumcised in a ceremony known as *brit milah,* or "the covenant of circumcision." God also makes a covenant with **Moses** as he prepares to receive the **Ten Commandments**. God tells Moses: "If you obey me faithfully and keep My covenant, you shall be treasured among all the peoples." Many scholars regard acceptance of the teachings of the Ten Commandments as an example of the Israelites' covenantal relationship with God. God also made a covenant with Noah, a non-Jew, after the Great Flood, giving him the **Noahide Laws** and promising never again to destroy the world. God created the rainbow as a sign of this covenant.

crain   See *khreyn.*

crowning ceremony n. English The ceremony held during a wedding reception to honor parents who have married off their last child. While the parents are seated on the dance floor, guests dance around them offering hugs, kisses, and *mazel tovs.* Sometimes the parents are "crowned" with wreaths of flowers, giving the ceremony its name in English, "crowning." The **Yiddish** song "Die Mezinke Oysgegeben" (The Youngest Daughter Is Given) is commonly played during this ceremony. Called *krenzel* in Yiddish.

Dan   The fifth son of **Jacob**, and the first of Bilhah, who was Jacob's concubine and **Rachel**'s maidservant. Dan is also the name of one of the 12 **tribes of Israel,** whose members were said to be descended from him.

dafina   n. from the Arabic word for "covered" (da-FEE-nah)   A **Sephardic** slow-cooked stew often served on Shabbat. *Dafina* is similar to the **Ashkenazi** *cholent. Dafina,* also called *hamin,* includes beef, potatoes, chickpeas, or beans. There are many variations. Moroccan *dafina* includes cumin, coriander, and veal bones; in the Egyptian version, whole eggs are cooked in the stew.

dati   n. Hebrew (dah-TEE); pl. **datim** (dah-TEEM)   The word used by Israelis to describe **modern Orthodox** Jews who follow the laws of **Judaism** while allowing some modifications in response to modern society. For example, *dati* children may go to a public high school, while most ultra-Orthodox **(haredim)** would send their children to a **yeshivah.** *Dati* is contrasted with *Masorti,* the Israeli name for **Conservative Jews.**

daven   v. Yiddish (DAH-ven)   Literally, "pray." Traditional Jews *daven* three times a day—evening, morning, and afternoon—in private or at **synagogue** services. This **Ashkenazic** term brings to mind the image of a traditional Jew in prayer, wearing a **tallit** and *kippah* and swaying back and forth in a *shuckling* motion. "Don't phone him Saturday morning. He'll be in shul *davening.*"

David   The second king of Israel, who reigned from 1010 to 970 B.C.E. As a young man, David, armed with only a slingshot and faith in God, gained fame for defeating the Philistine giant Goliath. As king, David united the warring tribes into the nation of **Israel,** with **Jerusalem** as its capital. Today, Jerusalem is still called the City of David, and it remains the physical and spiritual capital of Israel. David is also acknowledged as the author of the Book of Psalms.

davka   int. Hebrew (DAV-kah)   Similar in meaning to "can you believe it?" but with an ironic or unlucky twist. Used as an interjection to comment on an unimaginable event. "The one day I decided to dress casually for work was—*davka*—the day the regional manager made a surprise visit to our office."

Dayan, Moshe (1915–1981)   Israeli military commander and politician. The first child born on Kibbutz Degania Aleph in the **Galilee,** Dayan fought in World War II with the British Forces battling the Vichy French in Syria. He lost his left eye in battle and began wearing a black eye patch that became his signature. During the 1948 **War of Independence,** he was commander of several military units, including those defending Jewish settlements in the Jordan Valley. In 1959, he left the **Israel Defense Forces** (IDF) and was elected to the **Knesset.** As defense minister in 1973, Dayan and the government received much of the blame for the surprise attacks of the **Yom Kippur War.** He was also an amateur archaeologist who amassed an enormous collection of artifacts.

Dayenu   int. Hebrew (dye-AY-noo)   Literally, "it would have been enough." One of the most familiar songs of the **Pesach seder.** Each verse recounts a miracle or good deed that God performed and is followed by the chorus of "Dayenu"—"that would have been enough!" For example, "Had he helped us 40 years in the desert and not fed us manna, *dayenu*." The chorus of the song is a favorite among children because the word *dayenu* is broken up and repeated many times, making it an easy tune to learn and sing.

Day of Atonement   n. English   Another name for **Yom Kippur.**

Day of Judgment   n. English   **1.** Another name for **Rosh Hashanah.** According to the **Talmud,** the **Book of Life** is opened for the righteous on Rosh Hashanah so that God can inscribe their names for the coming year. Judgment for all others is on hold until **Yom Kippur. 2.** The future day at the end of the world, when all who have lived will be resurrected and judged by God as to whether or not they are worthy of eternal life. Also called End of Days.

Day of Remembrance   See **Yom ha–Zikaron.**

Days of Awe   pl. n. English   Another name for the 10-day period of introspection and repentance beginning with **Rosh Hashanah** and ending with **Yom Kippur,** called **Yamim Noraim** in Hebrew. See **High Holy Days.**

Days of Repentance   n. English   The name given to the 10 days beginning with **Rosh Hashanah** and ending with **Yom Kippur.** According to tradition, on Rosh Hashanah, God opens the **Book of Life** for the coming year. These days are an opportunity for introspection, repentance, prayer, charity, and resolutions, with the hope for a positive outcome when one's fate is sealed on Yom Kippur.

day school   n. English   The general name given to private Jewish schools in the United States. Some day schools are affiliated with particular movements in **Judaism,** like the Conservative movement's **Solomon Schechter** schools;

others are independent institutions. "They sent their daughter to day school so she could learn Hebrew as part of the language curriculum."

Dead Sea   n. English   The mineral–rich, landlocked lake in the valley southeast of **Jerusalem,** between **Israel** and Jordan. A super salty body of water, the Dead Sea is also the lowest place on earth—1,348 feet below sea level. Heavy with potash, salts, magnesium, iodine, and other minerals, the Dead Sea does not support any life. Visitors enjoy its buoyancy and the therapeutic benefits of the waters and surrounding mud. The minerals are commercially harvested for various uses including cosmetics, bath salts and other beauty products. In Hebrew, its name is *Yam ha-Melah,* Sea of Salt.

Dead Sea Scrolls   pl. n. English   Leather and papyrus scrolls containing partial texts of the Torah. In 1947, a Bedouin shepherd wandered into a rocky cave on a cliff at **Qumran,** an area northwest of the **Dead Sea,** and discovered pottery urns containing fragments of the oldest known copy of the **Bible.** Over the next nine years, more than 15,000 writings dating from the late **Second Temple** period (200 B.C.E. to 68 C.E.) were uncovered. The Dead Sea Scrolls are written in Hebrew and Aramaic. They contain pieces of nearly every book of the Bible, including the Book of Isaiah and Psalms, along with non-biblical writings, including a copper scroll that appears to be a list of hidden treasures from the Temple in Jerusalem, a story of a struggle between the Sons of Light and the Sons of Darkness, and rules for daily life. These rules led scholars to believe that the scrolls were written by the **Essenes,** a monastic, separatist sect of Judaism that took refuge at Qumran when Jerusalem was conquered by the Romans. The scrolls are now housed in the Shrine of the Book at the Israel Museum complex in Jerusalem.

Decalogue   n. Greek (DECK-ah-log)   Literally, "ten words." Another name for the **Ten Commandments.**

derash   n. Hebrew (duh-RAHSH)   From the root that means "to interpret." The symbolic, not obvious, interpretation of a Jewish text, in which the presence of certain words or phrases gives added meaning to a passage. *Derash* is contrasted with *peshat,* the literal meaning of the words.

derekh eretz   n. Hebrew (DER-ek EH-rets)   Literally, "way of the land." Good conduct; normal, polite behavior in a social setting. "We try to teach the kids that when they're working in a group they should treat each other kindly, with *derekh eretz.* "

Deuteronomy   n. English   The fifth and final book of the **Torah,** known in Hebrew as Devarim. It takes its name from the first sentence of the book, which begins "These are the words." Deuteronomy contains **Moses'** last words and thoughts to the **Israelites,** spoken when he blesses the 12 **tribes of Israel** as they prepare to cross to the **Promised Land.**

Devarim n. Hebrew (deh-var-EEM) The Hebrew name for the Book of **Deuteronomy,** the fifth and final book of the **Torah.**

devar Torah n. Hebrew (deh-VAR toe-RAH) A short speech that explains and comments on an issue related to the weekly **Torah** portion. Sometimes a *devar Torah* is given as part of the opening remarks to a meeting. It is also common for a **Bar** or **Bat Mitzvah** to give a *devar Torah* after reading from the Torah and **haftarah.** It is considered an honor to deliver a *devar Torah.*

deveikut n. Hebrew (deh-vay-KOOT) Literally, "cleaving" [to God]. The concept of coming close to God by prayer and contemplation. *Deveikut,* an important concept in **kabbalistic** thought, is described as the soul's highest step on the spiritual ladder during its ascent to the Divine.

Diaspora n. English From the Greek for "dispersion." The term for Jewish communities and their residents who live outside of the **State of Israel.** The term originated in the 6th century B.C.E. with the expulsion of the Jews from Palestine to Babylonia. Through the ages, Jews were forced to leave their homes many times because of persecution; as a result, they live in places as far-flung as Brazil, South Africa, and Australia. The term "wandering Jew" refers to the Jew's continuing search for a safe place to live. Today, Jews in the Diaspora lend financial and moral support to fellow Jews living in Israel. Much of that financial support is channeled through the **United Jewish Communities.** adj. **diaspora.**

draydel See **dreidel.**

draykop n. Yiddish (DRAY-cup) Literally, "turn head." A nutty, illogical person; someone who twists and confuses things. The term has been Anglicized in the expression "Don't dray your cup," meaning don't worry about it.

dreck n. Yiddish (DREHK) Literally, "shit." Vulgar expression to describe something that's shoddy, cheap, or of inferior quality, comparable to the English word "crap."

dreidel n. Yiddish (DRAY-duhl) A small, four-sided spinning top used in a game during **Hanukkah.** Every dreidel has a **Hebrew** letter on each side—*nun, gimmel, hay,* and *shin*—that together stand for the phrase *nes gadol hayah sham,* meaning "a great miracle happened there [Israel]." Dreidels made in **Israel** replace the Hebrew letter *shin* with a *pey* for the Hebrew word *po,* meaning "here" (a great miracle happened here). This phrase reminds Jews of the **Maccabees'** battle for religious freedom and the Hanukkah miracle of the oil.

Dreidels can be made of almost any material. Children make them of clay or paper; artists make them of silver, wood, or porcelain. In the game of dreidel, each player takes a turn putting money, candy, or some other small object in the center of a circle. Then each spins the dreidel to find out what he or she wins: *nun* means none, *gimmel* means all, *hay* means half, and *shin* means put one in. In the story of Hanukkah, legend has it that when **King Antiochus** forbade Jews to study **Torah,** they would do their lessons with a dreidel close at hand. When soldiers approached, they could quickly begin to play dreidel so as not to be caught studying Jewish texts. Today, dreidels and foil-wrapped chocolate coins **(gelt)** are traditional Hanukkah gifts.

dreykop   See *draykop.*

Druse   n. English   A separatist religious sect of approximately one million people who live chiefly in Israel, Syria, and Lebanon. About 20,000 Druse live in the United States. The Druse religion began in the 10th century as a branch of Islam and incorporates elements of Judaism and Christianity. The Druse were persecuted by mainstream Moslems because of their belief that Tariq al Hakim was an incarnation of God. Rather than try to change Islam, the Druse withdrew; today their beliefs and practices remain secret from those not in the community. The Druse in Israel are unique in that they are an Arab people who are mostly loyal Israeli citizens, even serving in the army and the Knesset.

dukhan   n. Hebrew (doo-KHAN)   Literally, "platform." The platform in front of the **Ark of the Covenant** from which the **Temple** priests would bless the people each day in ancient times. See *Birkat ha-Kohanim.*

dukhening   v. Hebrew (DOO-khen-ing)   To recite *Birkat ha-Kohanim,* the Priestly Benediction.

Dyanu   See **Dayenu.**

dybbuk   n. Hebrew (DIB-ick)   An evil spirit, often thought to be the soul of a dead person, that wanders the earth looking for a living body to inhabit. Dybbuks can be exorcised from the people they possess. These demons were associated with the tradition of the **Kabbalah** and popularized in Jewish folklore. Old-fashioned usage.

Eban, Abba (1915–2002) Israeli statesman and diplomat. Born in Cape Town, South Africa, he fought with the British Army in **Palestine** during World War II. Eban was a member of the Jewish Agency delegation to the United Nations before the founding of the **State of Israel.** In 1948, he was **Israel's** first representative at the U.N. Fluent in 10 languages and a learned historian, Eban spoke eloquently and passionately in support of Israel to a U.N. body that was often openly hostile. He also served as Israel's ambassador to the United States, as president of the Weizmann Institute of Science, and as a member of the **Knesset.**

Ecclesiastes n. English One of the five books, referred to as a scroll or **megillah,** that is contained in **Kethuvim,** the third section of the **TANAKH.** It is read in **synagogue** on **Sukkot.** Ecclesiastes offers a discourse on the meaning of life. It was originally thought to have been written by King **Solomon** in his old age, but its author is now described simply as Kohelet, "the preacher." In Hebrew, the book is named **Kohelet.** It is the source of many famous sayings, including "there is nothing new under the sun."

Eden, garden of n. English See **Gan Eden.**

Eikhah n. Hebrew (AY-khah) The Hebrew name for **Lamentations,** the **megillah,** or scroll, that is read on **Tisha b'Av.**

Eilat n. Hebrew (ay-LOT) The southernmost resort town in **Israel,** located on the Red Sea at the northern end of the Gulf of Aqaba. Eilat boasts many luxurious hotels and restaurants, a bustling beachfront boardwalk, coral reefs prized by scuba divers, boating, fishing, and birdwatching. Eilat is also one of Israel's commercial ports. It is bordered by Jordan on the southeast and Egypt's **Sinai** Peninsula on the west.

Ein Keloheinu n. Hebrew (AYN keh-loe-HAY-noo) A well-known song exalting God, it is sung toward the end of Saturday morning **synagogue** services. The prayer has a recurring theme that praises God with slightly different words in each verse: "There is none like our God/There is none like our Master/There is none like our King...." The melody of "Ein Keloheinu" is one of the most familiar to Jews.

Ein Sof   n. Hebrew (AYN SOFE)   Literally, "without end." The infinite un-knowable God; the One who cannot be comprehended by the human mind, according to **kabbalistic** theory. The four worlds of *atzilut, beriah, yetzirah,* and *asiyah* emerge from the *Ein Sof's* infinite light and culminate in the finite physical universe. The 10 Divine emanations, or *sefirot,* also issue forth from the *Ein Sof.*

El Adon   n. Hebrew (el ah-DOAN)   An acrostic prayer recited at the begin-ning of the **Shabbat** morning service that praises **God** as the creator.

Elijah   (eh-LYE-jah)   A prophet of the 9th century B.C.E. who, according to **talmudic** lore, ascended to heaven in a chariot and will reappear one day to announce the arrival of the **Messiah.** An angry prophet, Elijah often thought God had forsaken him and that he was the last righteous man. According to tradition, Elijah is a spiritual visitor at every **Pesach seder** and *brit milah.* Because of his pessimism about the fate of the Jewish people, he bears witness to the vitality and continuity of the Jewish people by attending these family gatherings.

Elijah's Chair   n. English   A special chair set aside at every *brit milah* for the mystical spirit of the Prophet **Elijah,** who is supposed to make sure that Jews are still faithful to the **covenant.** The Hebrew term is *Kisse Eliyahu.*

Elijah's Cup   n. English   A special goblet filled with wine and placed on the **seder** table for the Prophet **Elijah.** At a certain point in the seder, guests stand while someone opens the front door. All wait quietly for a moment to see if the prophet appears and takes a sip of wine. It is traditional that Elijah's Cup look different from a regular wine glass. It is often larger and decorative, a work of **Judaica.** The cup also symbolically fulfills the ancient injunction to welcome strangers and others who have no seder of their own. The Hebrew term is *Koss Eliyahu.* See also **Miriam's Cup.**

Eliyahu Hanavi   n. Hebrew (aye-lee-AH-hoo hah-nah-VEE)   Literally, "**Elijah** the Prophet." An ancient song traditionally sung during the **Pesach seder,** often when the door is opened to welcome the Prophet Elijah. Legend says that the Prophet Elijah will bring peace to the world, so the song is also sung at *Havdalah,* as a wish for the peace of **Shabbat** to linger through the work week.

El Male Rachamim   n. Hebrew (EL mah-LAY rah-khah-MEEM)   Liter-ally, "God full of compassion." A memorial prayer that asks for the repose of the soul of the departed. *El Male Rachamim* is recited at the burial service, at the **un-veiling,** in the synagogue on the anniversary of the death **(yahrzeit),** and dur-ing the *Yizkor* service.

Elohim   n. Hebrew (eh-loe-HEEM)   One of the many names used to refer to God. *Elohim* is used in the **Torah** and has an ancient biblical tone to it, whereas *Adonai* is the term most often used in prayer.

Elul   n. Hebrew (eh-LOOL)   The sixth month in the **Jewish calendar,** it falls in August or September, right before the **High Holy Days.**

ema   n. Hebrew (EEE-mah)   Literally, "mother." Some Jewish children are taught to use the word "Ema" instead of "Mommy" when referring to their mother. "Ema, can I clean my room after the cartoons are over?"

emet   n. Hebrew (eh-MET)   **emes**   n. Yiddish (EH-miss)   Literally, "truth." **1.** Truth, honesty. The word embodies a larger principle of speaking the truth, dealing honestly, and acting properly. **2.** adj. A word used in prayers to describe God, such as "true King," or "true Judge." **3.** int. When used colloquially, *emet* or *emes* is similar to "Are you putting me on?" or "Is that the truth?" "Dinner really costs $95 a person? *Emet?*"

emunah   n. Hebrew (eh-MOO-nah)   Faith. A deep, abiding belief, particularly in God and the **Torah.**

End of Days   See **Day of Judgment.**

Ephraim   Second son of **Joseph** and his wife Asenath, an Egyptian. Ephraim is also the name of one of the 12 **tribes of Israel,** whose members were said to be descended from him. Joseph was given a double portion of land, which he later gave to his two sons, **Menasseh** and Ephraim. The tribe of Ephraim occupied the central region of **Canaan.** When lighting Shabbat candles, it's customary in some homes to bless a son with the words, "May you be like Ephraim and Menasseh."

Eretz Mitzrayim   n. Hebrew (EH-rets meets-RYE-eem)   The land of ancient Egypt. This phrase appears many times in **Torah** and in the **Pesach haggadah** as the story of the **Exodus** from Egypt is told.

Eretz Yisra'el   n. Hebrew (EH-rets yis-rah-ALE)   Literally, "Land of Israel." It refers to both the ancient biblical land that God promised to **Abraham** and the modern geographic region known as the **State of Israel.**

erev   n. Hebrew (EH-rev)   Literally, "evening." The name for the evening of any holiday or **Sabbath.** The Jewish day runs from sunset to sunset, and all Jewish holidays begin just before sundown the night before. The night before **Yom Kippur,** for example, is called *erev* Yom Kippur.

erusin   n. Hebrew (eh-roo-SEEN)   The first half of the Jewish wedding ceremony, representing the betrothal; also called *kiddushin.* This, the legal part of the service, includes the ring ceremony and is traditionally separated from the *nissuin* by the reading of the *ketubbah.* In early times, this formal betrothal took place a year before the marriage. Today, the *erusin* and *nissuin* rituals have been combined into one ceremony, all conducted under a *huppah.*

eruv   n. Hebrew (EH-roov)   A string hung high in the air from telephone poles to form an unbroken circle around the houses and buildings of a community of traditional Jews. Many of the laws of *melakhah,* which prohibit specific activities on **Shabbat,** allow these activities within a private domain. Traditional Jews believe that constructing an *eruv* to encircle a neighborhood converts the public area into a "private" one. On Shabbat, traditional Jews within an *eruv* can move a bit more freely and engage in activities like pushing a baby stroller or carrying a child, which would otherwise be forbidden. In the **State of Israel,** whole cities are surrounded by an *eruv.*

Esau   Twin brother of **Jacob,** son of **Isaac** and **Rebecca.**   Esau was a skillful hunter and Isaac's favorite. Because he was the older twin, he was to inherit Jacob's birthright, but he sold it to Jacob for a bowl of stew. Later in **Genesis,** when Isaac was near death and nearly blind, Esau lost out on his father's final blessing because Jacob disguised himself as his brother and served his father the food that Isaac had requested of Esau.

eshet chayil   See **woman of valor.**

Essene   n. Hebrew (es-SEEN)   A member of a monastic Jewish sect that lived in ancient Israel in **Qumran** near the **Dead Sea** during the time of the **Second Temple** (538 B.C.E. to 70 C.E.) The Essenes did not marry and lived apart from mainstream society. They had very strict rules that governed every aspect of daily life, including hygiene, eating, and study. It is believed that the Essenes were the scribes and perhaps writers of the **Dead Sea Scrolls.**

Esther   The Jewish girl who became queen of ancient Persia, the second wife of **King Ahasuerus,** during the time of the **Purim** story in the 5th century B.C.E. The story of the Purim holiday is retold in a scroll called *Megillat Esther.* Purim celebrates the rescue of the Jewish community of ancient Persia from persecution by **Haman,** an evil adviser to King Ahasuerus. The Hebrew name for Esther is **Hadassah.**

Esther, Scroll of   n. English   One of the five books, referred to as a scroll or **megillah,** that is contained in **Kethuvim,** the third section of the **TANAKH.** Known as *Megillat Esther* in Hebrew, it is read in synagogue on **Purim.** It tells the story of how **Esther,** a Jew, became the wife of **King Ahasuerus** of Persia and stopped wicked **Haman** from destroying the Jews.

eternal light   n.   English   The light fixture in front of the **ark** in every **synagogue.** This lamp is always lit. Tradition says that the eternal light is a reminder of the **menorah** in the ancient **Temple** as well as a reminder that God is always with us. The eternal light may be a hanging lamp in front of the ark or mounted on the wall above the ark. It can be a simple light fixture or an elaborate sculpture. In Hebrew, it is called ***ner tamid.***

Ethics of the Fathers   n.   English   The English name for *Pirke Avot,* one of the sections of the **Mishnah.** It contains many ethical teachings, rabbinical sayings, and moral maxims from the ancient Jewish sages, including **Hillel, Akiva,** Ben Zoma, and others. It includes the well-known quote from Hillel: "If I am not for myself, who will be for me? And if I am only for myself, what am I? And if not now, when?"

etrog   n.   Hebrew (EHT-rogue)   Literally, "citron." A yellow citrus fruit larger than a lemon. The *etrog* is part of the celebration of the harvest holiday of **Sukkot.** It is always partnered with the *lulav.* Symbolic of the fruits of the harvest, it also represents the heart in the human body. On Sukkot, the *lulav* and *etrog* are marched around the synagogue and passed around the **sukkah** for all to see, smell, and hold. It is customary and preferable to use only an unblemished *etrog,* one that has no obvious bruises and has its stem *(pitom)* still intact.

Eve   The first woman. In Genesis it says, "God cast a deep sleep upon the man and while he slept, He took one of his ribs and fashioned the rib into a woman." Eve and the first man, **Adam,** lived in paradise, the Garden of Eden, and God provided for all their needs. The serpent tempted Eve with the forbidden fruit of the Tree of Knowledge of Good and Evil. She ate the fruit and gave some to Adam. When God found out what they had done, He punished them and banished them from Eden. Eve was the mother of Cain and Abel. See *Gan Eden.*

Exodus   n.   English   **1.** The second book of the **Torah,** called **Shemot** in Hebrew. Exodus contains the story of the holiday of **Pesach** — how the **Israelites** were slaves in Egypt, the account of the **Ten Plagues,** and the Israelites' flight from Egypt; the giving of the **Ten Commandments;** and the story of the Golden Calf. **2.** The term used to describe the Israelites' flight to freedom from slavery in Egypt.

F

falafel   n. Hebrew (fuh-LAH-full)   A mixture of mashed chickpeas, spices, and flour that is shaped into patties and deep fried. It is usually served in pita bread with lettuce, cucumber, tomato, and **tahini,** a creamy sesame seed sauce. Falafel sandwiches are street food in **Israel,** and falafel stands are a common sight, much like sidewalk hot dog carts are in cities in the United States.

Falasha   n. Amharic (fuh-LAH-shah)   Literally, "stranger" or "immigrant" in the language of Ethiopia. An Ethiopian who practices a form of Judaism, using the **Old Testament** and some **apocryphal** books. Some of their traditions correspond to Jewish traditions. The word "Falasha" is considered derogatory; Falashas call themselves Beit Israel (House of Israel) and believe themselves to be descended from the tribe of Dan. They faced discrimination in Ethiopia, and in 1984 and 1991 thousands of these "Black Jews" were airlifted to the **State of Israel** in daring rescue missions. Some remaining Ethiopians, who want to immigrate to Israel, are facing discrimination and obstacles because of Israel's debate over the **Law of Return.**

fapitzed   adj. Yiddish (fah-PITZED)   All dolled up; overdressed for the occasion. Used to describe someone wearing too much jewelry or too many bows, or having too big a hairdo. "She came to brunch at our house wearing a new suit, high heels, and a diamond necklace. She was all *fapitzed*."

farbissen   adj. Yiddish (far-BISS-en) Bitter, obstinate, scrooge-like.   n. masc. **farbissener** (far-BISS-en-er);   fem. **farbisseneh** (far-BISS-en-eh)   A mean, unpleasant person; a sourpuss.

farblondjet   adj. Yiddish (far-BLON-jit)   Lost; having no idea where one is. "Between reading the directions and looking for the sign, I got so *farblondjet* that I turned off the turnpike at the wrong exit." Old-fashioned usage.

farbrengen   n. Yiddish (far-BRUNG-in)   From the root meaning "to spend time together." Generally, the term refers to a gathering of **Hasidic** men. It might include study, lessons, or a *devar Torah*. A *farbrengen* could also be an informal gathering for camaraderie and refreshments or a women's gathering that features topic of interest to them.

farchadat   adj. Yiddish (far-CHAH-det)   Confused, distracted, mixed up. "She's a little *farchadat* since her children bought her one of those new cell phones."

farfel   n. Yiddish (FAR-full)   Small pieces of noodles sautéed with mushrooms, onions, and beef or chicken stock. Farfel is served as a side dish, much like rice or couscous. For **Passover,** farfel is made with crumbled **matzah** instead of noodles and is used as a substitute for poultry stuffing, rice, and other *hametzdik* foods.

farkakteh   adj. Yiddish (far-COCK-tuh)   Lousy, messed up, ridiculous. *Farkakteh* is similar to "crappy." "What kind of *farkakteh* deal is that? It is worth much more."

farklempt   adj. Yiddish (far-KLEMPT)   Distraught, emotional, choked up with tears. Someone who is *farklempt* may describe the feeling as a spasm or tightening around the heart. Old-fashioned usage.

farmisht   adj. Yiddish (far-MISHT)   A little mixed up, confused. "I was so *farmisht* I put my brisket in the oven but never turned the oven on."

farshtay   v. Yiddish (far-SHTAY)   Understand, comprehend. Often followed by a question mark, the equivalent of "You got that?"

fast days   n. English   The Jewish calendar includes specific fast days that are observed as a sign of repentance or mourning. The two major fasts, **Yom Kippur** and **Tisha b'Av,** last from sunset until the stars come out the following day. These fasts include abstinence from food, drink, sex, and wearing leather. Minor fast days, such as the **Fast of Gedaliah,** last from sunrise to until the stars come out and involve abstinence from food and drink.

Fast of Esther   n. English   The day before **Purim;** a minor **fast day** on the 13th of **Adar** on the **Jewish calendar.** The Fast of Esther recalls how Queen **Esther** fasted and prayed to God for guidance before she agreed to go before **King Ahasuerus,** pleading with him to spare the Jews of ancient Persia. At the time, she requested that **Mordecai** and the Jews of their town of Shushan join her in prayer and fasting for three days. The day is also known by its Hebrew name, Ta'anit Esther. On minor fast days, fasting begins at dawn and ends when stars appear in the sky.

Fast of Gedaliah   n. English   A minor **fast day** that falls on the third of **Tishrei,** the day following the second day of **Rosh Hashanah.** It commemorates the assassination of Gedaliah ben Achikam, the Jewish man appointed by

King Nebuchadnezzar of Babylonia to govern the Jews remaining in Palestine after the destruction of the **First Temple** in 586 B.C.E. On minor fast days, fasting begins at dawn and ends when stars appear in the sky. Known in Hebrew as Tzom Gedalyah.

Feast of Esther   See **Purim.**

Feast of Lots   See **Purim.**

Feast of Tabernacles   See **Sukkot.**

Feast of Weeks   See **Shavuot.**

feh   int. Yiddish (FEH)   Yuck! Phew! Ugh! An exclamation of disgust. Old-fashioned usage.

fence around the Torah   The practice of being extra stringent to ensure that *halakhah* is observed. The phrase comes from a section of Mishnah where it is written to "take the laws . . . and make a fence around the **Torah.**" This was interpreted by traditional rabbis to mean that in order to keep from violating commandments, more stringent requirements than the Torah demands should be followed. Some of these "fences" have become a matter of Jewish law, such as not sounding the **shofar** on **Rosh Hashanah** if it falls on **Shabbat,** because of the prohibition against doing work on the Sabbath. Other "fences" are decisions of personal observance. For example, an **Orthodox Jew** might not go to a shopping area on Shabbat. Even if he were just going to walk around, he might be tempted to buy something, eat non-kosher food, or carry a package—all activities that are forbidden.

Festival of Booths   See **Sukkot.**

Festival of First Fruits   See **Shavuot.**

Festival of Lights   See **Hanukkah.**

Final Solution   n. English   The official Nazi government plan of annihilating the Jews of Europe during World War II. The Final Solution was a planned genocide formulated by Nazi leaders at a secret meeting in Berlin in 1942 and resulted in the establishment of extermination camps, such as Auschwitz and Treblinka, for mass killings of Jews. See **Holocaust.**

first fruits   pl. n. English   In ancient times, the portion of the harvest that was dedicated to God. **Shavuot** (the Festival of First Fruits), **Pesach,** and

Sukkot are also known as **Pilgrimage Festivals,** when ancient Israelites would travel to the **Temple** in Jerusalem with flowers, fruits, sheaves of grain, and other "first fruits" offerings to God. Although the practice of making offerings to God ended with the destruction of the Temple, today special prayers for a good harvest, for rain, etc. are recited on the Pilgrimage holidays, and many synagogues decorate the *bimah* with flower arrangements and fresh fruits.

First Temple   n. English   The most holy place of worship and sacrifice in ancient **Jerusalem.** The First Temple was built by King **Solomon** in the late 10th century B.C.E. and destroyed by the conquering Babylonians under King Nebuchadnezzar in 586 B.C.E. See also **Second Temple** and **Holy of Holies.**

Five Books of Moses   n. English   Another name for the **Torah,** the first five books of the Hebrew Bible, which include **Genesis, Exodus, Leviticus, Numbers,** and **Deuteronomy.** Also called the **Pentateuch.**

flanken   n. Yiddish (FLAHNK-in)   A cut of beef, usually fatty, taken from the front end of the short ribs. The meat is boiled or stewed and served with horseradish.

fleishig   adj. Yiddish (FLAY-shick)   The general term for food in the meat category, according to the Jewish dietary laws of **kashrut.** This includes beef and poultry and any byproducts of these, such as chicken broth, and beef and chicken fat. It also refers to utensils and dishes used for cooking, eating, and serving meat products. A person who keeps **kosher** does not mix fleishig and **milchig** ("milk") foods or eat both food groups at the same meal. For example, a cheeseburger is forbidden. Likewise, one wouldn't have a glass of milk with a roast beef sandwich. Many Jews who observe kashrut wait several hours after eating meat before eating dairy, and vice versa. Under the laws of kashrut, all food can be classified as either milchig, fleishig, or **pareve.**

forshpeis   n. Yiddish (FOR-shpeyes)   Hors d'oeuvres, appetizers. Used literally, forshpeis refers to a little **nosh** that is served—perhaps some shmaltz herring—before dinner. It's also used figuratively. For example "Shabbat forshpeis" is a little taste of Torah—a preview of the week's Torah portion.

four cups of wine   See *arba kosot.*

Four Questions   pl. n. English   The four questions asked during the **Pesach seder.** The answers to these explain the meaning and the symbols of the holiday. During the seder, it is traditional for the youngest child to read or chant the Four Questions in Hebrew or English. The leader of the seder answers each question by guiding the guests through the **haggadah,** which tells the story of the Israelites' **Exodus** from Egypt. The questions are introduced with the query "Why is this night different from all other nights?" and are as follows: (1) On all other nights we eat bread or **matzah.** Why on this night do we eat only matzah? (2) On all other nights we eat many vegetables. Why tonight do we eat bitter herbs? (3) On all other nights we do not dip our food. Why tonight do we dip food twice? (4) On all other nights we can sit any way. Why tonight do we recline? Also called **"Mah Nishtanah,"** which are the first two words in Hebrew of the Four Questions.

four sons pl. n. English   A passage in the **haggadah** that uses the metaphor of four sons—the wise son, the wicked son, the simple son, and the one who doesn't even know how to ask—to demonstrate that the story of **Pesach** and the **Exodus** from Egypt should be told to all children in all generations. In some modern, egalitarian *haggadot,* the story is known as the "four children." In Hebrew, four sons is *arba banim.*

Four Species See *arba minim.*

freilach adj. Yiddish (FRAY-lakh)   **1.** Happy, cheerful; usually used in reference to music, especially at weddings and other *simchot.* "Play something *freilach.* We want to dance more!" **2.** n. The name of a group dance that originated among the Jews of Eastern Europe. Today, a *freilach* might be done in a line or a circle at a **Bar Mitzvah** or wedding, ususally to **klezmer** music.

fress v. Yiddish (FRES)   To eat or snack, often in large quantities; to eat quickly or noisily, like an animal. n. **fresser.** A heavy eater. Old-fashioned usage.

fried matzah See *matzah brei.*

fringes See **tzitzit.**

frum adj. Yiddish (FROM)   From the German word for "religious"; used mainly in conversation between Jews to refer to someone who is **Orthodox** or very strict in his or her observance of Jewish law. "I didn't know she was so *frum* until I realized that she wears a long skirt and a hat every day."

fumfeh v. Yiddish (FUM-fuh)   To speak unclearly, to mumble. To hesitate before talking. "He's not used to speaking in public. I hope he doesn't *fumfeh* when he gets up to the podium."

Gad   The seventh son of **Jacob** and first son of Zilpah, who was Jacob's concubine and **Leah**'s handmaid. Gad is also the name of one of the 12 **tribes of Israel,** whose members were said to be descended from him. His tribe occupied the mountainous region northeast of the **Dead Sea.**

gabbai   n. Hebrew (GAB-eye)   **1.** Historically, a paid official at a **synagogue** who collected dues. Today, the term is used for the layperson who is responsible for keeping things in ritual order in the synagogue, for example, compiling the list of Hebrew names of the people who are receiving *aliyot* and preparing the **Shabbat** morning announcements. **2.** The name for the secretary or assistant to a **Hasidic rebbe.**

Galilee, Sea of   n. English   The freshwater lake in northeastern **Israel,** fed by a number of streams and springs. The Jordan River flows through it from north to south. The most ancient artifacts found in Israel have been found on the shores of the Sea of Galilee. According to the New Testament, the Sea of Galilee was the site of much of Jesus' activities and preaching. Many of his disciples were fishermen and baptisms are still performed on the lake. Tiberias, an ancient city founded by King Herod's sons, is now a popular beach resort town on the western shore. The area around the lake, called the Galil Valley, or Galilee, is rich farmland that grows dates, mangos, bananas, and apples. Israel's oldest kibbutz, Degania Aleph, is on the southern shore. In Hebrew, the Sea of Galilee is called "Yam (Lake) Kinneret," meaning "harp-shaped sea."

Galitzianer   n. Yiddish (gah-LIT-see-ah-ner)   A Jew who traces his or her ancestry to the region known as Galicia, which included southeastern Poland and parts of the USSR. Galitzianers are contrasted with the other ethnic subgroup of **Ashkenazic** Jews, the **Litvaks,** by geography, differences in **Yiddish** pronunciation, and interpretation of Jewish law. Galitzianers pride themselves on being higher class, better educated, and more religious than Litvaks. In 1941, there were 650,000 Jews living in Galicia, Poland. Only 11 percent of Polish Jews survived World War II. Even today, Jews still ask one another, "Are you a Galitzianer or Litvak?"

galut   n. Hebrew (gah-LOOT)   Literally, "exile." Any place outside of the **State of Israel** where Jews live. Its English equivalent is **Diaspora.** Historically, *galut* referred to the compulsory exile of the Jews from Israel after the destruction of the **Second Temple.**

gaon   n. Hebrew (gah-OWN)   pl. **geonim** (gay-oh-NEEM)   Literally "pride" in biblical Hebrew and "genius" in modern Hebrew. **1.** A title of honor for the rabbis and teachers who were the spiritual heads of the Babylonian **yeshivot** between the 6th and 11th centuries C.E. As the highest religious authorities, the *geonim* interpreted the Talmud, answered questions of *halakhah* from Jews in the **Diaspora** and presided over the *beit din.* They compiled a version of the Talmud known as the Babylonian Talmud. **2.** Gaon. The Vilna Gaon, the title given to Rabbi Eliyahu ben Solomon Zalman, the 18th century Lithuanian Jew, known as a great Talmudic and kabbalistic scholar and for his mathematical genius. He was an early opponent of Hasidic Judaism.

Gan Eden   n. Hebrew (GAHN AYE-den)   Literally, "Garden of Eden." **1.** The place on Earth where **Adam** and **Eve** resided. **2.** Paradise; the place of spiritual reward for the souls of the righteous. In the traditional Jewish view of the afterlife *(olam ha-ba),* only the very righteous go directly to *Gan Eden.* Less virtuous souls spend up to a year in **Geihinnom** before ascending to paradise. Descriptions of *Gan Eden* vary; one source compares the bliss of the afterlife to the warmth of a sunny day, while another describes it as the place where one finally understands the true nature of God. See **Tree of Life.**

gartl   n. Yiddish (GAR-tuhl)   Literally, "to gird." **1.** The cloth belt that many **Hasidim** and **Orthodox** Jews wear around their midsections, either at all times or while praying. A *gartl* is worn to fulfill the commandment to divide the upper and lower body. **2.** Another name for a **wimpel,** the long band of material that encircles and holds together the two rolls of a **Torah** scroll, like a belt.

Gaucher disease   n. English (go-SHAY)   A rare inherited disorder that causes spleen and liver enlargement, bone and joint pain, anemia and impaired blood clotting. Gaucher's disease Type 1, the most prevalent Jewish genetic disease, occurs in one in every 1,000 **Ashkenazi** Jews. For most people, symptoms begin in childhood or early adulthood. Enzyme replacement therapy has been effective in reversing or reducing symptoms. Gaucher disease can be diagnosed with a blood test or prenatal testing.

Gaza   n. Hebrew (GAH-zah)   A small piece of land at the southwest corner of Israel, bordering the Mediterranean Sea. In 1967, Israel captured Gaza from Egypt during the **Six-Day War.** In August 2005, the Israeli government forced the Israelis who lived in Gaza to leave their homes and move from the area. Part of the **occupied territories,** it was turned over to the Palestinian Authority (PA) as the first independent Palestinian territory. Also called the Gaza Strip.

G-d   n. English (GEE-DASH-DEE)   Another way to write the name of God. This form is often used by traditional Jews, in keeping with Jewish law, to avoid writing God's name on paper or something else of a temporary nature that might be thrown away or erased. This is the reason that sacred texts, which do contain God's name, are traditionally stored in a *genizah.* Some people consider it unnecessary to use a hyphen in the word "God" because this is simply another name for the **Tetragrammaton**—the letters *yud, hay, vav, hay*—which is the name of God.

gefilte fish   n. Yiddish (guh-FILL-teh FISH)   Literally, "stuffed" fish. Deboned, ground up fish—usually carp, pike, and whitefish—that is mixed with eggs, seasonings, and **matzah meal;** shaped into small cakes; and simmered in broth. Served cold with horseradish, gefilte fish is a traditional appetizer at many Jewish holiday meals. Because fish is **pareve,** gefilte fish can be eaten with either meat or dairy foods at any meal. In earlier times, many Jewish women made their own gefilte fish from scratch, often from a fish bought live that was kept alive in a bucket or bathtub until the time came to cook it. Today, commercially produced gefilte fish is readily available in jars in supermarkets.

Gehenna   n. Greek (guh-HAY-nah)   See *Geihinnom.*

Geihinnom   n. Hebrew (gai-hee-NOHM)   Literally, "valley of Hinnom." An area outside **Jerusalem** where human sacrifices were offered to the god Moloch during certain periods in biblical history. In the traditional Jewish view of the afterlife *(olam ha-ba), Geihinnom* is the place of punishment and purification. The most righteous souls go directly to *Gan Eden;* the remainder to *Geihinnom.* Some consider it a place of severe punishment; in the **Talmud,** it is pictured as a dark region with fire and sulfurous fumes, perhaps because of the association with idol worship. Others describe it as a time when Jews review the actions of their lives and experience remorse for the harm they have caused. For most souls, punishment is not eternal; they ascend to *Gan Eden* within 12 months. Only the most wicked remain. Some sources believe the wicked souls are destroyed; others think they remain in *Geihinnom* forever. Also called *Gehenna.*

gelilah   n. Hebrew (guh-LEE-lah)   The honor of dressing the **Torah** after it has been read. The person who receives this honor rolls the Torah scrolls together and then fastens them with a sash, or *gartl,* before fitting the Torah cover over them. The scrolls are finally dressed with the *hoshen* and *keter Torah.*

gelt   n. Yiddish (GELT)   Literally, "money." **1.** Slang for money; cash. **2.** The foil-wrapped chocolate coins that are a traditional **Hanukkah** treat for children.

Gemara   n. Aramaic (guh-MAR-ah)   Literally, "learning." A compilation of 300 years of rabbis' legal and ethical commentaries on the **Mishnah,** edited in the 5th century C.E. Together, the Gemara and the Mishnah comprise the **Talmud,** the collection of ancient rabbinic laws, commentaries, and thoughts related to the teachings of the **Torah.**

gemar hatimah tovah   int. Hebrew (geh-MAR ha-tee-mah toe-VAH)   A customary greeting among Jews on **Yom Kippur** that wishes, "May you be sealed in the Book of Life." This reflects the wish that on Yom Kippur, when God closes and seals the Book of Life, your friend's name will be in it as one of the righteous.

gematria   n. Greek (geh-MAH-Tree-ah)   Literally, "geometry." An ancient system of **Hebrew** numerology, dating from the 2nd century C.E., in which each Hebrew letter was assigned a numerical value. Mystics believed there were hidden messages in the sacred Jewish texts and used *gematria* to decode them. The system was used in the Middle Ages and later by the **kabbalists;** it is still in use among some **Hasidim.** For example, *chai,* Hebrew for "life," consists of the letters *het* (equaling 8) and *yud* (equaling 10), giving *chai* the value of 18. This is why *tzedakah* is often given in multiples of 18 and why 18 is considered a lucky number.

gemilut hasadim   n. Hebrew (geh-mee-LOOT hah-sah-DEEM)   Literally, "acts of lovingkindness." The **Talmud** specifies six traditional kinds of *gemilut hasadim:* clothing the naked, providing for a bride, visiting the sick, comforting mourners, accompanying the dead to the grave, and extending hospitality to strangers. These deeds require personal involvement and should be done with no thought of motivation, reward, or thanks; performing *gemilut hasadim* is considered a **mitzvah.** In the *Pirke Avot,* it is written that *gemilut hasadim* is one of the three pillars on which the world stands. The others are **Torah** and *avodah*, service to and worship of God. An anonymous donation of groceries to a food pantry is an example of *gemilut hasadim.*

Genesis   n. English   The first book of the **Torah,** called **Bereshit** in Hebrew. The Book of Genesis includes the stories of the creation of the world, Noah's Ark, the **patriarchs** and **matriarchs,** and **Joseph** and his brothers.

genizah   n. Hebrew (guh-KNEE-zah)   Literally, "hidden away." A closet or storage space in a **synagogue** or religious institution, where old prayer books and religious articles are stored until they can be buried. Jewish law says that objects containing the word of God should be properly interred when they are no longer able to be used. This tradition has existed since ancient times. The most notable *genizah* is the Cairo Genizah.

gentile   n. English   The word Jews use to refer to anyone who is not Jewish. Unlike **"goy,"** the **Yiddish** word for non-Jew, gentile, has no negative connotations.

genug   adj. Yiddish (guh-NUG)   Enough. Often used in the expression *"Genug es genug!* (Enough is enough!)."When she got home from the Bar Mitzvah, she talked my head off and described every detail until I had to tell her *'genug!'"*

ger   n. Hebrew (GAIR)   Literally, "stranger." The old-fashioned, historical term for a convert to Judaism. See **Jew by Choice.**

geshmak   adj. Yiddish (guh-SHMACK)   Very tasty; delicious. "She made that stuffed capon just right. It was *geshmak*."

get   n. Hebrew (GEHT)   The Jewish divorce decree, traditionally written in **Aramaic.** According to Jewish law, in order for a couple to divorce, a husband must give his wife this deed, which nullifies their Jewish marriage contract, the **ketubbah.** A woman without a *get* is an **agunah** and cannot remarry. Many **Orthodox** and **Conservative** rabbis require a woman to obtain a *get* before she can remarry; most **Reform** and **Reconstructionist** rabbis do not.

gevalt   int. Yiddish (guh-VOLT)   A cry for help. An expression of surprise, as in "What happened?" or "How did this happen?" Often used with *oy,* as in *oy gevalt.*

gevurah   n. Hebrew (guh-voo-RAH)   Literally "strength." The fifth of the 10 *sefirot,* or aspects of God's creative nature. According to **kabbalistic** teachings, *gevurah* represents the determination and judgment of the **Ein Sof** and the power of Divine punishment. It is one of three *sefirot,* along with **chesed** and *tiferet,* in the category of the heart or emotions. Each *sefirah* is associated with a part of the body; *gevurah* corresponds to the left arm.

gezunt   n. Yiddish (guh-ZINT)   Literally, "health." Used in many Yiddish expressions, such as *gai gezunt,* "go in good health," or *abi gezunt,* "stay healthy." This is also the root of the word *gezuntheit,* the wish for good health after a sneeze.

gezuntheit   int. Yiddish (guh-ZUND-hite)   "God bless you" or "Be healthy." The common response uttered when someone sneezes.

ghetto n. English   Historically, the segregated section of a city or town where Jews were forced to live. From *geto,* the Italian word for "foundry"; the first ghetto in 1516 C.E. was simply a section of Venice where most of the Jewish community lived. Throughout history, as various governments discriminated against and persecuted Jews, ghettos changed. Physical barriers were erected, separating the Jewish population from the rest of the town and thereby severely limiting the economic, educational, and political opportunities for the Jews of Eastern Europe. During the **Holocaust,** life in the ghettos came to a murderous conclusion because the Nazis cut off food supplies to the ghettos and then rounded up the Jews to be taken to **concentration camps.** Today, the meaning of the word "ghetto" refers to a section of a city occupied by a particular ethnic or minority group, generally of a lower socioeconomic status. There are no physical barriers separating the residents of this part of the city from the rest. See **Warsaw Ghetto.**

gilgul n. Hebrew (gill-GOOL)   Transmigration of the soul. The concept of reincarnation is not a basic tenet of mainstream Judaism, but the belief is expressed in the **Zohar** and is an important part of the **kabbalistic** view of the afterlife. The theory holds that the soul is purified through *gilgul* and can be reborn—some scholars say three times, others say an infinite number of times—in another mortal or animal.

glatt kosher adj. Yiddish (GLOT CO-sher)   Strictly kosher. *Glatt* means "smooth"; it refers to a slaughtered animal's lungs, which must be found undamaged in order for the meat to be considered kosher. Although *glatt kosher* should be reserved for meat, the phrase has been broadened to refer to food or restaurants that meet the most demanding standards of **kashrut.**

God n. English   The Supreme Being, the Divine creator of the world and all that is in it. The belief in one God is the foundation of **Judaism.**

God, names of pl. n. English   Various Hebrew terms are used in the Torah, prayers, and other writings to refer to God. Sometimes the name is a variation on the **Tetragrammaton,** the four Hebrew letters (*yud, hay, vav, hay*) that compose the personal, inexpressible name of God, which Jews believe is sacred and must not be spoken aloud. Instead Jews call God *Adonai* (Lord), *ha-Shem* (the name), or *Elohim* (God). Other names of God are words for His attributes: *El Elyon* (Most High); *El Olam* (Eternal God); *El Shaddai* (God Almighty); *ha-Kadosh Baruch Hu* (the Holy One, Blessed Be He); *Ha-Rahaman* (The Merciful), and others. Some Jews believe that the name of God should not be written on a transient piece of paper that might be soiled or discarded, hence the tradition of writing G-d.

Golan n. Hebrew (go-LAN)   The mountainous, rocky region of north and northeastern Israel bordering Syria. The Golan was captured during the

Six-Day War, and it is of critical, strategic advantage to Israel. When the high-elevation area belonged to Syria, the Syrians could fire rockets and bombs literally "down the mountainside" onto Israeli kibbutzim and towns in the valleys. There are many hiking trails and beautiful mountain streams that form the source of the Jordan River, but much of the land is still unusable because of buried land mines. Mount Hermon, the tallest mountain in Israel and the only ski slope in the Middle East, also lies in the Golan region. The area is also called the Golan Heights.

goldene medina n. Yiddish (GOLE-deh-neh meh-DEE-nah)   Literally, "golden country." The term used by Eastern European Jews to refer to America, where the streets were thought to be paved with gold.

golem n. Hebrew (GO-lum)   A creature of Jewish medieval folklore, a golem is a figure made into the form of a human and given life; the creature is then slave to its master's commands. The most famous golem was the one created from a mound of clay by Rabbi Judah Loew of Prague in the 17th century to protect Jews from **anti-Semitism.**

gonif n. Yiddish (GAH-niff)   Literally, "thief." A clever but shady character, someone who might cheat you but without criminal or evil intent. "He wanted $6,000 for that old car. He told me it was 'gently used' by an old lady. What a gonif!"

gornisht n. Yiddish (GORE-nisht)   Nothing, zilch, zero. Can be used to describe someone who has nothing—no money, no personality, etc. *Er hot gornisht*—"He has nothing"—is similar in meaning to the English phrase, "He's so poor he doesn't have two sticks to rub together."

Gotenyu int. Yiddish (GAWT-en-you)   An exclamation meaning "Oh dear God." *Gotenyu* is used when other words fail to describe one's feelings; it can describe great joy or despair. "My daughter just got married. Was I thrilled? *Gotenyu!*"

gotkes n. Yiddish (GOT-kiss)   Long johns, winter underwear. "Put on your *gotkes*, and then we'll go out and play in the snow."

goy n. Hebrew (GOY); pl. **goyim** (GOY-eem)   Common biblical word meaning "nation" or "people." Today, it is most often used among Jews to refer to someone who is not a Jew. Unlike **"gentile,"** it is often used disparagingly.

goyish adj. Yiddish (GOY-ish)   In the manner or style of a non-Jewish person; like a **goy.** Used to describe something that would be unlike or unfamiliar to a Jewish person. "When she dressed her daughter in that plaid skirt and beret, it was cute, but she looked so goyish."

grager n. Yiddish (GROG-er) From the word for "rattle." A small noise-maker that is used during the reading of the *Megillat Esther* on **Purim.** It is traditional for congregants to stomp their feet, shake their *gragers,* and make noise to drown out **Haman**'s name every time it is mentioned. In **synagogues,** *gragers* are often distributed as families come in for the reading of the *Megillah.* Most *gragers* are metal cases that spin on a ratchet mounted to a handle. Some children make their own out of beans or rice in a can. Other *gragers* are elaborate works of **Judaica.**

gribenes n. Yiddish (GRIH-bin-ess) The fatty skin of a chicken or goose that is cooked with onions, chicken or goose fat **(shmaltz),** and salt until it is browned and crispy. Also called cracklings. Before today's concern over cholesterol, *gribenes* was eaten as a snack or mixed in with *kasha varnishkes,* noodle **kugel,** mashed potatoes, or chicken livers.

grogger See *grager.*

gut Shabbos int. Yiddish (GUHT SHA-bos) Literally, "Good Sabbath." Sabbath greeting commonly said after the candles are lit or at the end of services. May also be said as "Good Shabbos." *Shabbos* is the old-fashioned **Ashkenazic** pronunciation of **Shabbat.**

Habad See **Lubavitch movement** (Chabad).

hadas n. Hebrew (hah-DASS) A branch of a myrtle bush that is part of the *lulav* used on **Sukkot.** See *arba minim.*

Hadassah n. Hebrew (hah-DAS-sah) **1.** Founded in 1912 by Jewish scholar and activist **Henrietta Szold,** Hadassah is a women's charitable organization. In the **State of Israel,** it initiates and supports a variety of health care, education, and **Zionist** youth programs, including some of the biggest hospitals and medical research and education facilities in the nation. Hadassah's American chapters support these programs. **2.** The Hebrew name for **Esther.**

Had Gadya n. Aramaic (HOD GOD-yah) Literally, "one little goat." A popular **Pesach** song sung at the end of the **seder** and found in almost every **haggadah.** The pattern of the song is similar to those in the children's rhyme "There Was an Old Lady Who Swallowed a Fly."

haftarah n. Hebrew (hoff-TOE-rah) Literally, "conclusion." A reading from the biblical book of **Nevi'im (Prophets)** that is recited in **synagogue** immediately following the reading of the **Torah.** The passage, which consists of a chapter or two, is relevant to that week's Torah portion. Unlike the Torah, the haftarah is usually read from a bound book that contains Hebrew vowels. It is an honor to read the haftarah. A child becoming a **Bar** or **Bat Mitzvah** will usually read both a Torah and a haftarah portion.

Haganah n. Hebrew (hah-gah-NAH) Founded in 1920, the Haganah was the army of volunteers and civilians formed to protect the lives of Jews living in **Palestine** before it was the **State of Israel.** In 1948, with the establishment of Israel, the Haganah became the national army. Today it is known as the **Israel Defense Forces (IDF)** or by the Hebrew acronym **TZAHAL.**

Hagar (HAY-gar) The mother of **Ishmael.** Egyptian handmaiden to **Sarah,** Hagar conceived Ishmael with **Abraham.**

hagbah   n. Hebrew (HAHG-bah)   Literally "lifting." The ceremony of lifting the **Torah** aloft after it has been read and before it is dressed (*gelilah*). Though Torah scrolls are delicate and fragile, they are often quite heavy; a Torah can weigh 30 to 40 pounds. It's considered a job well done if the person receiving the *aliyah* of *hagbah* can hold the two Torah poles apart so the congregants can see several columns of writing on the parchment. Congregants usually say a hearty *"yasher koach"* when the *aliyah* is complete.

haggadah   n. Hebrew (hah-GAH-dah);   pl. **haggadot** (hah-gah-DOTE) Literally, "telling." The small book of liturgy, prayers, songs, and rituals used at a **Pesach seder.** The haggadah recounts the story of the **Exodus** from Egypt, explains the meaning of the **seder plate,** answers the **Four Questions,** and illustrates the other traditional rituals included in the seder. This fulfills the injunction, mentioned in the haggadah, to tell the Passover story from generation to generation. Every movement of Judaism has at least one version of the haggadah. There are many versions of the text, songs, and rituals; new *haggadot* are printed every year. Some focus on the role women played; others include songs and explanations appropriate for children. The haggadah, the most widely reprinted book in Jewish history, was first printed in Spain in about 1482.

Hagiographa   n. Greek (hah-gee-AH-grah-fah)   Literally, "holy writings." Another name for the third of the three sections that comprise the **TANAKH**, along with **Torah** and **Nevi'im.** It is known in English as **Writings** and in Hebrew as **Kethuvim.**

hag sameach   int. Hebrew (HAG sah-MAY-ach)   Literally, "Happy Holiday." The traditional, all-purpose greeting exchanged on almost any Jewish holiday.

hai   See *chai.*

Haifa   n. Hebrew (HIGH-fah)   **Israel**'s third largest city, Haifa is a major industrial and commercial port located on the Mediterranean Sea at the foot and on the slopes of Mount Carmel. Israel's world-renowned scientific research institute, the Technion, and the Baha'i Shrine and Gardens are located in Haifa.

haimish   adj. Yiddish (HAY-mish)   Unpretentious, homey; from the German word for "home." *Haimish* implies someone or something that is informal and friendly and that puts you at ease. "You'd think their daughter's Bat Mitzvah would have been formal and fancy, but it was really *haimish.*"

ha-Kadosh Baruch Hu   n. Hebrew (hah-kah-DOASH bar-RUKH HOO) Literally, "the Holy One Blessed Be He." Another way of referring to God. This phrase is used most often in prayers.

hakafah n. Hebrew (hah-kah-FAH); pl. **hakafot** (hah-kah-FOTE)   From the Hebrew word for "circle." The parade of persons carrying **Torah** scrolls around the **synagogue** on **Simchat Torah.** During the joyous parade, congregants may join in the march and dance, sing, or clap hands. Others gather on the aisles to see and touch the Torah scrolls as they pass by. Traditionally, there are seven *hakafot*. The parade, which goes around the perimeters of the sanctuary "circling" the congregation, is symbolic of the Torah's belonging to the entire community.

hakham n. Hebrew (huck-HUM) Yiddish (HUCK-hum)   Literally "wise." **1.** In ancient times, a title used for Jewish scholars who had not received their rabbinical ordination. **2.** In **Sephardic** communities, the title given to the local **rabbi. 3.** A title of respect for a wise person or a sage. **4.** In Yiddish, it is used ironically to mean a smart aleck or a wise guy.

hakhnasat kallah n. Hebrew (hakh-nah-SAHT kah-LAH)   A gathering of the bride and certain female guests prior to the wedding ceremony. *Hakhnasat kallah,* also known as attending the bride, may be observed at traditional weddings. Friends will greet and bless the bride, who is seated in a special chair, and may sing and dance around her. At the same time, the groom and his guests will be gathered for the *chossen's tish.*

hakhnasat orchim n. Hebrew (hakh-nah-SAHT or-KHEEM)   Literally, "welcoming guests." Hospitality. The **mitzvah** of *hakhnasat orchim* embodies the larger principle that Jews should make people feel welcome in the Jewish community. A couple's introducing themselves to someone they don't recognize at **synagogue** services or inviting a college student for **Shabbat** dinner are two examples of this mitzvah. Jews who are traveling and would like to find a local Jewish home in which to spend Shabbat can do so easily because of *hakhnasat orchim.*

halakhah n. Hebrew (hah-lah-KHAH)   Jewish law. The general term for the many rules, prohibitions, and requirements that govern almost every aspect of daily Jewish life, such as how to observe **Shabbat** and what foods to eat. *Halakhah* is the entire body of Jewish law, covering business, religion, agriculture, marriage, etc. These laws are defined in the **Torah** and interpreted in the commentaries of the **Talmud.** *Halakhah* is the opposite of *minhag* (custom or tradition).

halevai int. Yiddish (hah-leh-VAI)   Literally, "would that." An expression meaning "I hope" or "I wish," often said along with a wish, desire, or blessing to ward off the evil eye. "*Halevai,* she should make me a grandmother before I die."

hallah See **challah.**

Hallel   n. Hebrew (HAH-lail)   Joyous psalms of praise. Special prayers of thanks expressing gratitude to God, which are recited in synagogue on **Rosh Hodesh** (the beginning of the month on the Jewish calendar) and on the holidays of **Sukkot, Pesach, Shavuot, Hanukkah, Rosh Hashanah** and at home during the **Pesach seder.**

halutz   n. Hebrew (hah-LOOTS); pl. **halutzim** (hah-loo-TSEEM)   A pioneer, specifically an early settler to **Palestine** (before 1948). These ardent **Zionists,** many of whom left professional careers in Europe, founded and joined **kibbutzim,** drained swamps, planted trees, and cultivated the desert to develop the future **State of Israel.**

Haman   (HEY-man)   An adviser to **King Ahasuerus** of ancient Persia, Haman was the bad guy in the story of **Purim.** According to *Megillat Esther,* Haman hatched a plot to kill the Jews of Persia. But his plot was found out and stopped by Queen **Esther.**   During Purim services, it is traditional to make noise—for example, by stomping one's feet or twirling *gragers*—whenever Haman's name is mentioned. Tradition says this is done so that his evil name is never heard again and because it is the Jews' responsibility to "make noise," to speak up when they see evil.

hamantashen   n. Yiddish (HUH-min-TOSH-in)   Literally, "Haman's hats." Small, triangular-shaped cookies filled with fruit or jam that are eaten on **Purim.** It is traditional to give hamantashen to family and friends, often as part of a *shalach manot* gift basket. Common fillings for hamantashen include *lekvar* (prune), *mun* (poppy seed), cherry, and apricot.

hametz   n. Hebrew (hah-MAYTS)   Literally, "leaven." The general term used to describe all food and beverages, including wine, that are forbidden on **Pesach.** Specifically, this includes any regular bread or bakery product as well as any leavened or fermented food made with one of five prohibited grains: wheat, corn, barley, rye, or oats. Like most areas of Jewish observance, the definition of what is considered *hametz* depends on how religious a person is, where he or she lives, and the family's traditions. For example, **Sephardic** Jews do not consider legumes and rice, staples of their Mediterranean diet, *hametzdik,* while most **Ashkenazic** Jews do not eat these items. Very traditional Jews forbid consumption of any manufactured food product during Pesach that does not specifically have a **"kosher for Passover"** stamp on it, even foods like milk and cheese. Many Jews symbolically "sell" their *hametzdik* items to a non-Jewish person. Others donate *hametzdik* foods to charity, like a food bank, as Pesach *tzedakah.*

For more liberal Jews, it may be enough to simply put away the bread, cookies, cold cereal, and other products made with flour for the week of Pesach. They may be put in a sealed closet or basement before the ceremony of **bedikat hametz.**

hametzdik   adj. Hebrew (hah-MAYTS-dick)   Anything that can't be eaten on **Pesach;** any food made with prohibited ingredients like flour or leaven. For example: "Those cookies look too good to be made with **matzah meal.** They must be *hametzdik.*"

Hamishah Asar b'Shevat   n. Hebrew (hah-mee-SHAH ah-SAR buh-sheh-VAHT)   The old-fashioned name for **Tu b'Shevat.**

ha-Motzi   n. Hebrew (hah-MOE-tsee)   The most well known and commonly recited **bracha,** or blessing, it is recited over bread before a meal is eaten. Often, at a holiday or *simcha* meal, someone is given the honor of saying *ha-Motzi* over the **challah.** The person so honored will stand at the front of the room or at the head of the table; guests can join in or say **"amen"** at the end. The bread is then cut and pieces are distributed to all. The translation of *ha-Motzi* is "Blessed are you, *Adonai* our God, Ruler of the Universe, who brings forth bread from the earth." It is sometimes referred to simply as "the *Motzi.*"

hamsa   n. Arabic (HAHM-sah)   From the word "five," an amulet or good luck charm shaped like a hand. Popular in Middle Eastern countries, including Iran, Syria, and **Israel,** the *hamsa* is thought to symbolize the protective "hand of God" which keeps the wearer safe from the evil eye.

Hanukkah   n. Hebrew (HAH-noo-kah)   Literally, "dedication." Beginning on the 25th of **Kislev,** which corresponds to late November or sometime in December, Hanukkah is a joyous holiday that celebrates the victory of the **Maccabees** over the Syrians and the rededication of the **Second Temple** in **Jerusalem** in ancient times. Hanukkah is often called the Festival of Lights. The Syrian king, **Antiochus,** who ruled ancient **Israel** from 175 to 163 B.C.E., wanted to wipe out Judaism and convert the population to his Greek ways. Citizens were forced to speak Greek and worship Greek gods. It was forbidden to practice Judaism, celebrate Jewish holidays, or study **Torah.** A Jew named Mattathias, and his son Judah, known as **Judah Maccabee,** led a revolt against the Syrian army. Called Maccabees, the revolutionaries fought for three years against the much stronger Syrian army and finally prevailed. Jerusalem was liberated and the Temple returned to Jewish control. But when the Jews entered the Temple, they found that it had been desecrated with statues of Greek gods and discovered that there was only enough pure oil to rekindle the eternal flame, the **ner tamid,** for one day. Miraculously, the oil lasted for eight days, long enough to purify new oil and rededicate the Temple.

Today, Hanukkah is celebrated for eight days. Each night another candle is lit and placed in a special eight-branched candelabra called a **menorah** or *hanukkiah.* A *shamash* candle is lit first and used to kindle the others. Families often place their menorahs in a window or other visible spot to bear witness to the miracle. Special blessings are said to thank God for the wondrous events and religious freedom that Hanukkah recalls. Families exchange gifts; play **dreidel,** a traditional game that uses a spinning top; and give Hanukkah **gelt** to children. It is also traditional to eat foods cooked in oil, like **latkes** (potato pancakes) or *sufganiyot* (Israeli jelly donuts), to remember the miracle of the oil. Also spelled Hanukah, Hannukkah, and Chanukah.

hanukkat ha-bayit   n. Hebrew (hah-noo-KAHT hah-BYE-eet)   Literally, "dedication of the home." The ceremony of affixing a **mezuzah** to the doorpost of a new home while reciting two special prayers. It is customary to do this within 30 days of moving in.

hanukkiah   n. Hebrew (hah-noo-kee-AH); pl. **hanukkiyot** (hah-noo-kee-OTE)   The modern Israeli word for a **Hanukkah menorah,** the eight-branched candelabra used to hold lighted candles on Hanukkah. Also spelled *chanukiah.*

haredim   n. Hebrew (ha-RAY-dim)   Literally, "those who tremble in fear of God." The name Israelis use for the extremely pious **ultra-Orthodox** Jews. The **Hasidim,** who separate themselves from the secular world and shun modern life, are the most visible of these sects. *Haredim* are distinguished by their old-fashioned dress, which includes black hats and coats, untrimmed beards, and *payot. Haredi* women dress modestly and, if married, keep their heads covered.

haroset   n. Hebrew (hah-ROE-set)   The mixture of apples, sweet red wine, and chopped nuts that is placed on the **seder plate** at **Pesach.** *Haroset* is symbolic of the mortar and bricks the ancient Israelites used to build the pyramids when they were slaves in Egypt. Specific recipes for *haroset* differ according to geography: **Ashkenazic** Jews usually use almonds or walnuts, cinnamon, and apples. A **Sephardic** family recipe might include pistachio nuts, chopped figs, cardamom, honey, and cloves. At the seder, *haroset* is first tasted on a small piece of **matzah.** Later, it is eaten with *maror.*

Harvest Festival   See **Shavuot** and **Sukkot.**

ha-Shem   n. Hebrew (hah-SHEM)   Literally, "the name." A euphemism for God, used by traditional Jews, usually in conversation. This comes from the belief that the name of God should only be said in prayer and with reverence, so in conversation and casual writings another name is often used. See *Adonai* and *Adoshem.*

Hasidism n. Hebrew (HAH-see-dizm) A mystical religious movement founded in Poland by the 18th-century teacher Israel ben Eliezer, also known as the **Baal Shem Tov.** His teachings, based on **Kabbalah,** promoted the holiness of the common man and the importance of attachment to God and **Torah.** He stressed the role of joy in worship and encouraged feasts. Hasidim, counted among the **ultra-Orthodox**, are differentiated from **modern Orthodox** Jews by their devotion to a leader, called a **tzadik** or **rebbe,** and their exuberant worship, which includes dancing, singing, and feasting. They also believe in dressing much as their ancestors did: men in black fur hats and long black coats; women in long sleeves and long skirts, and with their heads covered. There are numerous Hasidic groups that follow different charismatic leaders and identify themselves by their particular style of dress, with the **Lubavitch movement** being among the better-known sects. n. **Hasid;** pl. **Hasidim.** Literally, "pious one." Follower of Hasidism.

Haskalah n. Hebrew (hah-skah-LAH) The Jewish Enlightenment. A movement among Eastern and Central European Jews in the 18th and 19th centuries to update Judaism and bring some of its precepts into the "modern world." It was begun in Germany by Moses Mendelssohn. His followers, known as *maskilim,* found much of Judaism to be old-fashioned and were in favor of Jews' experiencing what secular culture had to offer. They were opposed to having Jewish children attend **yeshivot** and study only Jewish texts. There was also a stress on modern dress. Another focus was to make services less "foreign"; the eventual result of this was the rise of the **Reform movement,** which originated in Germany. One of Mendelssohn's major feats, for example, was the translation of the **Bible** into German. The *maskilim* were opposed by the **Orthodox,** who did not wish to change or modernize Judaism.

Hasmoneans n. Hebrew (has-muh-KNEE-ins) Another name for the descendants of Hashmon, a Jewish dynasty that included the **Maccabees.** The Hasmoneans ruled ancient Israel from 142 to 63 B.C.E. See Maccabees.

hatafat dam brit n. Hebrew (hah-tah-FAHT dahm BREET) The ritual drawing of a single drop of blood from the penis, performed by a *mohel,* as part of the conversion ritual. The **Orthodox, Conservative,** and **Reconstructionist movements** require a male convert to be circumcised in a *brit milah* ceremony. If he was already circumcised at birth, he undergoes *hatafat dam brit* as a symbol of his acceptance of Judaism. The ritual is also used for male infants who are born to a non-Jewish woman or adopted and already circumcised, to show they have been converted to Judaism according to *halakhah.*

hatan n. Hebrew (hah-TAHN) The bridegroom.

Hatikvah   n. Hebrew (hah-TICK-vah)   Literally, "the hope." The national anthem of the **State of Israel**. Before 1948, "Hatikvah" was a popular song in the **Zionist** movement.

Havah Nagilah   n. Hebrew (HAH-vah nuh-GEEL-ah)   Literally, "let's rejoice." Traditional Jewish melody, often played at *simchot* (**Bar** and **Bat Mitzvah** celebrations and weddings). Guests often dance the **hora,** a circle dance, to the tune.

Havdalah   n. Hebrew (hav-DOLL-ah)   Literally, "separation." The ceremony that marks the end of **Shabbat** on Saturday evening, separating Shabbat from the remaining days of the week. Traditionally, *Havdalah* is observed when three stars appear in the sky. The ceremony, usually celebrated at home with family, has three main components: a cup of wine; a tall, braided candle with several wicks; and a box filled with fragrant spices *(besamim).* The person performing *Havdalah* lights the candle, says *Kiddush,* sips the wine, and extinguishes the candle in the wine. It is traditional to pass around the **spice box,** a fragrant reminder of Shabbat that will stay with the family through the coming week. Another *Havdalah* tradition says that one should worship God with all five senses. Participating in *Havdalah* by tasting the wine, seeing the candle flame, touching the candle, smelling the spices, and hearing the prayers and songs accomplishes this. Legend says that the Prophet **Elijah** will bring peace to the world, so one traditional *Havdalah* song is **"Eliyahu Hanavi."** A **synagogue** *Havdalah* service is another time when a **Bar** or **Bat Mitzvah** can be celebrated.

haver   n. Hebrew (hah-VAIR)   pl. **haverim** (hah-vay-REEM)   Literally, "member." **1.** Friend, comrade. **2.** In ancient Israel, the term for a Jew who observed the strict laws of ritual purity and tithing. The opposite of *am ha-eretz.*

havurah   n. Hebrew (hah-voo-RAH); pl. **havurot** (hah-voo-ROTE)   A Jewish fellowship group that meets informally for discussion, worship, and Jewish celebrations. Some *havurot* offer a creative, free-thinking interpretation of prayers and holiday rituals, while others are strictly traditional. The earliest groups included **Hasidic** practices, such as group dances, chanting, and meditation, in their worship services. *Havurot* were originally a counterculture movement of Jews who were not affiliated with a **synagogue,** although it is now common for synagogues to sponsor *havurot* for congregants with particular interests, such as equal participation for women or a **Zionist** perspective. Some *havurot* get together every **Shabbat,** others only on holidays or for festive meals.

hazeret   n. Hebrew (hah-zer-ET)   A bitter vegetable, often romaine lettuce, sometimes placed on the **seder plate** during the holiday meal for **Pesach**. *Hazaret* is sometimes used in addition to *maror*, bitter herbs. During the **seder,**

hazeret may be added, along with **maror**, to the **Hillel sandwich.** Most seder plates have a spot for *hazeret.*

hazzan   n. Hebrew (HAH-zin)   The Hebrew word for **cantor.** Originally, the *hazzan* was the **synagogue** caretaker, given the job of announcing the times for prayer and **Shabbat** observance from the roof. He also chanted the prayers at services.

Hebrew   n. English   **1.** The scholarly and holy language of the Jews, used in prayer. It is the language of the **TANAKH.** A **Semitic** language, Hebrew was spoken by the ancient **Israelites** until the 2nd century B.C.E., when **Aramaic** took its place as the everyday language. It was not spoken again in the vernacular until modern times, when the **State of Israel** adopted Hebrew as its national language. **2.** The term for Israelites and Judeans before the Babylonian exile in 586 B.C.E. From the Hebrew root *ivri*, perhaps meaning "one from the other side (of the Jordan River)."

Hebrew Bible   n. English The term non-Jews sometimes use when referring to the **Old Testament,** which Jews commonly call the **TANAKH.**

Hebrew Immigrant Aid Society   See **HIAS.**

Hebrew school   n. English   The common name for a **synagogue**-based religious school, usually attended outside of regular public school hours—after school and on Sundays. The curriculum includes prayers, holiday rituals, Jewish values, and the **Hebrew** language. Children usually begin Hebrew school in kindergarten or first grade and continue through **Bar** or **Bat Mitzvah** and on to **Confirmation.**

heder   n. Hebrew (HAY-der)   Literally, "room." Historically, the small elementary school where Jewish boys met to study **Talmud** and prepare for the **yeshivah.** In the **shtetl,** these were one-room schoolhouses. The *heder* was the first step in Jewish education. Today, the term may be used for a traditional **synagogue**-based **Hebrew school.**

heksher   n. Hebrew (HECK-sure)   An official seal of approval of **kashrut** on food that is issued by a *mashgiach*. The most common *heksher* on manufactured foods is the letter **"U"** in a circle, the trademark of the **Union of Orthodox Jewish Congregations.** It can also be the letter **"K"** or the word **"kosher."** Around **Pesach,** foods that are *pesachdik* and contain no leaven are marked with a special *heksher* that says **"kosher for Passover."** A *heksher* can also be a certificate, such as those posted in restaurants, to assure diners that the food served therein is kosher.

helzel n. Yiddish (HELL-zuhl) Literally "neck." An old-fashioned recipe in which the neck skin of a goose or chicken is filled with stuffing (usually made of **matzah meal** or bread crumbs, onion, **shmaltz,** and eggs), and then sewn together at the ends. Helzel is boiled and then roasted.

Herzl, Theodor (1860–1904) A Hungarian Jew acknowledged as the founder of modern **Zionism.** When Herzl was a newspaper correspondent, he covered the trial of Captain Alfred Dreyfus, a French Jew accused of treason who many believed to be the victim of **anti-Semitism.** Herzl became convinced that the establishment of a Jewish homeland was the only solution to European anti-Semitism. In his writings, he described in detail his vision for a Jewish state; he is remembered for his optimistic quote: "If you will it, it is no dream." He campaigned tirelessly on behalf of Zionism, meeting with kings, government leaders, and the pope. Herzl organized the first World Zionist Organization in 1897 and presided over five Zionist Congresses before his death. After the creation of the **State of Israel** in 1948, Herzl's remains were brought to the new Jewish state. His imposing black granite tomb sits on Mount Herzl in **Jerusalem.**

Heshvan n. Hebrew (HESH-vahn) The eighth month in the **Jewish calendar,** Heshvan falls in October or November.

hevrah kadishah n. Hebrew (HEV-rah kah-DEE-shah) Literally, "holy society." The society of laypeople who prepare a deceased body for burial according to Jewish law. In ancient times, members of the *hevrah kadishah* were honored volunteers. Although these societies still exist and function in some Jewish communities, it is more likely that the preparation and purification of the body *(tohorah)* will be done by an employee of a Jewish funeral home.

heychal n. from the Portuguese (heh-KHALL) The **Sephardic** term for the **ark** where **Torah scrolls** are kept in the **synagogue.** The *heychal* is most commonly located at the center of the eastern wall of the synagogue.

HIAS n. English (HIGH-iss) An abbreviation for the Hebrew Immigrant Aid Society. A non-profit Jewish organization dedicated to the rescue, protection, and movement of refugees and émigrés. HIAS offers assistance in matters of citizenship, government benefits, job training, navigating bureaucracy, and other issues that concern immigrants to the United States. HIAS worked extensively, and still does, to reunite family members who lost each other during the **Holocaust.**

hiddur mitzvah adj. Hebrew (hee-DOOR mits-VAH) Literally, "beautifying the **mitzvah**." The tradition of putting extra time, style, or resources into a mitzvah so that it is performed as beautifully as possible. *Hiddur mitzvah* is often given as the reason for traditions such as creating handcrafted **Judaica** or decorating the *bimah* with flowers on holidays. It is why Jews recite *Kiddush* over a fancy goblet instead of a paper cup.

High Holidays   n. English   A contraction of the phrase "High Holy Days."

High Holy Days   n. English   The holidays of **Rosh Hashanah** and **Yom Kippur,** and the days in between. Together these make up the solemn period of repentance, prayer, and redemption, known as the **Days of Awe,** that are the most important dates on the **Jewish calendar.**

Hillel   (HIL-lel)   Perhaps the best-known Jewish scholar and sage of all time, Hillel was a Palestinian **rabbi,** interpreter of biblical law, and president of the **Sanhedrin** who lived from about 60 to 9 B.C.E. He was said to possess a love of both learning and his fellow man. His commentaries on **Torah** law, bits of wisdom and advice, and interpretations of ethical dilemmas are still quoted today by rabbis and scholars 2,000 years after he wrote them. Scholars believe that Hillel helped write the contents of the **Passover haggadah** in the 1st century B.C.E. Many of his sayings and quotations are contained in *Pirke Avot.* Hillel wrote the famous saying, part of which later became known as the Golden Rule: "What is hateful to you, do not do to your neighbor. All the rest is commentary. Go and study."

Hillel sandwich   n. English   A sandwich, made by putting *maror* between two pieces of **matzah,** which is eaten during the **seder** on **Pesach.** The sandwich is named for Hillel, the 1st century sage and rabbi who, unlike other rabbis, ate the holiday's three symbolic foods together: matzah, *maror,* and the Paschal lamb that was sacrificed at the **Temple** on the eve of Passover. Today at the seder, Jews eat a Hillel sandwich—minus the lamb, but sometimes with haroset. Some say the Hillel sandwich combines the bitterness of slavery *(maror)* with the bread of freedom (matzah), showing that even in difficult times, God is always with us.

Hillel: The Foundation for Jewish Campus Life   n. English   Founded in 1923, Hillel sponsors a network of Jewish student organizations on college campuses around the world. The foundation provides opportunities for students to explore and celebrate their Jewish identity through social events, informal education, religious services, community service, and political action. Some Hillel organizations provide kosher meal plans. Hillel embraces all movements of Judaism. Any student may participate; no membership is required.

hillul ha-Shem   n. Hebrew (hee-LOOL hah-SHEM)   Literally, "profaning of God's name." An action that brings disgrace to God's name. In the Jewish community, an individual's transgression brings disgrace not only to that person but to the entire Jewish community and to Judaism. *Hillul ha-Shem* is the opposite of **kiddush ha–Shem.**

hiloni   n. Hebrew (hee-loe-NEE)   The word used by Israelis for secular Jews who are not affiliated with any branch of Judaism. Also called *lo* **dati.**

Hineni   n. Hebrew (hee-NI-nee)   Literally, "here I am." A prayer, sung by the **cantor** on **Rosh Hashanah,** which describes the congregations' humility before God. The words of the prayer call out to God, "Here I am."

hod   n. Hebrew (HOED)   Literally "majesty." The eighth of the 10 *sefirot,* or aspects of God's creative nature. According to **kabbalistic** teachings, *hod* represents devotion and humility and the lower channel through which the **Ein Sof**'s judgment comes down to the world. It is one of three *sefirot,* along with **netzach** and **yesod,** in the category of nature or the functional world. Each *sefirah* is associated with a part of the body; *hod* corresponds with the left leg.

hok a tchynick   int. Yiddish (HOCK A CHYE-nick)   Literally, "striking a teakettle." This expression refers to making meaningless noise, like chatter, or nagging. "Stop *hocking my tchynick*" is similar to the expression "don't talk my ear off."

hokhmah   n. Hebrew (HOOK-mah)   Literally "wisdom." **1.** The second of the 10 *sefirot,* or aspects of God's creative nature. According to **kabbalistic** teachings, *hokhmah* represents vision and the contemplative aspect the **Ein Sof.** It is one of three *sefirot,* along with **keter** and **binah,** in the category of the intellect. Each *sefirah* is associated with a part of the body; *hokhmah* corresponds to the eyes. **2.** The catch or trick needed to figure out a puzzle or problem.

hol ha–moed   n. Hebrew (HOLE hah-MOE-ed)   The intermediate days of the weeklong holidays of **Pesach** and **Sukkot.** These middle days are less restrictive, though all the rituals, like not eating *hametz* on Pesach, are still observed. The one or two days at the beginning and end of both Pesach and Sukkot are considered "more important" days of the holiday.

Holocaust   n. English   Genocide. Although holocausts have occurred throughout history, today the word has come to refer specifically to the systematic elimination of European Jewry from 1933 to 1945 by the Nazi Third Reich. During these years, Jews were first excluded from community life, then forced to live in **ghettos,** and later transported to **concentration camps** where they were killed. Six million Jews were slaughtered by the Nazis during World War II; entire Jewish communities were wiped out. The Holocaust is called *Shoah* in Hebrew. In the **State of Israel** and throughout the **Diaspora,** the Holocaust is commemorated on an annual memorial day, **Yom ha-Shoah,** on the 27th of **Nisan.**

Holy Ark   See **ark.**

Holy Land   n. English   The ancient land on the east coast of the Mediterranean Sea, once also known as **Canaan** and, later, **Palestine.** It is called the "Holy Land," because it is the site for many biblical stories, such as Abraham's sacrifice of Isaac and Jacob's dream of a ladder to heaven, as well as New Testament stories such as the miracle of the loaves and fishes. Today, the term Holy Land is generally used by Christians; Jews call it the **State of Israel.**

Holy of Holies   n. English   The inner sanctum in the ancient **Temple,** where the **Ark of the Covenant**—the chest containing the **Ten Commandments**—was kept. The Holy of Holies was entered only once a year, by the high priest on **Yom Kippur.**

hora   n. Hebrew (HOE-rah)   A traditional Romanian circle dance. This folk dance is the national dance of the **State of Israel.** The hora is a favorite dance at Jewish weddings and at **Bar** and **Bat Mitzvah** receptions. It is often danced to the song **"Havah Nagilah."**

hoshanah   n. Aramaic (hoe-shah-NAH)   pl.   **hoshanot** (hoe-shah-NOTE) Prayers recited on **Sukkot** while circling the **synagogue** and waving the *lulav.* The prayers are said for the land of Israel, for fertility and rain. Each begins with the word "*hoshanah*," which means, "Save, I pray."

Hoshanah Rabbah   n. Hebrew (hoe-SHAH-nah RAH-bah)   The seventh day of **Sukkot,** when it is traditional for worshipers to parade around the sanctuary carrying the *lulav* and *etrog* and to engage in all-night study of Jewish texts.

hoshen   n. Hebrew (HO-shen)   The breastplate, usually made of silver, that beautifies the **Torah.** Modern breastplates are reminiscent of the one worn by the High Priest in biblical times, which had 12 precious stones engraved with the names of the 12 **tribes of Israel.** The *hoshen* is attached to a chain and draped over the *atzei chayim* after the scrolls have been "dressed." Usually a small box is soldered to the plate; it contains silver nameplates for each holiday and special **Shabbatot.**

Humanistic Judaism   n. English   A nontheistic philosophy that combines the celebration of Jewish identity and culture with humanistic values. The movement was founded in Detroit in 1963 by Rabbi Sherwin Wine. Adherents reject dependence on a supernatural diety and focus instead on self-determination and a universal morality not focused on a particular religious ideology. The movement has about 30,000 members with congregations (often called communities) around the world, many under the umbrella of the Society for Humanistic Judaism. These communities celebrate Jewish holidays and life cycle events with ceremonies that draw upon traditional literature.

Humash   n. Hebrew (hoo-MAHSH); pl. **Humashim**   (hoo-mah-SHEEM) Derived from *hamesh*, the Hebrew word for "five." A bound book containing the **Five Books of Moses** that is used in **synagogue** or for study. A *Humash* contains the weekly **Torah** portions in Hebrew, along with commentaries and explanations of the portions in English. It also contains the weekly **haftarah** portions in Hebrew and English. In synagogue, congregants use it to follow the Torah readings. See **Pentateuch.**

hummus   n. Arabic (HUM-iss)   A paste of ground-up chickpeas that is blended with oil and spices to make a creamy dip. Hummus is often eaten with **tahini** (ground sesame seeds) or as a dip with vegetables or pita bread. Hummus and **falafel** in pita bread is a popular Israeli sandwich.

huppah   n. Hebrew (HUH-pah)   The Jewish wedding canopy; that is, the cloth under which the Jewish wedding ceremony is conducted. The *huppah* can be anything from a **tallit** stretched over the bridal party to a personalized, embroidered cloth of silk, satin, or velvet. It might be fashioned from flowers or made to resemble a gazebo. The *huppah* is said to variously symbolize God's presence, the couple's new home, the marriage wreath worn by the bride and groom in **talmudic** times, and the ancient tent life in **Israel.** Sometimes friends are given the honor of holding the four support poles.

hutzpah   See **chutzpah.**

IDF   The English acronym for the **Israel Defense Forces,** the military units of the **State of Israel.** The Hebrew acronym is **TZAHAL.**

Inquisition, Spanish   n. English   An ecclesiastical court of the Catholic Church, established in Spain in the late 15th century, which investigated and prosecuted heretics. In 1483, King Ferdinand II and Queen Isabella appointed Tomas de Torquemada as Grand Inquisitor to oversee trial and punishment of **Conversos,** the name for Jews and Muslims who claimed to have converted to Catholicism but continued to practice their true religions in secret. In total, more than 13,000 Conversos were tried—and many were sentenced to imprisonment or death—from 1480 to 1492. The Inquisition culminated in the expulsion of all of the Jews from Spain in 1492.

intermarriage   n. English   The word Jews use for a marriage between a Jew and a non-Jew. **Orthodox** and **Conservative rabbis** will not officiate at an intermarriage ceremony, although some more liberal rabbis will do so. In modern times, as more and more Jews are intermarrying, some movements of Judaism are striving to welcome and include intermarried families by sponsoring education programs, family holiday celebrations, and other opportunities for their family to participate in Jewish life. Sometimes called a "mixed marriage."

intifada   n. Arabic (in-tee-FAH-dah)   An organized campaign of violence and unrest against the Israeli government and its citizens by **Palestinian** Arabs and others in Israel. Acts of violence and terrorism committed in the name of the *intifada* include stone throwing, street demonstrations, and suicide bombings and are often directed at civilian targets such as buses, markets, or restaurants. Participants in *intifada* violence are agitating for the formation of a new Arab Palestinian state within the borders of Israel, the withdrawal of Israel from some **occupied territories,** and its most radical members work toward the destruction of the State of Israel.

Isaac   The second of the three **patriarchs** of the Jewish people; son of **Abraham** and **Sarah;** half-brother of **Ishmael.** Isaac was born when his mother was 90. When he was a young man, his father was ready to sacrifice Isaac to show obedience to God, but God sent an angel to intervene and Isaac was saved. Isaac married **Rebecca** and fathered twin sons, **Esau** and **Jacob.** See *Akedah.*

Ishmael   (ISH-mah-ail)   Son of **Abraham** and **Hagar;** the **patriarch** of the Muslim people.

Israel   n. English   **1.** The modern nation, also called the **State of Israel,** or *Medinat Yisra'el* in Hebrew. It was established in what was **Palestine** in May 1948. Israel is located in southwest Asia on the Mediterranean Sea and borders Egypt, Lebanon, and Jordan. Its capital is **Jerusalem.** Jewish ties to the Land of Israel go back 4,000 years, when tradition holds that God told **Abraham** to go there and promised him and his descendants that land. The creation of the modern State of Israel was the culmination of the **Zionist** dream for a Jewish homeland.   **2.** In ancient times, the northern kingdom of the Jews, home to 10 of the 12 **tribes of Israel.** It was part of the kingdom united by **David** and held by **Solomon.** Israel broke off from Judah, which was home to the remaining two tribes.   **3.** The new name given to **Jacob** after he wrestled the angel (in the Book of **Genesis**).

Israel Defense Forces (IDF)   n. English   Established in 1948 to protect **Israel,** the **IDF** includes the air force, infantry, tank corps, navy, intelligence, and civil defense units. The IDF has three main components: officers, a mandatory corps of servicemen (ages 18–21) and servicewomen (ages 18–20), and a reserve of citizens who must serve 30 to 60 days a year until age 55. The continued compulsory reserve duty keeps most Israelis in a constant state of readiness and accounts for the IDF's outstanding record. Exemptions from service are granted to married women and **Orthodox** Jews.

Israel Independence Day   See **Yom ha-Atzmaut.**

Israelites   n. English   The ancient term for the Jewish people, thought to be descended from the 12 **tribes of Israel.** In ancient times, these descendants of **Jacob** inhabited the land then known as **Canaan,** which is present-day **Israel.**

Issachar   The ninth son of **Jacob** and the fifth son of **Leah.** Issachar is also the name of one of the 12 **tribes of Israel,** whose members were said to be descended from him. The tribe occupied the west bank of the Jordan River. During the time of King **David,** the tribe was known for its wise men, and its descendants were considered men of learning.

Ivrit   n. Hebrew (ee-VREET)   Literally, "Hebrew." The word for the **Hebrew** language.

Iyar   n. Hebrew (EE-yar)   The second month in the **Jewish calendar,** it falls in April or May.

Jacob   The third of the three **patriarchs** of the Jewish people; the second son of **Isaac** and **Rebecca.** Jacob tricked his twin brother, **Esau,** into handing over Esau's birthright; later, with the help of his mother, he intercepted his father's blessing for Esau. Jacob worked for Laban for seven years in order to marry Rachel, Laban's younger daughter, but on the wedding night, Laban tricked Jacob into marrying **Leah,** his older daughter. Jacob married Rachel one week later and worked for Laban for seven more years as a condition of his father-in-law's approval of the marriage. Jacob had 12 sons with Leah, **Rachel,** Bilhah, and Zilpah, and these sons became the leaders of the 12 **tribes of Israel** (Israel is the name God gave to Jacob when appearing to him a second time).

JAP   n.   English   Acronym for "Jewish American Princess." Derogatory slang for a young Jewish woman who is spoiled or showy with material possessions. The term is considered offensive and insulting.

Jehovah   n.   English   A name for God in modern Christian use. Jehovah is not, and never has been, the Jewish name for God. The word "Jehovah" comes from reading the consonants of the **Tetragrammaton** (*yud, hay, vav, hay*)—the four letters that compose the name of God. Traditionally, God's name is so sacred it is not spoken, so Jews generally use *Adonai, Elohim,* or *ha-Shem* instead.

Jerusalem   n.   English   The capital city of the **State of Israel** since 1950. Since biblical times, Jerusalem has been regarded as a holy city by Jews and later by Christians and then Muslims. King **David** made Jerusalem his capital (hence its nickname, the City of David), and the ancient Jewish **First** and **Second Temples** were built here. The modern city of Jerusalem has grown to encompass many neighborhoods, including the ancient walled section, often called the Old City, as well as outlying suburbs of apartment buildings, universities, museums, and hospitals. As part of the cease-fire in 1949 that ended Israel's **War of Independence,** Jerusalem was partitioned. The Old City, including the **Western Wall,** came under Jordanian control and was closed to Jews. In 1967 during the **Six-Day War,** Israel captured the Old City and reunified Jerusalem, opening the holy sites, churches, and mosques to people of all religions.

Jerusalem Talmud   See **Talmud.**

Jew   n. English   A person whose religion is Judaism. Historically, a scattered group of people who trace their lineage to the ancient **Israelites.** The term came into use after the Babylonian Exile (586 B.C.E.) to refer to those people from **Judea** as well as to the **patriarchs, matriachs,** and descendants of **Jacob** and all converts to their faith. Today, there is much debate among the branches of Judaism as to who is a Jew. Traditionally, a person is Jewish if he or she is born to a Jewish mother or converts according to Jewish law. More liberal branches of Judaism recognize children born to either a Jewish mother or a Jewish father and have less stringent rules about conversion and adoption of children who will be raised in Jewish homes.

Jew by Choice   n. English   The modern, politically correct term for someone who has converted to Judaism. While a pending marriage or childbirth might be an impetus for someone to consider conversion, Judaism stresses that the convert must make the decision for him- or herself. In fact, the ancient **rabbis** advised turning away the prospective convert three times. If he or she came back, then the would-be Jew could study for conversion. Most people convert under the auspices of the Jewish movement in which they feel most comfortable, and study requirements vary. The ceremony differs among the movements, but for all it includes the bestowing of a Hebrew name on the convert and his or her pledge to fulfill the commandments. Conversion rituals in the **Orthodox movement** strictly follow *halakhah* and take place in the presence of a *beit din* (rabbinical court of three). The ceremony includes *tevilah* (ritual immersion in a *mikveh*) and, for a male, *brit milah* (ritual **circumcision**). If a boy or man has already been circumcised, *hatafat dam brit* is performed instead. The **Conservative** and **Reconstructionist movements** follow *halakhah* for the most part. The **Reform movement** insists on religious instruction, but does not require *tevilah* or *brit milah*. In **Israel,** only conversions performed by Orthodox rabbis are recognized.

Jewish   adj. English   Pertaining or related to the Jewish people; characteristic of Jews or Judaism.

Jewish calendar   n. English   A lunar calendar, used by Jews, that has 12 months and between 353 and 355 days (except for leap years). The Jewish calendar, which was instituted by Hillel II in the 4th century C.E., counts the years beginning with the supposed creation of the world, calculated to be 3761 B.C.E., as opposed to the Gregorian calendar, which begins counting with the birth of Christ. For example, the 29th of **Nisan** 5760 C.E. on the Jewish calendar corresponds to A.D. May 2, 2000, on the Gregorian calendar.

   Nisan, the first month of the Jewish calendar, is in the spring; **Passover**

begins on the 15th of Nisan. However, the Jewish New Year, **Rosh Hashanah,** falls on the first of **Tishrei,** the seventh month (in August or September). This is when the year number is increased. The months, in order, are Nisan, **Iyar, Sivan, Tammuz, Av, Elul,** Tishrei, **Heshvan, Kislev, Tevet, Shevat,** and **Adar**. Instead of adding a leap day in February, the Jewish calendar adds a leap month, **Adar II,** seven times in every 19 years. The Jewish day runs from sunset to sunset, rather than from midnight to midnight, and holidays begin just before sundown, not the following morning. Jews use it in addition to the Gregorian calendar to mark their religious holidays throughout the year.

Jewish Defense League (JDL)   n. English   Founded in the United States in 1968, the JDL is an organization of Jewish activists dedicated to fighting **anti-Semitism** and defending Jewish interests. The JDL is often in favor of "fighting back" rather than discussion when anti-Semitism or violence against Jews is involved.

Jewish Federation   n. English   The name given to the central organization that oversees Jewish social services, recreational facilities, and fund-raising in most North American cities. Programs and institutions affiliated with Jewish Federation include day care, family counseling, Jewish community centers, geriatric facilities, and employment services. Fund-raising efforts support these local efforts and similar programs in the **State of Israel.** Usually, a local federation bears the name of the city in which it functions, such as the Jewish Federation of Cleveland. Volunteer leaders from the community serve on agency boards, manage projects, and oversee fund-raising appeals. Jews often make a donation to their local Jewish Federation, which collects and distributes the funds. In 1997, the Council of Jewish Federations merged with the United Jewish Appeal and the United Israel Appeal. The combined agency is now called the **United Jewish Communities.**

Jewish National Fund (JNF)   n. English   Founded in 1901 as Keren Kayemeth L'Yisrael, the Jewish National Fund purchases, reclaims, irrigates, and cultivates land in **Israel.** Since its inception, the JNF has been best known for its "blue boxes." These small, blue-and-white metal *tzedakah boxes* featuring a map of Israel are distributed to Jews worldwide to encourage donations that go toward fulfilling JNF's **Zionist** ideals. JNF's major project is planting trees; if you donate money, you can visit your tree in a JNF forest in Israel. JNF is the largest single landowner in Israel, second only to the government.

Jewish Reconstructionist Federation (JRF)   n. English   The official congregational arm of the **Reconstructionist movement.** The JRF serves over 100 congregations and *havurot* in North America. Under its sponsorship is the Reconstructionist Press, the No'ar Hadash youth programs, and a summer camp.

Jewish Renewal   n. English   A movement born in the early 1970s that emphasizes a hands-on, participatory, and intimate form of Judaism. The Jewish Renewal movement is epitomized by the *havurah* and inspired by the neo-**Hasidism** of Martin Buber, Zalman Schachter-Shalomi, and others. Important tenets include equality for men and women in Jewish life, rediscovery of meditative traditions in Judaism, the healing of the earth and society, and respect for learning from other spiritual paths. The umbrella organization is ALEPH: Alliance for Jewish Renewal, formed from the merger of P'nai Or Religious Fellowship and The Shalom Center. ALEPH publishes a quarterly journal, *New Menorah*, and oversees a network of Jewish Renewal communities with about 40 local *havurah* and **synagogue** affiliates in the United States.

Jewish star   n. English   The six-pointed star that is used as a symbol of Judaism. Also called the **Magen David** and the **Star of David.**

Jews for Jesus   See **Messianic Jew.**

Joseph   The 11th son of **Jacob** and the firstborn son of **Rachel.** Joseph was his father's favorite. He was sold into slavery in Egypt by his jealous brothers and eventually, because of his ability to interpret dreams, became a confidant of Pharaoh and later the viceroy of Egypt. When Joshua divided the land of **Canaan** among the **12 tribes of Israel,** he gave Joseph a double portion of land, which Joseph passed on to his two sons, **Menasseh** and **Ephraim.** The story of Joseph is told in the Book of **Genesis.**

Jubilee   n. English   **1.** A special year of rest and forgiveness observed every 50th year by the ancient Israelites, when slaves were set free, property given back, and the fields left unplanted. It might be described as a "super *shemitah*." **2.** The celebration of a special anniversary.

Judah   **1.** Fourth son of **Jacob** and **Leah.** Judah was one of the 12 **tribes of Israel,** whose members were said to be descended from him. The tribe inhabited **Jerusalem** during the reign of kings **David** and **Solomon. 2.** The southern part of the Israelite kingdom. The land was divided in two after the death of King Solomon in 930 B.C.E.

Judaica   n. English   The general term for Jewish ritual objects, such as *Kiddush Cups,* **mezuzot, menorahs,** and such. Objects of Judaica come in all shapes, styles, and forms of expression. There are *Kiddush Cups* embellished with jewels and *yads* made of olive wood from **Israel, Hanukkah** menorahs with cartoon characters and *kippot* with sports motifs. Many times, ritual objects are made as original, beautiful works of art to fulfill the tradition of *hiddur mitzvah.* They are common gifts for a wedding, housewarming, **naming,** or other *simcha.*

Judaism   n. English   The monotheistic religion that traces its roots back more than 5,000 years to the **patriarch Abraham,** making it one of the world's oldest religions. Followers of Judaism, called **Jews,** base their beliefs on the body of writings and doctrines contained in the **Torah** and **Talmud.** All movements of Judaism share certain principles, among them a belief in one God, who is incorporeal (without a shape or body); a belief in the **Ten Commandments** and the Torah; observance of the **Shabbat;** celebration of Jewish festivals and holidays; and male **circumcision.** Different movements in Judaism vary in their interpretations of *halakhah* (Jewish law), levels of observance of those laws, and reevaluations of the laws and rituals throughout history.

Judea and Samaria   n. Hebrew (joo-DAY-uh and suh-MAR-e-uh)   The biblical name of the land on the west bank of the Jordan River. This area was captured from Jordan and became part of **Israel** during the **Six-Day War** in 1967. In recent years, it has been more commonly referred to as the **West Bank.** Someone who uses the biblical name Judea and Samaria is emphasizing Israel's ancient ties to this land, which includes Jerusalem's Western Wall, Hebron's tomb of the Patriarchs, and other sites that are vital parts of Jewish history. Today, the West Bank includes several Jerusalem suburbs and Israeli towns and settlements amidst a Palestinian Arab population.

Judeo-Spanish   n. English   The Romance language spoken by **Sephardic** Jews, especially in Turkey, the Balkans, and North Africa. Also called Judezmo. When Spanish Jews were expelled from Spain in 1492, they settled in new countries around the Mediterranean; their 15th-century Castilian Spanish fused with Turkish, Arabic, Greek, and **Hebrew** words to create Judeo-Spanish, which is considered the Sephardic counterpart to **Yiddish.** The term **"Ladino"** is commonly used in place of Judeo-Spanish, although Ladino is actually the written liturgical language of the Sephardim.

Judezmo   n. Spanish (joo-DEHZ-moe)   Another name for **Judeo-Spanish.**

K   n. When in a circle, usually a symbol of **kosher** certification found on packaged, prepared food.

Kabbalah   n. Hebrew (kah-bah-LAH)   Literally, "to receive." The Jewish mystical tradition. Through the ages, Kabbalah has been primarily transmitted orally from a teacher to a disciple who was over 40 and well versed in the teachings of the **Torah** and **Talmud. Rabbis** worried that the Kabbalah would be misinterpreted or used for superstitious practices if it were studied by someone unfamiliar with Jewish texts; in its early years, it was practiced in secret. Kabbalists have developed meditative practices and distinctive theories on heaven, reincarnation, the coming of the **Messiah,** and creation. They use a system called *gematria,* in which each **Hebrew** letter is assigned a numerical value, to uncover the secrets that they believe are hidden in the Torah.

Kabbalists believe that these teachings were revealed to **Moses** at **Mount Sinai** as a secret part of the **Oral Law.** In the 2nd century C.E., Rabbi **Akiva ben Joseph** was a leading figure in Jewish mysticism; his search for paradise is mentioned in the Talmud. The earliest known kabbalistic text is *Sefer ha-Bahir,* edited in Provence in the mid-12th century. It describes the 10 *sefirot,* through which the hidden God is revealed. Around 1290, the Spanish mystic Moses de Leon compiled the teachings of Kabbalah in the **Zohar,** which remains the classic text of this tradition. He credited the Kabbalah teachings to the 2nd-century writings of the talmudic sage Shimon bar Yochai. Kabbalah was practiced by large numbers of Jews following their expulsion from Spain and Portugal in the 1490s. In Safed, in the mid-16th century, Rabbi **Isaac Luria** furthered kabbalistic thought with theories about the *Ein Sof,* the creation of the universe, the origins of evil, and how to repair the world *(tikun olam).* Lurianic Kabbalah played a major role in the development of **Hasidism.** Today, there is revived interest in Jewish mysticism among **Orthodox** Jews and those in the **Jewish Renewal** movement; synagogues and schools offer courses on Kabbalah and other topics of Jewish mysticism.

kabbalat panim   n. Hebrew (kah-bah-LAHT pah-NEEM)   Literally, "receiving faces." The welcoming of guests prior to the wedding ceremony. At a traditional wedding, the *kabbalat panim* usually consists of two separate ceremonies, the **chossen's tish** (for the groom and his male guests) and the **hakhnasat**

kallah, for the bride and her female guests. These ceremonies precede the *be-deken.* In some non-**Orthodox** communities, the bride also has a *tish.*

Kabbalat Shabbat n. Hebrew (kah-bah-LAHT shah-BAHT) Special prayers and songs included as part of Friday night services to welcome in **Shabbat.**

Kaddesh Urechatz n. Hebrew (kah-DAYSH oor-KHATS) A rhyming song chanted on **Pesach** that sums up the parts of the **seder.** It is sung at the beginning of the seder, thereby giving a preview of what is to come. *Kaddesh* (making *Kiddush,* or saying the blessing over wine) and *Urechatz* (washing the hands) are the first two steps performed at a Pesach seder.

Kaddish n. Aramaic (KAH-dish) From the Hebrew word for "holy." The ancient prayer customarily recited by Jewish mourners. Ironically, the *Kaddish* makes no mention of death; rather, it praises God and speaks to God's greatness. With slight variations in wording—and different names (the Learner's *Kaddish* and the Reader's *Kaddish*)—the *Kaddish* is recited several times during daily and **Shabbat synagogue** services. Some say the prayer became associated with death because mourners were given the honor of reciting the final *Kaddish* during services. Usually, while mourners stand, the congregation joins in reciting the prayer. In some congregations it is customary for everyone, not just mourners, to rise during the prayer as a declaration of faith. The words to the *Kaddish,* which begins in Aramaic with *"Yitgadal ve-yitkadash Shmei rabbah,"* are among the most well recognized. Many times, Jews who are not familiar with other prayers know the *Kaddish* because they have said it in memory of a loved one. According to Jewish law, the *Kaddish* can only be said if there is a **minyan,** so in a way, the mourner is forced to seek out the comfort and support offered by praying with others. During the **shivah** period, *Kaddish* is recited in the mourner's home. It is also recited at the graveside, in synagogue daily for 11 months after the death of a parent, and during *Yizkor* services. The prayer is also known as the Mourner's *Kaddish* or *"Mourner's Prayer."*

kallah n. Hebrew (KAH-lah) **1.** A bride; a young newly married woman **2.** A metaphor that describes **Shabbat** as a lovely bride. It is found in the song **"Lekhah Dodi":** "Go, my beloved, to meet the bride. Let us welcome the Sabbath." **3.** A study session, over several days in length, set aside for learning. A kallah is often sponsored by a **synagogue.**

kamishbread n. Yiddish (kah-MISH-bread) A crunchy, dry cookie, similar to biscotti. It is made by forming dough into a loaf, baking it, and then slicing the loaf into oblong cookies and baking them again. Each baker has his or her own variation; common additions include cinnamon or chocolate chips. Kamishbread is **mandelbread**'s plainer cousin. Also called *komishbrodt.*

Kaplan, Mordechai (1881–1983)   American rabbi, educator, and philosopher. The founder and leader of the **Reconstructionist movement** of Judaism, Kaplan was a dean at the Jewish Theological Seminary of America, the rabbinical school of the Conservative movement. His Society for the Advancement of Judaism, established in 1922 in New York, was a synagogue for disaffected Jews who were committed to "reconstructing" American Judaism to make it more meaningful in modern times. It's considered the forerunner of the Reconstructionist movement, which was officially founded in 1935.

kapparah   n. Hebrew (kah-pah-RAH)   Literally, "atonement." **1.** An ancient custom performed on the eve of **Yom Kippur,** the Day of Atonement to symbolically transfers one sins—and punishment of death—to another object, particularly a chicken. The custom involves swinging a chicken over one's head while reciting verses from the Yom Kippur *machzor.* The ritual is still practiced by some traditional Jews. **2.** Any act of atonement that makes up for past transgressions and cleanses the soul; used in connection with the penitent atmosphere of **Yom Kippur.** The Yiddish term is *kaparos.*

Karaite   n. Hebrew (KAR-eh-ite)   A member of a sect of **Judaism** founded some time after 760 C.E., which rejected the **Oral Law** and any rabbinical interpretations or innovations. Karaites based their religious beliefs entirely on the written **Torah.**

karpas   n. Hebrew (CAR-pas)   A green vegetable, usually celery or parsley, placed on the **seder plate** during the holiday meal for **Pesach.** The green vegetable is symbolic of the coming of spring and the hope that a new season brings. During the **seder,** the green vegetable is dipped in salt water, a reminder of the tears the **Israelites** shed as slaves in Egypt.

kasha   n. Yiddish (KAH-shah)   Cracked buckwheat or barley grain that is usually sautéed with mushrooms or onions and served hot as a side dish, much like rice. Kasha is often mixed with bow-tie shaped noodles to make a dish called *kasha varnishkes* (KAH-shah VAR-nish-kahs).

kasher   v. Hebrew (KAH-shur)   Literally, "fit" or "proper." To make **kosher.** Often used when referring to the process of making meat kosher by washing, soaking, and salting it in a prescribed fashion. This must be done before it can be cooked, to drain the flesh of as much blood as possible. Today, most kosher meat comes already kashered, ready to be cooked and eaten. Kasher also refers to the process of heating and cleaning utensils and dishes so that they can be used for kosher cooking. It can also refer to cleaning a kitchen and its contents of *hametz* in preparation for **Pesach.** For example: "He poured boiling water over all the silverware to kasher it for Pesach."

kashrut   n.   Hebrew (KOSH-root)   The body of Jewish dietary laws and regulations that specify what and how a Jew who keeps **kosher** can eat. Usually used in the phrase "to keep kashrut."

kavanah   n.   Hebrew (kah-vah-NAH)   Intense concentration; devotion; personal inspiration. The frame of mind needed for praying or performing a **mitzvah.** Jews are required to "pray with *kavanah,*" to bring true feeling, understanding, and inspiration to the *keva,* the fixed order of the prayer. The beginning of the *Shema* and the *Amidah* are considered high points of *kavanah.* The concept of *kavanah* is important to **Hasidic** Jews, who are known for their ecstatic praying, which they believe elevates the soul toward God. Hasidim also say special meditations *(kavanot)* before performing all kinds of mitzvot.

kavod   n.   Hebrew (kah-VODE)   **1.** Honor, dignity, respect; used in reference to people. In the fifth of the **Ten Commandments,** Jews are called on to "honor" their mother and father. Judaism demands special *kavod* to parents, grandparents, elder siblings, teachers, **rabbis,** and the dead. Honor is defined as showing mutual respect for the dignity of another. **2.** When said with the Yiddish pronunciation **(KUH-vid),** the meaning is more casual, as in "paying respects" or giving honor to the leader of an organization or community.

kavod ha-met   n.   Hebrew (kah-VODE hah-MET)   Literally, "honor for the dead." The concept behind all Jewish burial customs. This showing of respect traditionally includes quick burial of the dead; the use of a *shomer;* and prohibitions against embalming, cosmetology, and an open casket, which might be interpreted as being undignified or irreverent.

kedushah   n.   Hebrew (keh-doo-SHAH)   **1.** Holiness, sanctity. In Judaism, the notion of *kedushah* extends not only to sacred objects, such as a **Torah** scroll, but also to abstract concepts such as the separateness and uniqueness of **Shabbat. 2.** *Kedushah* (keh-DOO-shah)   A responsive prayer sung by the *shaliach tzibbur* and congregation as part of the *Amidah* during synagogue services. The *Kedushah* praises God with the words: "Holy, holy, holy is God, Ruler of Hosts. The whole earth is full of God's glory."

kehillah   n.   Hebrew (keh-HEE-lah)   A Jewish community that revolves around a **synagogue** and its school. This use of the term originated in Poland and referred to the autonomous communities where Jews had their own school systems and law enforcement; the *kehillah* controlled all aspects of religious life. Today, the term is sometimes used to describe **Orthodox** communities.

keppe   n.   Yiddish (KEH-pea)   Head. An informal, Anglicized variation of the Yiddish word "*kop.*" "Lay your little *keppe* down and take a nap."

keriah n. Hebrew (keh-REE-ah)   The ritual tear made in a mourner's garment before the funeral, signifying the rending apart that the death has caused in the mourner's life. Traditionally, the tear is made to a woman's dress and a man's vest or jacket. The left side is torn for parents; the right side, for a son, daughter, brother, sister, or spouse. The tearing is done by the officiating **rabbi,** although in **Orthodox** circles, women perform this ritual for one another. The modern custom is for mourners to pin a black ribbon on their lapel, which is then cut instead.

keter n. Hebrew (keh-TER)   Literally, "crown." The first of the 10 *sefirot,* or aspects of God's creative nature. According to **kabbalistic** teachings, *keter* represents the superconscious realm of experience. The highest level or sphere, *keter* encompasses all of the *sefirot* and is sometimes considered the intermediary between *Ein Sof* and the *sefirot.* It is one of three *sefirot,* along with *hokhmah* and *binah,* in the category of the intellect. Each *sefirah* is associated with a part of the body; *keter* corresponds to the essence and potential.

keter Torah n. Hebrew (KEH-tair toe-RAH)   The large decorative crown, often made of silver, that fits over the wooden poles of a **Torah** scroll. Along with the cloth cover and the *hoshen,* the *keter Torah* is used to dress a Torah. See *gelilah.*

Kethuvim n. Hebrew (keh-two-VEEM)   The third of the three sections that comprise the **TANAKH,** along with **Torah** and **Nevi'im.** Kethuvim, known by the English name **The Writings,** is a collection of ancient texts: liturgical poetry (Psalms and **Lamentations**), love poetry (**The Song of Songs**), wisdom literature (Proverbs, Job and **Ecclesiastes**), historical works (**Ruth, Esther,** Ezra, Nehemiah, Chronicles), and history and prophecy (Daniel). Ruth, The Song of Songs, Lamentations, Ecclesiates, and Esther, collectively known as *megillot,* are often grouped together because they are read on specific holidays. Kethuvim is also called **Hagiographa.**

ketubbah n. Hebrew (keh-TOO-bah); pl. **ketubbot** (keh-too-BOTE)   The Jewish marriage contract, traditionally written in **Aramaic.** This legal document details the obligations of the husband to his wife. It must be signed before the marriage ceremony by two witnesses who are not related to the bride or groom. It is customary for the **rabbi** to read parts of the *ketubbah* aloud during the wedding ceremony. Today, many egalitarian *ketubbot* are written in both English and Hebrew; these include mention of the bride's rights and responsibilities as well as those of the groom, and are signed by both bride and groom. Modern *ketubbot* are often embellished with calligraphy and personalized artwork and are framed and hung in the home of the bride and groom.

keva n. Hebrew (KEH-vah)   Literally "fixed." The fixed order of a prayer. *Keva* is distinct from *kavanah,* the intention one brings to praying. Jews strive to create a balance between *keva* and *kavanah,* which are equal requirements in *tefilah.*

khreyn n. Yiddish (CRANE) Horseradish. Khreyn might be eaten straight from the root or more commonly grated and bottled as it is (white) or with beets (red). It is an essential condiment for gefilte fish.

kibbe n. Hebrew (KIH-bee) A Middle Eastern recipe for meatballs, usually made from lamb and served in a pita pocket.

kibbutz n. Hebrew (kih-BOOTS); pl. **kibbutzim** (kih-boot-SEEM) A collective farm or settlement in the **State of Israel.** The first kibbutz, Degania Alef, was established in 1909 as an efficient way to farm the land. Originally, many kibbutzim were based on principles of socialism, with all members of the kibbutz sharing equally in the work and the profits. Today, the organizational philosophies of kibbutzim vary, but most still provide members with services such as day care, group meals, and community-wide recreation. Many kibbutzim not only produce agricultural products but also manufacture goods as varied as sunglasses, tractors, and computer chips.

kibbutz galuyot n. Hebrew (kih-BOOTS gah-lee-OAT) Literally "in-gathering of the exiles." **1.** The tenth blessing of the **Amidah. 2.** A term for Jews in the **Diaspora** returning to the land of **Israel.** The establishment of the Jewish state is considered to be the fulfillment of a biblical prophecy, made by Ezekiel during the Babylonian exile, that Jews would one day return to their ancestral homeland. Operation Magic Carpet, in 1949, when Israeli government planes brought 45,000 Yemenite Jews "home" to make *aliyah* and live in Israel, is an example of *kibbutz galuyot.*

kibbutznik n. Yiddish (kih-BOOTS-nik) A term for a person who lives on a **kibbutz** or one who was born or raised there.

kibitz v. Yiddish (KIB-its) **1.** To fool around, joke, or make wisecracks, particularly while others are trying to work or be serious. "Enough kibitzing! Will you get out of my office already? I have to finish this work." **2.** To give unsolicited but good-natured advice. The word was originally used to describe a spectator at a card game, who would make comments and give advice. "My father-in-law always kibitzes about what I serve for dinner. He wants a fancy dessert." n. **kibitzer** One who kibitzes.

kichel n. Yiddish (KIKH-ul) Literally, "cookie." A small, plain, puffy cookie made with unsweetened dough and many eggs. Kichels may be sprinkled with sugar or poppy seeds, or baked plain.

Kiddush n. Hebrew (KID-ish)   Literally, "sanctification." **1.** The blessing recited over wine. The *Kiddush* is said on all Jewish holi-
days, including **Shabbat,** and before celebratory meals. The wording, which
changes for various holidays, is of several parts. The first part is a verse from
Genesis. The middle section is a blessing over wine, thanking God for creating
the fruit of the vine. The last portion thanks God for the blessings of the day,
whether it be Shabbat or a holiday. At a holiday meal, most Jews do not begin
to eat until all the blessings over food and wine have been said. The expression
"Let's make *Kiddush*" can also mean "Let's sit down, we're ready to eat." **2.** The
refreshments, usually including wine, juice, and pastries, that are offered after
Shabbat and holiday services in the **synagogue.** The snack, also called an **Oneg
Shabbat,** got its name because it begins with the recitation of the *Kiddush*.

Kiddush Cup n. Hebrew/English (KID-ish CUP)   A special wine goblet set
aside for "making *Kiddush*," or saying the blessing over wine. One of the most
recognizable objects of **Judaica,** *Kiddush Cups* are often forged of silver and engraved with Hebrew words or **brachot.** Modern artists of Judaica fashion them of
painted ceramic, colored glass, or precious metals. Making decorative *Kiddush
Cups* from plastic cups is a favorite children's craft. There are no laws specifying
how *Kiddush Cups* must look, but they, like other Jewish ritual objects, are often
embellished because of the tradition of *hiddur mitzvah,* "beautifying the mitzvah."

kiddush ha-Shem n. Hebrew (kee-DOOSH hah-SHEM)   Literally, "sanctification of the Name." Any prayer, conduct, or martyrdom that brings honor to
God's name. Jews are called upon to sanctify God's name in everything they do;
a generous, righteous, or selfless deed is thought to bring honor to Judaism and
to the Jewish community. Martyrdom, as demonstrated by Jews during the
Christian Crusades and the **Holocaust,** is thought to be the ultimate expression
of *kiddush ha-Shem. Kiddush ha-Shem* is the opposite of *hillul ha-Shem.*

kiddushin n. Hebrew (kee-doo-SHEEN)   Sanctification; holiness. Another
name for the betrothal part of the Jewish wedding ceremony; see *erusin.* This is
also the name given to the state of matrimony.

kike n. English (KIKE)   A slang and derogatory term for a Jew. There's much
conjecture about this ethnic slur. It's thought to come from *kikel,* the Yiddish
word for circle, the symbol that illiterate Jews wrote on immigration documents—because they didn't want to draw a cross or "x"—when they arrived at
Ellis Island. It is thought that the term was first used by assimilated German Jews
to refer to the poorer immigrants from Eastern Europe.

kinder n. Yiddish (KIN-der)   Children. The word is often said with senti-
mentality and pride. "The *kinder* bring us joy."

kine-ahora int. Yiddish (KIN-eh-HORE-ah) An expression said to ward off the evil eye or bad luck in general; the verbal equivalent of knocking on wood. "I've felt good all summer, *kine-ahora.*" One might also say, "Don't give me a *kine-ahora!*" when paid an extravagant compliment so that the evil eye isn't tempted to make the opposite happen. The word **"canary"** is sometimes used as a slang contraction for *kine-ahora.*

Kinneret, Yam (Lake) n. English/Hebrew (KEY-ner-et) The Hebrew name for the Sea of Galilee. See **Galilee.**

kinyan n. Hebrew (kin-YAHN) A groom's formal acceptance of the terms of the **ketubbah.** At a traditional wedding, this ritual takes place during the **chossen's tish,** when the **rabbi** or a witness, acting on behalf of the bride, offers the groom a handkerchief or some other object. When the groom accepts it, he is symbolically accepting the obligations detailed in his marriage contract. The *ketubbah* is then signed. This ceremony is a vestige of ancient times, when marriage was a business transaction between the bride's father and the groom. That transaction was confirmed by the passing of a handkerchief and/or sealed with the payment of a silver or gold coin.

kippah n. Hebrew (KEE-pah); pl. **kippot** (kee-POTE) The small, round head covering worn as a symbol of respect and religious observance in **synagogue.** Since the 12th century, Jewish men have worn *kippot.* Some traditional men wear a *kippah* all the time; others wear it only during prayers and at meals because of the blessings recited before and after eating. Today, in liberal congregations, *kippot* are worn by both men and women. In the entrance to many **Conservative** and liberal synagogues, there is a basket of *kippot,* so that anyone who didn't bring his or her own can put one on before entering. There may also be a basket of lace head coverings and bobby pins for women who wish to cover their heads but are not comfortable wearing a *kippah.* In most **Reform** synagogues, the covering of one's head is optional for both men and women. *Kippot* can be made from almost any type of fabric. Many are knitted or crocheted; others are painted on leather or machine-made and quite plain. Special *kippot,* imprinted with the names of the bride and groom or the **Bar** or **Bat Mitzvah,** are often given to guests at a *simcha.* A *kippah* is also known as a **yarmulke** (Yiddish) or skullcap.

Kisse Eliyahu See **Elijah's Chair.**

kishka n. Yiddish (KISH-kah) **1.** Animal intestine or casing stuffed with a savory mixture of flour, onion, **shmaltz,** and spices; the old-fashioned Jewish version of sausage. Also called stuffed derma. Today, with cholesterol concerns, traditional, fat-laden kishka has all but disappeared. In its place are vegetarian versions that use **matzah meal,** onions, and seasonings to mimic the taste. **2. kishkas:** slang for guts, or intestines. "It took *kishkas* to stand up to him like that."

Kislev   n. Hebrew (KISS-lev)   The ninth month in the **Jewish calendar,** it corresponds to November or December.

kitel   n. Yiddish (KIT-ell)   Literally, "gown." The long white robe, usually made of linen, worn by **rabbis** and other prayer leaders on important occasions, including **Rosh Hashanah** and **Yom Kippur,** and sometimes for the marriage ceremony. The *kitel* was the popular wedding garb for grooms in 19th-century Eastern Europe, a practice that is still followed today by some traditional Jewish grooms who, like their brides, wear white as a symbol of purity. Some men are buried in the *kitel* they wore throughout their lifetime.

kitniyot   pl. n. Hebrew (kit-knee-OTE)   Literally, "legumes or beans." The term used for certain foods that are restricted during **Pesach** in some Jewish communities. *Kitniyot* include rice, corn, soybeans, string beans, peas, lentils, and peanuts. Most **Ashkenazic** Jews follow the prohibition against *kitniyot,* which was instituted in 13th-century France to avoid confusion about what was and was not *hametzdik.* While Jewish law prohibits Jews from having *hametz* in their homes during **Pesach,** they can own *kitniyot* and even use it (for example, baby powder with cornstarch). **Sephardic** Jewish communities did not adopt this custom, because these foods are staples of their diet. Likewise, the *Masorti* **(Conservative)** movement in Israel permits Ashkenazic Jews to eat *kitniyot* during Pesach.

klaf   n. Hebrew (KLAHF)   The parchment, from the skin of a **kosher** animal, on which the **Torah** is written by a *sofer.* It is also the name for the handwritten scroll placed in a **mezuzah,** containing verses from the *Shema.*

klal Yisra'el   n. Hebrew (KLAL yis-rah-ALE)   Literally, "oneness of Israel," a synonym for the Jewish people. The term is usually used in the context of shared values or unity among Jews. "When the Jewish Federation designated a 'mitzvah day,' all the synagogues worked together to send volunteers to the shelter and collect toys for charity. It was a great example of *klal Yisra'el.*"

klezmer   n. Yiddish (KLEZ-mur)   A joyous, Eastern European style of instrumental music; the music most often associated in the U.S. with "sounding Jewish." It features a clarinet accompanied by a combination of trumpets, flutes, violins, cellos, or drums. Klezmer music, which is enjoying a revival, is often played at weddings and *simchot;* it is the music for traditional Jewish circle dances. The klezmer tradition started with informal bands of self-taught musicians who traveled from village to village in Eastern Europe playing a lively mixture of folk tunes, military marches, famous melodies, and dance tunes. Like jazz, klezmer music is characterized by improvisation and instrumental solos.

klop   v. Yiddish (KLOP)   **1.** To smack or hit. "Stop teasing her or I'll *klop* you!" **2.** n. Blow; hit. "The little boy gave his friend a *klop* for taking his teddy bear."

klutz   n. Yiddish (KLUTZ)   A clumsy or awkward person, a clod. Used more endearingly than negatively these days. "He really means well, but he is such a klutz. Don't let him unpack your good china."

knaidel   n. Yiddish (kuh-NAY-dull); pl. **knaidlach**   (kuh-NAID-lock)   A dumpling made of **matzah meal** and beaten eggs, usually served in chicken broth, often at the **Pesach seder.** Also called a **matzah ball.**

Knesset   n. Hebrew (kuh-NESS-et)   The governing, law-making body of the **State of Israel.** Created in 1949 and located in Jerusalem, the Knesset's 120 elected members represent numerous political parties, including Labor, Likud, and Gush Emunim. These differing political groups must work together and form ever-shifting coalitions to govern the nation. Similar to the U.S. Congress, the members of the Knesset represent different geographical regions of the country; others are members at large.

knish   n. Yiddish (kuh-NISH)   A baked, fist-sized pocket of dough filled with meat or vegetables and served hot, often as a snack or appetizer. Common varieties include potato, spinach, kasha, and liver.

k'nocker   n. Yiddish (kuh-NOCK-er)   A showoff. A big shot who is boastful and cocky. Old-fashioned usage.

koach   n. Hebrew (CO-akh)   Strength, fortitude.

Kohan   See **Kohen.**

Kohelet   n. Hebrew (co-HELL-let)   The Hebrew name for **Ecclesiastes,** the **megillah,** or scroll, that is read on **Sukkot.**

Kohen   n. Hebrew (CO-hane); pl. **Kohanim**   (co-hah-NEEM)   A Jew who can trace his ancestry to the ancient priestly tribe descended from **Aaron.** Today, a Kohen is traditionally honored with the first *aliyah* during a **Torah** service. *Kohanim* are also called on to perform other ritual functions in traditional Judaism. At a *pidyon ha-ben* ceremony, a father symbolically redeems his son from a Kohen. The **Reform movement** does not make distinctions as to heritage when it calls congregants for an *aliyah*. Most Jews with the last name Cohen or Kohen—as well as Kaplan, Katz, and variations of these—are *Kohanim,* but last names are not the final word. Only family history and detailed lineage can determine from what tribe each Jew is descended.

kol ha-kavod   int. Hebrew (coal hah-kah-VODE)   Literally, "all of the honor." An expression of congratulations or acknowledgement offered to someone who has completed an *aliyah* in synagogue, read from the **Torah,** or performed some other accomplishment. Like *yasher koach*, it may be said of the person, rather than directly to him. "Did you hear that he raised all that money for breast cancer research? *Kol ha-kavod* to him."

kollel   n. Hebrew (koh-LELL);   pl. **kollelim** (koh-lel-LEEM)   **1.** An institute for advanced **Talmudic** and *halakhic* study, often attached to an established **yeshivah,** where married men pursue full-time postgraduate work. **2.** A community program for adult Torah education for the surrounding Jewish community. Though many are run by **Orthodox** Jews, there are some **Reform** and **Conservative**-affiliated *kollelim.*

Kol Nidrei   n. Aramaic (coal KNEE-dray)   Literally, "all vows." **1.** An ancient solemn **Aramaic** prayer recited in **synagogue** on the eve of **Yom Kippur.** In the *Kol Nidrei* prayer, one asks to be excused and released from vows made but not kept during the past year and in the new year to come. *Kol Nidrei* is sung in a distinctive, haunting melody. It ushers in the repentance and inner reflection of Yom Kippur. **2.** The name for the synagogue service on *erev* Yom Kippur.

kol tov   int. Hebrew (coal TOEV)   Yiddish (coal TOOV)   Literally "all good." An expression of farewell, similar to wishing someone "all the best."

komishbrodt   See **kamishbread**.

kosher   adj. Hebrew (CO-sher)   **1.** The general term used to describe foods that are acceptable according to the Jewish dietary laws. The basic laws of **kashrut** are set forth in the book of **Leviticus** in the **Torah,** which contains a list of all kosher and non-kosher animals. Meat must come from an animal with split hooves that chews its cud (for example, cow, lamb, deer) and that is slaughtered in a ritual way by a *shochet.* Pork is forbidden. Fish must have both fins and scales. Thus shellfish, shrimp, and lobster are forbidden. Foods made with milk **(milchig)** cannot be eaten or mixed with foods that contain meat **(fleishig)** products. This comes from the biblical injunction that says: "You shall not seethe a kid in its mother's milk." Thus, combinations like cheeseburgers are not kosher. All fruits, vegetables, and grains (including pasta) are neither milk nor meat. Such foods are called **pareve** and may be eaten or mixed with either milk or meat. Eggs are also pareve.

If a Jewish homemaker keeps kosher, the kitchen will have two sets of dishes (one milchig, one fleishig), two sets of silverware, two sets of pots and pans, and so forth. When foods are prepared, they are cooked and served with the appropriate utensils. Manufactured packaged foods are designated kosher by a *heksher* on the label.

Levels of observance of kashrut and the interpretations of the law vary widely among movements of Judaism and even among families. Some families who keep kosher at home will eat anything when in a restaurant. Some eat only vegetarian dishes or fish in a restaurant to ensure that the food is kosher (even if the tableware is not). Others will only eat in a kosher restaurant that is certified and watched over by a *mashgiach.* Some persons who keep kosher will eat in another person's home; some will not unless they are sure the other person also keeps kosher.

2. Permissible, proper, or legitimate. Often used when referring to ritual objects such as **mezuzot** or **tefillin** that are "correct" according to Jewish law and can be used. "Kosher" may also refer to situations and things outside of Jewish life. For example: "He wants to have a coed sleepover party, but I don't think that's kosher."

kosher for Passover   The seal of approval *(heksher)* found on manufactured foods that are *pesachdik* and contain no leaven, making them acceptable for eating during **Pesach.**

kosher style   adj. English Jewish home-style cooking, including favorite foods such as **brisket,** corned beef, **matzah ball** soup, **kugel,** or **blintzes**. As the name implies, "kosher-style" food is not the same as ritually acceptable **kosher** food. Although the fare may be similar, the laws of **kashrut** are not observed in a kosher-style restaurant.

Kotel   n. Hebrew (CO-tell) Literally, "wall." Short for *Kotel ha-Ma'arivi,* Hebrew for the **Western Wall.** The Kotel is the archaeological site in **Jerusalem** that is believed to be the remaining retaining wall of the **Second Temple,** which was destroyed by the Romans in 70 C.E.

krechz   v. Yiddish (KREKHTZ) To sigh, moan, and grunt about a little ache or pain or minor discomfort. The sounds are often accompanied by *"oy."* Old-fashioned usage.

krenzel   n. Yiddish (KREN-zel) The Yiddish name for the **crowning ceremony** that is held during a wedding reception to honor parents who have married off their last child.

kreplach n. Yiddish (CREP-lokh) Small, folded dough pockets that are stuffed with meat, cheese, or vegetables. Kreplach may be fried and eaten as a side dish, or boiled and served in broth. They are the Jewish version of wontons or pierogies.

Kristallnacht n. German (CRYS-tal-nacht) Literally, "the night of broken glass": November 9, 1938. During this government-sponsored **pogrom,** the Nazis shattered the windows of more than 1,000 synagogues in Germany, desecrating **Torah** scrolls and burning prayer books. They destroyed Jewish hospitals, cemeteries, businesses, and homes. Ninety-one Jews were murdered, and 30,000 were arrested and sent to **concentration camps.** Kristallnacht marked a turning point in Hitler's campaign against the Jews. This escalation of violence is considered to be the beginning of the horrors of World War II.

kugel n. Yiddish (COO-gull) or (KEE-gull) A baked casserole made with eggs and other ingredients. It is a traditional dish for both **Shabbat** and holidays. A noodle kugel is often made with fruit, nuts, sugar, and raisins. Kugels can also be made with potatoes, carrots, zucchini, or other vegetables. On **Pesach,** cooks traditionally use crumbled **matzah** or the new **kosher for Passover** noodles in their kugels.

kuni lemel n. Yiddish (KOO-knee LEM-mel) from the German "lummel," meaning bumpkin. A simple person; a yokel; similar to a nebbish. The term comes from the Yiddish theater; *Kuni Lemel* is the title of a comedic operetta written by playwright Abraham Goldfaden in the early 1900s.

kuntz n. Yiddish (KUNTZ) Peculiarity, particular oddness. Often used in the context of "his own *kuntz.*" "He stayed indoors when everyone else took a walk on this beautiful day. He has his own *kuntz* going."

kvater n. Yiddish (kuh-VAH-ter) The name given to an infant's godfather. The *kvater* participates in the **brit milah** by taking the infant from the *kvaterin* (godmother) and handing him to the father. It is an honor to be asked to serve as a child's *kvater.*

kvaterin n. Yiddish (kuh-VAH-ter-in) The name given to an infant's godmother, who participates at the **brit milah** by taking the baby from the mother and passing him to the **kvater** (godfather). It is an honor to be asked to serve as a child's *kvaterin.*

kvell v. Yiddish (KVELL) To be extraordinarily pleased; to be delighted. From the German for "gush," *kvell* means to burst with pride, particularly over the accomplishments and achievements of one's children. "Congratulations on your daughter's getting into Harvard. You must be *kvelling*."

kvetch v. Yiddish (KVETCH) To chronically complain or gripe to others over minor issues and exaggerated aches and pains. "Stop kvetching about your sore ankle like it's a broken leg." n. **kvetcher** One who kvetches.

labreoot   int. Hebrew (lah-bree-OOT)   Literally, "to health." The expression Israelis commonly use to wish one well after a sneeze; similar to *gezuntheit*.

Ladino   n. Spanish (lah-DEE-noe)   **1.** The semisacred written language of the **Sephardic** Jews. Ladino, which predates the Jews' expulsion from Spain in 1492, is a variation of Spanish written with **Hebrew** characters. A number of texts were created this way; an example is the famous Ladino translation of the Bible, the Biblia de Ferrara, written in 1553. Ladino is one of the languages, including **Aramaic,** Hebrew, and **Yiddish,** written with Hebrew characters, although unlike these languages, it is written in **Rashi script. 2.** adj. The term most commonly used to refer to the music, culture, and language of the Sephardic Jews; though their spoken language is more accurately called Judeo-Spanish or **Judezmo.** Like Yiddish, Ladino is undergoing somewhat of a revival these days. There are singers who specialize in keeping Ladino music alive, an Internet chat room where only Ladino is "spoken," and courses given at universities around the country.

Lag ba-Omer   n. Hebrew (LOG bah-OH-mare)   A minor holiday celebrated on the 18th of **Iyar.** This holiday occurs on the 33rd day after **Pesach** (see **Omer**). No scholar is really sure what Lag ba-Omer commemorates: Some say it was a military victory; others say it marks the end of an ancient plague. The "Lag" in the name of the holiday comes from the Hebrew letters *lamed* and *gimmel,* which add up to 33 (days of counting the Omer).

Lamentations   n. English   One of the five books, referred to as a scroll or **megillah,** that is contained in **Kethuvim,** the third section of the TANAKH. Known as **Eikhah** in Hebrew, Lamentations is read in synagogue on **Tisha be-Av.** Chanted to a sad melody, the book tells the story of the Babylonian destruction of **Jerusalem** in 586 B.C.E. and the exile of the Jewish people.

landsman   n. Yiddish (LAHNDS-mahn)   A person whose ancestors came from the same town or region as another; a compatriot. Used more generally to describe a fellow Jew. Old-fashioned usage.

landsmanshaft n. Yiddish (LAHNDS-mahn-SHOFT) A fraternal organization, often called a club or circle, made up of immigrants from the same region. Old-fashioned usage.

lashon ha-ra n. Hebrew (lah-SHONE hah-RAH) Literally, "bad tongue." Gossip. Similar to the English expression "to bad-mouth" someone. In the **Torah,** *lashon ha-ra* is specifically forbidden. According to Jewish tradition, one should not repeat negative comments or rumors about another person, even if they are true.

latke n. Yiddish (LOT-kah) A fried pancake. The most common type is the potato latke, traditionally eaten on **Hanukkah.** These latkes are fried in oil to remind Jews of the Hanukkah miracle of the rededication of the **Temple,** when a tiny bit of oil lasted for eight days. There are many other varieties of latkes, such as carrot, zucchini, and sweet potato. On **Pesach,** latkes are made from **matzah meal.**

Law of Return n. English The very first law passed by the **Knesset** after the establishment of the **State of Israel.** The Law of Return guarantees all Jews throughout the world the right to immigrate to Israel and become a citizen. In many respects the law was a reaction to the horrors of the **Holocaust,** when Jews trying to escape the Nazis were denied entry to many countries, including the United States. The Law of Return was seen as a guarantee that this would never happen again: Israel would be a homeland for all Jews. In recent years, arguments within Israel regarding who is a Jew have complicated application of the Law of Return. Different movements of Judaism have varying views of who is Jewish, and therefore, who will be allowed to immigrate, because of differences in conversion rituals and interpretation of Jewish law. For example, Ethiopian Jews who want to immigrate to Israel are facing discrimination and obstacles because of questions of their lineage and legitimacy as Jews. To date, the Law of Return, without any stipulations, is still in effect.

l'chaim int. Hebrew (luh-KHYE-eem) Literally, "to life." An age-old Jewish toast—"to your health"—said over wine or liquor with glasses raised.

Leah One of the four **matriarchs** of the Jewish people; the first wife of **Jacob,** one of the three **patriarchs.** Leah was wed when her father, Laban, tricked Jacob into marrying her instead of his true love, her younger sister, **Rachel.** This deception is said to have inspired the wedding custom of *bedeken*. Leah had seven children: **Reuben, Simeon, Levi, Judah, Issachar, Zebulun,** and Dinah.

leaven See *hametz.*

lehitraot   int. Hebrew (leh-HEET-rah-OAT)   The modern Israeli expression for "goodbye for now, see you again soon." The Hebrew equivalent of the Italian word *ciao.*

lekakh   n. Yiddish (LECH-huck)   Honey cake, traditionally served on **Rosh Hashanah.** The dark, moist spice cake is made with honey, eggs, cinnamon, and, often, coffee.

Lekhah Dodi   n. Hebrew (leh-KHAH doe-DEE)   Literally, "come, my beloved." The song sung by Jews worldwide at dusk on Friday evenings to welcome **Shabbat.** The words of the first stanza are: "Come, my beloved, to meet the bride. Let us welcome the Sabbath."

lekvar   n. Hungarian (LECK-var)   Pureed, cooked prune filling used in **hamantashen;** from the Hungarian word for "jam."

le-shanah ha-ba'ah be-Yerushalayim   int. Hebrew (leh-shah-NAH hah-bah-AH beh-yeh-ROO-shah-LYE-eem)   Literally, "Next year in **Jerusalem!**" The traditional phrase said to end the **Pesach seder.** It expresses the wish that all Jews will one day have the opportunity to visit Jerusalem. The most traditional interpretation of this phrase is that by next Pesach the **Messiah** will come, gathering all Jews to Jerusalem.

le-shanah tovah tikatevu   int. Hebrew (leh-shah-NAH toe-VAH tee-kah-TAY-voo)   Literally, "May you be inscribed [in the Book of Life] for a good year." This is the customary greeting among Jews on **Rosh Hashanah.** These words also commonly appear on the "Happy New Year" greeting cards Jews send to family and friends at this time of year. According to the **Talmud,** God inscribes the names of the righteous in the **Book of Life;** the fate of all others is on hold until **Yom Kippur.** How one behaves—repenting, performing acts of charity, and praying—can influence God's decree during the days between Rosh Hashanah and Yom Kippur.

Levi   Third son of **Jacob** and **Leah.** Levi's daughter, Yocheved, was the mother of Moses and Aaron. Levi is also the name of one of the 12 **tribes of Israel,** whose members were said to be descended from him. His descendants are known as **Levites.**

Levite   n. Hebrew (LEE-vite)   A member of the tribe of **Levi.** Levites carried the **Tabernacle** and later assisted at the **Temple** by serving as gatekeepers, teachers, musicians, and assistants to the priests *(Kohanim).* The Levites were chosen for service to God because, in Exodus, they refused to worship the Golden Calf. The

Levites had no tribal land of their own but were spread among the other tribes. Today, the second *aliyah* in a traditional **Torah** service is reserved for someone who traces his family lineage to Levi. Most Jews with the last name of Levy, Levine, or variations are Levites, but last names are not the final word. Sometimes a vessel of water or a cup pouring water is carved on a tombstone as a symbol of a Levite, because assisting the **Kohen** in washing was an ancient duty of this tribe.

Leviticus   n. English   The third book of the **Torah,** called **Va-yikra** in Hebrew. The Book of Leviticus includes laws concerning **Temple** sacrifices in ancient days and the laws of **kashrut,** as well as the famous admonition to "love your neighbor as yourself."

levivot   pl. n. Hebrew (leh-vee-VOTE)   Potato pancakes. The Hebrew word for the **latkes** traditionally eaten on **Hanukkah.**

Litvak   n. Yiddish (LIT-vock)   A Jew who traces his ancestors to Lithuania, which was part of Poland before it became part of czarist Russia. Lithuania includes the cities of Vilna, Minsk, Bialystock, and Grodno. At the turn of the century, more than 1.5 million Jews lived in this area. Today, the Jewish population is negligible. Litvaks are contrasted with the other ethnic subgroup of **Ashkenazic** Jews, the **Galitzianers,** by geography and their pronunciation of **Yiddish.** For example, a Litvak would call a noodle pudding "COO-gull," while a Galitzianer would say "KEE-gull."

loch in kop   int. Yiddish (LAWKH in kawp)   Literally, "a hole in the head." Used to describe something you don't need. "I need another errand to run today like a *loch in kop.*" Old-fashioned usage.

lokshen   n. Yiddish (LAWKSH-en)   Noodle. Often refers to noodles in soup. *Lokshen kugel* is a casserole made with noodles. Old-fashioned usage.

lost tribes of Israel   n. English   The 10 **tribes of Israel** that disappeared from biblical accounts after the northern kingdom of **Israel** was conquered by the Assyrians in 721 B.C.E. The tribes lost their separate identity during their exile and captivity and are thought to have intermarried with the Assyrians. Throughout history, various groups around the world have claimed that they are descendants of the lost tribes, pointing to their ancient Hebraic customs and beliefs as proof. Perhaps the best known of these are the **Falashas** of Ethiopia and the **Samaritans** of Nablus.

lox   n. Yiddish (LOCKS)   Thinly sliced smoked salmon. Bright orange in color, lox can be salty or sugar cured (this latter is called nova lox, short for Nova

Scotia lox). It is often served for breakfast along with bagels and cream cheese. From the Scandinavian word *lax* (salmon).

Lubavitch movement   n. Hebrew/Yiddish (luh-BOVE-itch)   One of the most famous and powerful **Hasidic** sects, it was founded in the late 1700s in the Russian town of Lubavitch; today its headquarters is in the Crown Heights section of Brooklyn, New York. These **ultra-Orthodox** Jews dress modestly and follow the most stringent requirements of *halakhah.* The group was originally called Lubavitch; in later years, the word Chabad, an acronym for the Hebrew words for wisdom, understanding, and knowledge, was added to the name. The movement is based on the teachings of the **Baal Shem Tov** and Rabbi Schneur Zalman (the Alter Rebbe), who wrote the compilation of Jewish mystical concepts known as the *Tanya.* The most recent Lubavitch **rebbe** was **Rabbi Menachem Mendel Schneerson** (1902–1994), who some hailed as the **Messiah** until his death. His followers, who are known as Lubavitchers or Chabadniks, still regard his teachings, sayings, and writings with reverence.

Today, the movement, sometimes called Chabad or Chabad-Lubavitch, is known for its outreach programs to the larger Jewish community. For example, the sect sponsors "Mitzvah Mobiles"; secular Jews are invited inside these vans to learn the blessings for various Jewish rituals, given objects of **Judaica,** and reconnected with their heritage. Lubavitch Houses, which host **Shabbat** dinners, **Torah** study groups, and social gatherings, can be found in cities and towns throughout the world as well as on college campuses with significant Jewish populations.

luftmensch   n. Yiddish (LOOFT-mench).   Literally "air man." A dreamer, someone with his head in the clouds. A *luftmensch* is optimistic with no good reason and has big goals but doesn't take action. "He took one screenwriting class and already that *luftmensch* thinks his play is going to Hollywood."

lukshen   See *lokshen.*

lulav   n. Hebrew (LOO-lav); pl.   **lulavim**   (loo-lah-VEEM)   Literally, "palm." **1.** A ritual object used on **Sukkot.** A *lulav* is a branch of palm that is tied together with two branches from a willow tree *(aravot)* and three from a myrtle bush *(hadas).* The *lulav* is always partnered with an *etrog,* a citrus fruit. On Sukkot, both in **synagogue** and in the **sukkah,** it is traditional to hold the *lulav* in the right hand and the *etrog* in the left, and then shake the *lulav* while reciting a blessing. Jews wave the *lulav* in all directions—up, down, east, west, north, and south—to symbolize that God is all around. These four species—the three parts of the *lulav* and the *etrog*—are called *arba minim.* **2.** The part of the *arba minim* that is the palm branch.

Luria, Isaac ben Solomon   (1534–1572)   A **Jerusalem**-born kabbalist; also known as ha–Ari, "the (sacred) lion." In 1570, Luria settled in Safed, **Palestine,** where he led an important school of mysticism and taught disciples his unique kabbalistic system, which came to be known as Lurianic **Kabbalah.** His concepts of repairing the world *(tikun olam)* and identifying with the Divine spirit through intense concentration *(kavanah)* were influential on the **Hasidic** movement.

Ma'ariv   n. Hebrew (mah-ah-REEV)   Literally, "evening." The evening prayer service, conducted after sundown. Many **synagogues** have two services a day, one in the morning for *Shacharit* services and one in the early evening when both *Mincha* and *Ma'ariv* prayers are said.

ma'asim tovim   pl. n. Hebrew (mah-ah-SEEM toe-VEEM)   Good deeds. See *gemilut hasadim.*

macaroon   n. English   A flourless, chewy ball-shaped cookie made with ground nuts, coconut, egg whites, and other ingredients. Macaroons come in many flavors, such as chocolate chip, chocolate covered, and almond. Because they contain no flour or yeast, macaroons are *pesachdik* and therefore a favorite **Pesach** treat.

Maccabee, Judah   (JOO-dah MACK-ah-bee)   The third son of Mattathias, Judah led the rebellion against **King Antiochus** of Syria in the 2nd century B.C.E. after his father died. Nicknamed "Maccabeus"—the hammer—because of his strong fighting style, Judah led the revolt against the Syrians that eventually returned control of **Jerusalem** and the **Temple** to the Jews. The Maccabean rebellion and the rededication of the Temple are the basis for the story of **Hanukkah.**

Maccabees   n. (MACK-ah-bees)   The band of Jewish revolutionaries, led by **Judah Maccabee,** who fought from 167 to 165 B.C.E. for religious freedom and the right to reclaim **Jerusalem** from **King Antiochus** and Syrian control. Their victory is the story of **Hanukkah.**

Maccabiah Games   n. Hebrew/English (mah-KAH-bee-AH GAMES)   A series of athletic competitions for Jewish athletes from around the world, held in the **State of Israel.** Like the Olympics, the Maccabiah Games take place every four years. Unlike the Olympics, amateur Maccabiah athletes range in age from teens to senior citizens. Each summer, Jewish community centers around the United States sponsor Maccabiah-like athletic competitions for teenage athletes to promote physical fitness and *ruach.*

macher n. Yiddish (MAKH-er) From the German word for "maker" or "doer." A big wheel, an operator; someone who can use his or her connections to make things happen. Also refers to someone who is active in an organization. "He just joined our **synagogue** and already he's a big *macher* in the **men's club.**"

machetayneste n. Yiddish (makh-eh-TAY-nis-teh) Mother-in-law.

machetunim n. Yiddish (makh-eh-TUH-num) The members of a spouse's extended family; particularly the in-laws. "My daughter just got engaged. I guess I have to invite the *machetunim* over for dinner soon."

machuten n. Yiddish (mah-KHOO-ten) Father-in-law.

machzor n. Hebrew (MAKH-zore); pl. **machzorim** (makh-zor-EEM) A special prayer book used in **synagogue** on **Rosh Hashanah** and **Yom Kippur.** A *machzor* contains the seasonal prayers, melodies, and readings for **High Holy Day** services.

maftir n. Hebrew (MAHF-teer) The final three or four verses of the weekly **Torah** reading. The *maftir* is the Torah portion that is most often recited by a **Bar** or **Bat Mitzvah,** although many teens read more of the **parashah.**

maftir aliyah n. Hebrew (MAHF-tear uh-LEE-ah) An additional and final *aliyah* that follows the seven prescribed *aliyot* on **Shabbat** and on holidays when the **haftarah** is read. The person who recites the *maftir aliyah* also reads a portion of the haftarah. On Shabbat, this honor is usually given to a **Bar** or **Bat Mitzvah.**

Magen David n. Hebrew (mah-GEN dah-VEED) Literally, "Shield of David." The six-pointed star that has become the symbol of Judaism. See **Star of David.**

Mah Nishtanah n. Hebrew (MAH nish-tah-NAH) The Hebrew name for the **Four Questions,** recited at the **Pesach seder.**

mahzor See *machzor.*

maideleh n. Yiddish (MAY-deh-leh) Unmarried woman; little girl. Used endearingly. Old-fashioned usage.

Maimonides, Moses (1135 1204) A Jewish philosopher and **rabbi** who is considered to be one of the greatest thinkers, scholars, and prolific writers on

Jewish history and sacred texts. Maimonides was born in Spain; his family fled persecution to Egypt, where he served as court physician to the sultan. He was the leader of the Jewish community of Cairo in the Middle Ages. His *Guide of the Perplexed* attempted to put many of the philosophies of Judaism in simple terms that the general populace could understand. His **Mishneh Torah** is a systematic code and compilation of Jewish law that he hoped would make it easier to observe **halakhah**, since Jews would not have to search the **Talmud** to find the reference point for each law. His *Book of Commandments,* a compilation of the Torah's 613 commandments, is still one of the primary texts used by **yeshivah** students. His most noted work, the **Thirteen Principles of Faith,** contains the famous quote "I believe with complete faith in the coming of the **Messiah.** Even though he may tarry I will wait for him on any day that he may come." He is so renowned that a Jewish expression of the time compared him with the biblical hero: "From **Moses** (of the **Torah**) to Moses (Maimonides), there is no one like Moses." Maimonides is also known by the acronym Rambam (Rabbi Moses ben Maimon).

malchut   n. Hebrew (maal-HOOT)   Literally "kingdom." The last of the 10 *sefirot,* or aspects of God's creative nature. According to kabbalistic teachings, *malchut* represents accomplishment and realization of the Divine plan. The 10th *sefirah* is also identified with the **Shekhinah,** the feminine presence of God. Each *sefirah* is associated with a part of the body; *malchut* corresponds to the entire body.

mama loshen   n. Yiddish (MAH-meh LAW-shen)   Literally, "mother tongue." Used to refer to the **Yiddish** language itself. While **Hebrew** was taught only to men for their study of the holy books, Yiddish was the everyday language of the home and of women.

mameleh   n. Yiddish (MAH-meh-leh)   A term of endearment for a little girl. Old-fashioned usage.

mamzer   n. Hebrew (MOM-zer)   Literally, "bastard." **1.** An offspring of an illicit relationship, including adultery and incest. According to Jewish law, a *mamzer* can only marry another *mamzer.* This category does not include the child of an unmarried Jewish woman, who is considered legitimate. **Progressive** movements of Judaism have abolished this classification. **2.** Untrustworthy or cheating. It can be a slang term of grudging admiration for someone who is clever or shrewd.

mandelbread   n. Yiddish (MON-duhl-bread)   Literally, "almond bread." A crunchy, dry cookie, similar to biscotti. It is made by forming dough into a loaf, baking it, and then slicing the loaf into oblong cookies and baking them again. Each baker has his own variation; common additions include almonds, walnuts, or bits of fruit. It is the fancier cousin of **kamishbread.** At **Pesach,**

mandelbread can be made with **matzah meal** instead of flour. Also called *mandelbrodt.*

mandlen   pl. n. Yiddish (MOND-lynn)   Literally, "almonds." Small, baked, crackerlike balls with hollow centers that are floated in chicken soup. *Mandlen* can be made with **matzah meal** so they are *pesachdik.* Because they taste like dry bites of air, few people ever eat them—except maybe on **Pesach.** *Mandlen* can be store-bought; they're often called "soup nuts."

manna   n. Hebrew (MAH-nah)   Food that was miraculously supplied to the **Israelites** in the wilderness during the **Exodus** from Egypt. When the Israelites questioned **Moses** about his decision to flee slavery in Egypt to an uncertain future, he and Aaron told the people that God would provide. The next morning, God rained "bread from heaven"—manna—to sustain the Israelites. Manna was described as white in color and delicious to eat. The tamarisk bush, which grows in the wilderness of **Sinai,** secretes a sweet juice that hardens into a white, fluffy, honeylike cloud. Perhaps this substance was the miracle of manna. Today, the expression "like manna from heaven" is used to describe an unexpected, bountiful gift.

maot hittim   n. Hebrew (mah-OAT hit-TEAM)   Literally, "money for wheat." A charitable collection taken right before **Pesach** to help poor Jews purchase **matzah** and the many other special foods required for the holiday's observance. Pesach can be very expensive because of the *pesachdik* foods and wine needed for the weeklong holiday. Today, many **synagogues** participate in this *tzedakah* project.

Maoz Tzur   n. Hebrew (MAH-oze TSOOR)   Literally, "rock of ages." An old Jewish folksong that praises God as **Israel**'s deliverer. "Maoz Tzur" is most often sung on **Hanukkah** after the candles on the **menorah** have been lit.

mappah   n. Hebrew (mah-PAH)   Literally, "tablecloth." **1.** The cloth placed over a table on which the **Torah** is read so that the Torah doesn't touch bare wood. During the **High Holy Days,** a white *mappah* is customarily used for this purpose. **2.** The decorative, embroidered cloth mantle used to protect and beautify the Torah. It has two openings at the top to accommodate the *atzei chayim.* The mantle is placed on the Torah before the breastplate and crown are put on, in a process known as dressing the Torah. **3. Mappah** The name of a set of **Ashkenazic** commentaries to the **Shulchan Arukh.**

maror   n. Hebrew (mah-ROAR)   A bitter herb, usually horseradish, placed on the **seder plate** at **Pesach** to symbolize the bitterness of slavery. During the **seder,** the story of the **Israelites'** slavery in ancient Egypt and the **Exodus,**

their journey to freedom, is told. A line from the **haggadah** reads, "Their lives were made bitter with the hard work and oppression of slavery." One of the **Four Questions** refers to *maror,* when it asks: "On all other nights we eat different vegetables. Why on this night do we eat bitter herbs?" During the seder, *maror* is also eaten between two pieces of matzah; this concoction is known as a **Hillel sandwich.**

Marrano n. Spanish (mah–RAH–no)   A historical but derogatory term for a Spanish or Portuguese Jew who was forced to convert to Christianity in the late Middle Ages during the Inquisition. The term comes from the Spanish word for "swine." See **Converso.**

Masada n. Hebrew (mah–SAH–dah)   The archaeological remains of a mountaintop fortress on the shores of the **Dead Sea** in the **State of Israel.** Masada, built by King Herod in the 1st century B.C.E., was the stronghold of the Zealots, a small group of Jews who fled Jerusalem after the Romans conquered the city and destroyed the **Second Temple** in 70 C.E. The Zealots held off the Roman legions for three years. In 73 C.E., rather than surrender to Rome, they committed mass suicide. Today, Masada is a popular tourist site. American teens sometimes hold their **Bar** or **Bat Mitzvah** services amid the stone ruins of the Zealot **synagogue** atop Masada.

mashgiach n. Hebrew (mahsh–GEE–akh); pl. **mashgichim** (mahsh-gee–KHEEM)   A person, usually an **Orthodox** Jew, who inspects and makes sure all the laws of **kashrut** are followed. *Mashgichim* are often employed by restaurants, supermarkets, **kosher** butchers, and food manufacturers. When food is certified by the *mashgiach,* a **heksher,** or certificate of kashrut, is issued.

Mashiach n. Hebrew (mah–SHEE–akh)   Literally, "the anointed one." The Hebrew word for **"Messiah,"** the person who will usher in a time of universal peace. Within Judaism, there are differing interpretations of exactly what the *Mashiach* will mean. A traditional **Orthodox** interpretation is that the Prophet **Elijah** will return, followed by a descendant of King **David** who will be chosen by God as the *Mashiach.* He will put an end to evil in the world, rebuild the **Temple,** and usher in the world to come *(olam ha–ba).* Jews will be "gathered in" and reunited in the Land of **Israel.** Many Jews believe that doing more **mitzvot** and leading a pious life will hasten the arrival of the *Mashiach.* **Reconstructionist** Jews do not believe that ancient Jerusalem will be restored; they believe in a **Messianic Age** rather than an embodied Messiah. The Jewish concept of a Messiah is very different from the Christian one. Jews do not believe that the Messiah has come yet.

maskilim pl. n. Hebrew (mahs–kee–LEEM)   Literally, "enlightened ones." The Eastern European Jews who were followers of the **Haskalah,** the Jewish

Enlightenment movement that was begun in Germany by Moses Mendelssohn in the late 18th century and lasted into the 19th century. The *maskilim* considered much of Judaism to be old-fashioned and wanted to experience what secular culture had to offer. They were opposed by the **Orthodox,** who did not wish to change or modernize Judaism.

Masoretic text   n. (mas-uh–RET-ik) from the Hebrew word *masorah,* which means "tradition."   The Hebrew text of the **TANAKH,** which is traditionally accepted as the authoritative version and most often used in synagogues. It was primarily compiled and edited by a group of Jewish sages known as the Masoretes between the 7th and 10th centuries C.E. It differs from the **Septuagint,** the Greek translation of the Bible.

Masorti   n. Hebrew (mah-SOR-tee)   Literally, "traditional." The word used by Israelis to refer to the **Conservative movement** of Judaism. The Masorti movement is growing larger and sponsors youth groups, camps, a kibbutz, and programs for new immigrants.

matriarchs   pl. n. English from Greek   The "founding mothers" of the Jewish people: **Sarah, Rebecca, Rachel,** and **Leah;** the wives of the three **patriarchs.** The names of the matriarchs are sometimes added to prayers in an effort to make liturgy more egalitarian. The matriarchs' names are also included in a blessing said at a naming for baby girls, a wish that they "grow up to be like Sarah, Rebecca, Rachel, and Leah." On **Sukkot,** the names of the partriarchs and matriarchs are invoked in the custom of *ushpizin.* The names of the matriarchs are still popular ones for Jewish girls.

Mattan Torah   n. Hebrew (mah-TAAN toe-RAH)   Literally "giving of the law." According to tradition, the term used to describe God's giving the **Torah** to **Moses** and the **Israelites** at Mount Sinai. **Shavuot** marks the anniversary of *Mattan Torah.*

matzah   n. Hebrew (MAH-tsah); pl. **matzot** (mah-TSOTE)   The unleavened, flat cracker made from flour and water that is eaten during **Pesach.** Matzah is symbolic of the haste with which the **Israelites** fled from slavery in ancient Egypt. Because they did not have time to allow bread to rise, they packed flat bread to take with them. There are many religious regulations regarding its manufacture. It must be mixed, kneaded, and baked within a time span of 18 minutes so that fermentation (and yeast rising) does not occur. Matzah has tiny holes in each sheet to retard the swelling during baking. Today, most matzah is made in factories and is available in supermarkets in a variety of flavors, including whole wheat, onion, and egg. Handmade matzah is often called *shemurah matzah.*

matzah ball   n. Hebrew/English (MAH-tsah BALL)   A combination of **matzah meal,** eggs, and salt that is rolled into a ball and cooked in boiling water or soup; it is similar to a dumpling. Matzah ball soup—chicken broth with matzah balls—is a traditional first course at **Shabbat** and holiday meals and at **Pesach sedarim.** A matzah ball can also be called a *knaidel.*

matzah brei   n. Yiddish (MAH-tsah BRYE)   A combination of water-softened **matzah** pieces and beaten eggs that is lightly fried. A popular choice for breakfast during **Pesach,** *matzah brei* is the *pesachdik* version of French toast. It is served sweet, with jam or syrup; or savory, with salt or sour cream. Also called fried matzah.

matzah meal   n. Hebrew/English (MAH-tsah MEAL)   Finely crumbled, crushed **matzah** used as a flour substitute in cooking during **Pesach.** Many *pesachdik* cakes and other foods use matzah meal as a primary ingredient. At Pesach, matzah meal can also be mixed with milk or water and eggs to make pancakes, called matzah meal **latkes.**

matzo   See **matzah.**

maven   n. Yiddish (MAY-vin)   An expert or connoisseur; a specialist. A maven is someone who has a certain interest or considers him- or herself to be an expert in a particular area. "Becca spends so much time sending e-mail; she's the computer maven."

mazel   n. Yiddish (MAH-zull)   Literally, "constellation." In the **Torah,** *mazel* referred to a favorable astrological sign; *mazel* implies that the stars are with you. The word has come to mean "good luck." "Last week, his son was sick and his wife had a fender-bender. He could use some *mazel.*"

mazel tov   int. Yiddish (MAH-zul TOVE)   "Good luck!" An expression of congratulations and best wishes used by Jews on happy occasions, **simchot,** and achievements. **Ashkenazim** shout *"mazel tov"* at the bride and groom at the end of a wedding ceremony.

mechayeh   n. Yiddish (muh-KHYE-yeh)   Literally, "resurrection." A feeling of pleasure, delight, or relief. Usually refers to physical pleasure, like loosening a belt after a big meal or cooling off on a hot day, or a simple enjoyment like watching a favorite movie. "After standing all day at work, it was a *mechayeh* to finally sit down and take off my shoes."

mechitzah   n. Hebrew (meh-KHEE-tsah)   The physical means of separation, usually a curtain or a small wall, between the men's and the women's sections in an **Orthodox** or very traditional **synagogue.** In some synagogues, the women's section is a balcony or raised gallery. In most Orthodox congregations, women have no public role in the service.

megillah   n. Hebrew (meh-gee-LAH); pl. **megillot**   (meh-gee-LOTE) **1.** Literally, "scroll." Each of these five books or stories, which are part of **Kethuvim,** tells a different historical tale. **The Song of Songs (Shir ha-Shirim)** is read on **Pesach; Ruth** is read on **Shavuot; Lamentations (Eikhah)** is read on **Tisha be-Av***; ***Ecclesiastes (Kohelet)** is read on **Sukkot;** and **Esther** is read on **Purim.** In ancient days the *megillot* were written on parchment, like the **Torah;** today most *megillot* are contained in a book. When the word "Megillah" is used without specifying which one, it is most often capitalized and usually refers to the Scroll of Esther, *Megillat Esther,* the most well known. **2.** Yiddish (meh-GILL-ah)   A long or complicated story; anything that is done in its fullest form, from start to finish. The phrase takes its meaning from *Megillat Esther,* a long and detailed historical story. On Purim, it is traditional to read and listen to the "whole megillah" from start to finish. "When they went out to dinner, they didn't just have an entree. Soup, salad, and dessert were included, so they had the whole megillah!"

Megillat Esther   n. Hebrew (meh-gee-LAHT ess-TER)   The Hebrew name for the Scroll of Esther, the **megillah** that is read on **Purim.** See **Esther, Scroll of.**

Meir, Golda (1889–1978)   Fourth Prime Minister, Foreign Minister, and one of the founding leaders of the **State of Israel.** Born in the Ukraine, Golda Meir immigrated with her family to Wisconsin when she was a child. She became a passionate **Zionist** and made *aliyah* in 1921 with her husband; she was active in the Histadrut, a powerful trade union. She often traveled abroad as a goodwill ambassador to solicit funds and support from the U.S. government and its citizens on behalf of the Jewish State. Between 1949 and 1974, Meir held various positions in the **Knesset,** including Foreign Minister under **David Ben Gurion.** Whenever she tried to retire, she was called back to government service. During her term as Prime Minister (1969–1974), she led the country through the surprise attacks of the **Yom Kippur War.** She is buried on Mount Herzl in Jerusalem.

melakhah   n. Hebrew (meh-lah-KHAH)   Work or actions forbidden on **Shabbat.** Like many aspects of Judaism, the interpretations and observances of these ancient laws vary widely, depending on a Jew's personal belief, how he or she was raised, and which movement of Judaism that individual follows. Set out specifically in the **Talmud,** the 39 labors forbidden on Shabbat include common activities like baking, sewing, and writing as well as actions like sheepshearing, kindling a fire, and tying a knot. Today, traditional Jews interpret these prohibited activities to include many modern inventions and conveniences that, although not mentioned, are related in some way to the ancient list. Thus, for example, most **Orthodox** Jews will not drive a car on Shabbat because starting an engine involves a spark, which is kindling a fire. Other Jews may observe some of the Shabbat prohibitions, such as not going to work, spending money, or drawing during children's services. Still others celebrate the spirit of Shabbat by engaging in family activities that, while they may violate traditional *melakhah,* encourage Jewish identity and culture and celebrate the spirit of the day.

melaveh malkah   n. Hebrew (meh-LAH-veh MAL-kah)   Literally, "accompanying the queen." **1.** The festive meal served on Saturday night following **Shabbat** as a way to bid farewell to the Sabbath Queen. Tradition says it began with King **David,** who had been warned that he would die on a Sabbath. At the end of each Sabbath, he celebrated his being alive with a feast. **2.** A term used by **Orthodox** women to refer to a party or gathering for women only.

Menasseh   First son of **Joseph** and his wife, Asenath, an Egyptian. Menasseh is also the name of one of the 12 **tribes of Israel,** whose members were said to be descended from him. Joseph was given a double portion of land, which he later gave to his two sons, Menasseh and **Ephraim.** The tribe of Menasseh occupied the mountainous region northeast of the **Dead Sea.** When lighting **Shabbat** candles, it's customary in some homes to bless a son with the words, "May you be like Ephraim and Menasseh."

menorah   n. Hebrew (meh-NOE-rah)   A branched candelabra, the menorah is an ancient and important symbol of Judaism. **1.** The seven-branched menorah, commonly displayed in **synagogues,** is said to symbolize the seven days of Creation. When the **Israelites** fled Egypt in the **Passover** story, they took with them a seven-branched golden menorah. The archaeological ruin of the Arch of Titus in Rome depicts the Romans sacking **Jerusalem** and carrying a menorah out of the **Second Temple** in 70 C.E. **2.** The eight-branched candle holder, also called a *hanukkiah,* is used to celebrate **Hanukkah.** A raised ninth candle, called the *shamash,* is used to kindle the others. On Hanukkah, menorahs are often placed in windows as a public testament to the miracle of the holiday. Menorahs can be made of almost any material, with all sorts of decorations and motifs. Children's Hanukkah menorahs often depict cartoon characters, animals, and the like. Other menorahs are hand-wrought works of **Judaica** made from metal, glass, or clay.

mensch   n. Yiddish (MENCH)   Literally, "person." A caring, decent person— man or woman—who can be trusted. It refers in a much larger sense to acting in an honorable, proper way. The term is bestowed as a compliment on someone who has done the right thing without asking for thanks or credit. For example, "Larry is a real mensch. Before he returned Peter's car, he filled the tank with gas!"

menschlikhkeit   n. Yiddish (MENCH-lekh-kite)   The code of behavior that involves acting like a **mensch** and living an honest, compassionate life. For example: "We try to teach our children not just to follow the rules and rituals of Judaism, but also to always act with *menschlikhkeit.*"

men's club   n. English   The men's auxiliary of a **synagogue.** Men's clubs sponsor educational, social, and social action programs; their fund-raising efforts support various synagogue projects. Programs might include hosting a monthly Sunday breakfast, organizing a blood drive, serving as ushers at **High Holy Day** services, or building a **sukkah.**

meshugge   adj. Yiddish (mch-SHOO-gah)   Crazy, nuts, cuckoo. "He took all the kids to the toy store on a **Hanukkah** spree. It was meshugge. The kids went crazy running in the aisles." n. **meshuggener** (male), **meshuggeneh** (female): An affectionate term for a crazy, nutty person.

Messiah   n. English   One who is promised and chosen by God to usher in a time of universal peace. Among Christians, the word "Messiah" refers to Jesus, but Jews use the term *Mashiach* to refer to the Messiah or the **Messianic Age** to come.

Messianic Age   n. English   The promised and expected time of universal peace, sometime in the future. It is said that in the Messianic Age, people will return to **Torah** and the land of Israel; the **Temple** in Jerusalem will be rebuilt; war and famine will end; and an era of peace and prosperity will come upon the earth. This concept is a tenet of the **Reconstructionist movement,** which distinguishes the Messianic Age, whether brought about by God's actions or human involvement, from the belief in a *Mashiach*, a personal Messiah who will be anointed by God.

Messianic Jew   n. English   A member of the religious sect that follows some of the beliefs of Judaism but also believes that Jesus is the son of God. Although Messianic Jews share some of the texts and ideas of Judaism, the central tenet of Messianic Jews—that Jesus is the **Messiah**—is diametrically opposed to the very foundations of Judaism. Many of their other beliefs also differ significantly and importantly from Judaism. For example, Messianic Jews believe that man can atone for sin and find redemption through Jesus, who can forgive all sin. Jews believe that God can forgive sin but also that people can forgive those who wronged them. Messianic Jews believe that Jesus is a deity to be worshiped as the son of God. The first commandment of Judaism is that there is only one God. Messianic Jews actively proselytize and work to recruit new members; Jews rarely do this. Although they often use Hebrew words—for example, they call Jesus "Yeshua"—no movement of Judaism considers Messianic Jews to be members of the Jewish faith. Also called Jews for Jesus.

mezinke   n. Yiddish (meh-ZEEN-kah)   A joyous **klezmer** melody. It sometimes refers to a dance done toward the end of a wedding reception during the **crowning ceremony,** which honors parents who have married off their last child. The parents sit while guests circle around them, traditionally to the song "Die Mezinke Oysgegeben" (The Youngest Daughter Is Given).

mezuzah   n. Hebrew (meh-ZUH-zah); pl. **mezuzot**   (meh-zoo-ZOTE) Literally, "doorpost." A parchment scroll that is inscribed with verses from the **Torah,** rolled up, inserted in a decorative case or tube, and attached to the doorway. Since biblical times, the presence of a mezuzah has marked a house as a Jewish home. Part of the tradition comes from the Book of **Deuteronomy,** a verse of which reads, "You shall write them [the laws of the Torah] upon the doorposts of your house and upon your gates" (6:9).

The parchment, or *klaf,* is handwritten by a scribe following the same rules that apply to writing a Torah scroll. The *Shema* prayer from Deuteronomy is handwritten on one side and the word *Shaddai,* another name for God, is written on the other side. When a mezuzah case has an opening, the parchment is positioned so that the word *Shaddai* shows through. The letter *shin* (for *Shaddai*) often appears on the outside of a mezuzah case. Jews attach a mezuzah, on an angle pointing inward, to the upper third of the doorway of their home (on the right as they enter). They often place mezuzot on some interior doorways as well. Some Jews gently touch the mezuzah and then kiss their fingers when entering a home as a gesture of reverence for God. An important article of **Judaica,** a mezuzah is often given as a gift for a wedding or housewarming. A mezuzah can also be worn, in miniature, as a piece of jewelry.

midrash   n. Hebrew (MID-rahsh); pl. **midrashim**   (mid-rah-SHEEM) Literally, "interpretation." Midrashim are written interpretations and discussions of the laws, customs, and rituals of Jewish life mentioned in the **Torah.** Ancient collections of midrashim date back thousands of years and are attributed to famous sages and **rabbis.** In these discussions, the rabbis dissect the Torah verse by verse, looking for explanations and meaning in each word. Other midrashim are more like sermons; they include fanciful stories that have a moral. There are even versions of midrashim for children, similar to fables, that are easier to read and understand. Midrashim are still being written today. The Midrash refers to the entire body of midrashic literature.

Mi Khamokha n. Hebrew (MEE khah-MOE-khah) An ancient prayer that asks the rhetorical question, "Who is like [as great as] God?" *Mi Khamokha* is sung by the congregation as part of **Shabbat** and festival services at almost every **synagogue.** This familiar song is thought to be one of the most ancient liturgies in Judaism, dating back to biblical times. Parts of *Mi Khamokha* were among the songs of joy and gratitude **Miriam** sang after the **Exodus** and the crossing of the Red Sea.

mikveh n. Hebrew (MICK-veh); pl. **mikvaot** (mick-vah-OTE) Ritual bath; a body of natural water used for ritual cleansing. Most *mikvaot* are located in a synagogue or other Jewish communal institution and look like small swimming pools; they are filled, however, with either rainwater or water from a spring or stream.

   The *mikveh* has several uses. A traditional married Jewish woman immerses herself to fulfill the laws of **taharat ha-mishpachah.** After her menstrual period has been over for seven days, she must cleanse herself in the *mikveh* before resuming sexual relations with her husband. At the *mikveh,* the woman undresses completely and female attendants help her clean her body and remove all jewelry, makeup, and other accessories before entering the water. Upon immersion, the woman recites a blessing to God. She might also visit a *mikveh* after giving birth. It is also traditional for a bride to visit the *mikveh* before her wedding day. Converts to Judaism are immersed in a *mikveh* as part of their conversion ceremony. Some men may use a *mikveh* to purify themselves before **Shabbat, Yom Kippur,** their wedding day, or other occasions.

   Today, the tradition of the *mikveh* has also been embraced by more liberal Jews. A bride might visit the *mikveh* before her wedding day; women also enter the *mikveh* after a life-changing event, such as divorce or the completion of chemotherapy.

milchig adj. Yiddish (MILL-khick) The general term for food in the "dairy" category, according to the Jewish dietary laws of **kashrut.** This includes milk, cheese, ice cream, and milk products that might contain whey. Milchig also refers to the utensils and dishes used for cooking, eating, and serving milk products. A person who keeps **kosher** does not mix **fleishig** (meat) and milchig foods or eat from both food groups at the same meal. This is why at a **kosher** meal, where chicken is the main course, you would be served coffee with nondairy creamer, and fruit, or perhaps a **pareve** frozen dessert instead of ice cream. Under the laws of kashrut, all food can be classified as either milchig, fleishig, or pareve.

Mincha n. Hebrew (MIN-hah) The afternoon prayer service. Originally held just after noon, it is often moved back to later in the day. Most **synagogues** have two services a day, one in the morning for *Shacharit* services and one in the late afternoon or early evening, when *Mincha* and ***Ma'ariv*** prayers are said.

minhag   n. Hebrew (MIN-hag)   Literally, "custom." A tradition that is not mentioned in the **Torah** or mandated by law, but nonetheless is followed. There is an expression that something is "either ***halakhah*** (Jewish law) or *minhag*." What is considered *minhag* varies greatly among branches of Judaism, according to family heritage, and even within families. One example is that **Ashkenazic** Jews consider it *minhag* to name a child after deceased relatives, while **Sephardic** Jews do not. The tradition of celebrating **Bar** and **Bat Mitzvah** is *minhag,* as is getting married under a ***huppah.***

minyan   n. Hebrew (MIN-yin); pl. **minyanim** (min-yah-NEEM)   Literally, "number." A gathering of 10 people, the minimum necessary for a communal religious service according to Jewish law. The *Kaddish* and *Birkat ha-Kohanim* prayers cannot be recited without a minyan, nor is the **Torah** read aloud without a minyan. For traditional Jews, a minyan is composed only of men, **Bar Mitzvah** age and above. In 1973, the **Conservative movement** ruled that women could be counted in a minyan. **Reconstructionists** follow the same policy. **Reform** congregations can conduct a prayer service even in the absence of 10 adult Jews.

Miriam   The sister of **Moses** and **Aaron.** Miriam watched her brother, the baby Moses, float down the Nile until he was safely rescued by Pharoah's daughter; she then brought their mother to the palace to serve as Moses' nurse. During the **Exodus** from Egypt, after the **Israelites** safely crossed the parted Sea of Reeds, Miriam led the women in joyful song and "dance with timbrels." Along with the **matriarchs,** Miriam, one of the few female leaders of ancient Israel, is the focal point for many feminist Jewish rituals. See **Miriam's Cup** and **Miriam's Well.**

Miriam's Cup   n. English   A special goblet, often handcrafted, that is filled with water and placed on the **seder** table in honor of **Miriam,** a central figure in the **Pesach** story. It represents the nurturing waters of Miriam's Well and Miriam's rejoicing after the **Exodus.** Many feminists have added a Miriam's Cup to the seder in recent years as a symbol of women's contributions throughout Jewish history. Women have also developed rituals and blessings for using a Miriam's Cup as part of **Shabbat,** *Havdalah,* and **Rosh Hodesh** celebrations and at the onset of menstruation.

Miriam's Well   n. English   The Bible tells of a mysterious well that would bring forth waters to sustain those in need. For 40 years, while the **Israelites** wandered through the desert after the **Exodus, Miriam** was guardian of the well. She used its miraculous waters to heal the sick and nourish the people. When Miriam was stricken with leprosy, Zipporah, **Moses'** wife, healed her with water from the well. When Miriam died, the well disappeared; some say it remains at the bottom of the Sea of **Galilee,** others say it is still with us somewhere. Today, Miriam's Well is used as a symbol of women's healing and nurturing abilities; a woman's tears, menstrual blood, and breast milk are links to the fluid of the well. Healing prayer groups, or *havurot,* sometimes take the name Miriam's Well.

misheberakh   n. Hebrew (mih-shah-BAY-rock)   Literally, "he who blessed." A prayer asking God for a special, specific blessing. There are many types of *misheberakh*; in some **synagogues** everyone who is called to the **Torah** for an *aliyah* receives a *misheberakh.* The prayer is often used after the birth of a child and on behalf of the sick; the **rabbi** may read a list of persons who are ill or ask the congregants for names they wish to be mentioned, and a *misheberakh* for a speedy recovery is recited.

mishegoss   n. Yiddish (mih-sheh-GOSS)   Foolishness, nonsense, craziness. Used often to refer to wasting time or effort on something not worthy. "Spending all that money on baseball cards? Such *mishegoss!* He already has hundreds."

mishkan   n. Hebrew (MISH-kahn)   See **Tabernacle.**

mishloach manot   pl. n. Hebrew (mish-LOW-ahkh mah-NOTE)   Literally, "delivery" or "sending of portions." Goodie bags or baskets containing **hamantashen,** candy, fruit, and other treats that are given to family, friends, and the needy on **Purim.** They are sometimes delivered by children dressed in costumes for the holiday. Also called *shalach munis* (Yiddish).

Mishnah   n. Hebrew (MISH-nah)   The section of the **Talmud** that contains rabbinical commentaries and laws that were passed down from generation to generation, starting with **Moses.** Known as the **Oral Law,** the Mishnah was written down in the 2nd century C.E. It was an attempt to put the commands and laws of the **Torah** into practical terms. Sections of the Mishnah deal with holiday observances, family life, agriculture, civil and criminal law, rituals, and more. One of the most famous books of the Mishnah is *Pirke Avot* (Ethics of the Fathers), which includes famous quotations from Jewish scholars and **rabbis** from ancient times. The Mishnah and the **Gemara** make up the two sections of the Talmud.

Mishneh Torah   n. Hebrew (MISH-neh TOE-rah)   A famous, comprehensive book of Jewish law completed in the 12th century C.E. by the rabbinic scholar and philosopher **Moses Maimonides.** The *Mishneh Torah* is a lengthy commentary and discussion of the **Torah**'s 613 commandments. It covers subjects such as Jewish rituals, customs, and holiday celebrations as well as business ethics and civil dealings.

mishpachah   n. Hebrew (mish-pah-KHAH); Yiddish pronunciation (mish-PUH-khah)   Literally, "family." Extended family; the whole clan. A *mishpachah* includes relatives by blood and marriage and sometimes even very close friends. The word conveys a warm feeling of friendship. "Let's invite the whole *mishpachah* to our seder this year."

miskeit   n. Yiddish (MEES-kite)   Ugliness. Can refer to someone who is ugly in appearance or character. Old-fashioned usage.

mission to Israel   n. English   An organized group excursion to the **State of Israel** sponsored by a **synagogue** or a Jewish communal agency such as **United Jewish Communities.** Trips usually include visits to educational, cultural, and religious institutions and behind-the-scenes looks at **kibbutz** life, the government, the military, and some of the projects that American Jews support in the State of Israel, like housing or hospitals. Fund-raising is frequently a part of the mission agenda.

mitnagdim   pl. n. Hebrew (mit-nahg-DEEM)   Literally, "opponents." The Eastern European **Orthodox** Jews who were opposed to the practices of the emerging sect of **Hasidism** in the 18th century. The *mitnagdim* differed from the Hasidim in how they observed **kashrut** and educated their children; they objected to the Hasidim's exuberant prayers, which were in contrast to their own disciplined study. These two Orthodox groups later overlooked their differences because they were both traditional when compared with the *maskilim,* the followers of the **Haskalah** Enlightenment movement that began at the end of the century.

mitzvah   n. Hebrew (MITS-vah); pl. **mitzvot** (mitz-VOTE)   Literally, "commandment." **1.** One of the 613 specific obligations required for leading a good Jewish life. Many of these mitzvot, which are detailed in the **Torah,** could be classified as "good deeds," like visiting a sick friend or giving to charity. Others have to do with leading a Jewish life, such as keeping **kosher** or reciting prayers. Some are ethical and moral obligations, such as the prohibition against incest. Tradition says that the 613 mitzvot include 248 positive commandments, corresponding to the number of bones in the human body, and 365 negative commandments (things not to do) corresponding to the number of days in the year. It is traditional that if one is going to perform a mitzvah, it should be done happily and not grudgingly, with true feeling *(kavana)* and as beautifully as possible. See *hiddur mitzvah*. **2.** The general term for any good deed or act of kindness. "You really did a mitzvah by watching their kids all day Sunday so that they could go to the funeral."

mizrach n. Hebrew (miz-RAHKH) A decorative sign containing the word "*mizrach*," meaning "east." It is traditional for Jews in the Western Hemisphere to pray facing east, the direction of **Jerusalem** and the **Temple.** So Jews who pray in their homes might hang a *mizrach* on an eastern-facing wall to indicate which way to face when they pray. This is also why the **ark** in an Ashkenazic **synagogue** is set in an eastern-facing wall.

moadim le-simcha n. Hebrew (moe-ah-DEEM le-sim-KHAH) Literally, "holidays for rejoicing." A greeting, similar to *"hag sameach,"* but used only during *hol ha-moed.*

Modeh Ani int. Hebrew (MOE-deh AH-knee) Literally, "I give thanks." A prayer recited upon waking in the morning.

modern   Orthodox n. English A movement, first called neo-Orthodoxy, that was founded in the late 19th century by Samson Raphael Hirsch to modernize **Orthodox** Judaism and come to terms with secular society. Today, the term is often used by other Jews to characterize the more modern members of the Orthodox movement and distinguish them from the **ultra-Orthodox.** Modern Orthodox Jews observe the laws of *halakhah* while participating in modern society. Some modern Orthodox children attend secular schools; others go to Jewish **day schools.** While women dress modestly, their long skirts may be the latest style, and their head covering may be a sequined scarf. Yeshiva University is the rabbinical school for the modern Orthodox; its rabbinical arm is the Rabbinical Council of America. In the **State of Israel,** modern Orthodox Jews are called *dati.*

mohel n. Hebrew (MOE-hel); Yiddish pronunciation (MOY-el) The person trained to perform ritual **circumcision,** or *brit milah.* In ancient times it was the father's obligation to circumcise his child. Today, a *mohel* is trained by an older *mohel* or a surgeon and then is certified by both medical and religious authorities. When performing a *brit milah,* the *mohel* often conducts the service, leads the appropriate prayers, and instructs the parents afterward in the post-circumcision care of their son.

momzer See *mamzer.*

mondelbrodt See **mandelbread.**

mondlen See *mandlen.*

Mordecai (MORE-deh-CHYE) A cousin of Queen **Esther,** Mordecai served as a palace official during the reign of **King Ahasuerus.** He is one of the heroes of the **Purim** story. Tradition says that Mordecai was responsible for Esther's Jewish upbringing and that he was the one who refused to bow down to **Haman,** thus incurring Haman's wrath upon the Jews.

Moses   Biblical prophet, lawgiver, and greatest leader of the ancient Jewish people. Son of Amram and Yocheved, brother of **Miriam** and **Aaron.** The story of his life is told in the Books of **Exodus, Numbers,** and **Deuteronomy.** After growing up in the Egyptian court, Moses was appointed by God to lead the **Israelites** out of slavery in Egypt. Moses received the **Ten Commandments,** the basis of Jewish law, from God on **Mount Sinai** and served as God's messenger to the people. Moses also led the Israelites in the wilderness for 40 years, preparing them to enter the land of **Canaan.** He died at the age of 120 in the land of Moab, overlooking Canaan. There are several explanations as to why God punished Moses by not allowing him to enter the **Promised Land,** including that he argued with God, he smashed the Ten Commandments when he saw the Israelites worshiping the Golden Calf, and he disobeyed God in the desert.

moshav   n. Hebrew (moe-SHAHV); pl. **moshavim**   (moe-shah-VEEM) A cooperative agricultural settlement in the **State of Israel.** The first moshav was established in 1921. The members of a moshav jointly own the land and farm machinery and work together in planning and marketing. Unlike on a **kibbutz,** members own their own homes and can use their income as they wish.

Motzi   See *ha-Motzi.*

Mount Sinai   n. English/Hebrew   **1.** According to the **Torah,** the mountain on which God gave **Moses** the stone tablets containing the **Ten Commandments.** The location of the mountain is not specified in the Torah. See *Torah mi-Sinai.* **2.** The tallest mountain in the **Sinai** Peninsula, which now belongs to Egypt; in Arabic it is called Jabal Musa ("Mount Moses").

Mourner's Kaddish   See *Kaddish.*

muktzeh   n. Hebrew (MOOK-tseh)   An object that should not be touched on **Shabbat** because it could be used for an activity that is prohibited according to the most stringent interpretation of Jewish law. Because *halakhah* forbids, for example, driving, writing, working, and shopping, the objects that go along with these activities—such as car keys, pens, tools, and money—are also off-limits. Thus, in an **Orthodox** Jewish home, if a child picks up a crayon on Shabbat, a parent might say, "Put that away, it's *muktzeh.*"

mun   n. Yiddish (MOHN)   A sweetened poppy seed mixture used to fill **hamantashen.**

Musaf   n. Hebrew (MOO-sahff)   Literally, "additional." The extra set of prayers tacked onto the morning service, usually after the reading of the **Torah** and **haftarah,** in honor of festivals, the **High Holy Days,** and **Shabbat.**

mutche   v. Yiddish (MOO-cheh)   Literally, "torture" or "torment." **1.** To nag or harass, as in "Don't *mutche* your sister." **2.** To struggle financially; to barely make ends meet. Old-fashioned usage.

nachas   n. Hebrew (NAH-khiss]   Fulfillment, proud pleasure, special joy, especially in the accomplishments of one's children or grandchildren. Used in the expression *shep nachas,* which roughly translates as "get joy," as in "She's getting straight A's. Her parents must **shep nachas** from her."

Nachmanides, Moses (1194–1270)   One of the great Jewish scholars of the Middle Ages, Nachmanides was a Spanish Talmudist, Kabbalist, and biblical commentator. Born Moses ben Nakman Gerondi, he is perhaps best remembered for his historic Jewish-Christian debates, where he posed such questions as whether Jesus was the **Messiah,** whether the Messiah had come yet, and if Jesus was Divine. These debates took place in front of King James I of Spain. Nachmanides was later tried for blasphemy and forced to flee the country. He settled in **Palestine** where he continued writing biblical commentaries.

naming   n. English   The Jewish ceremony and celebration welcoming the birth of a daughter, so called because it is traditional for the infant's Hebrew name to be announced publicly for the first time. A naming may be held in the family's home, weeks or even months after the birth. Sometimes the ceremony takes place in **synagogue** during the **Torah** service. If the ceremony is held during a Torah service, the baby's parents and/or grandparents, siblings, and friends may receive an *aliyah,* and special prayers are said for the well-being of the baby. Many parents include readings and personal observations about having a child, along with appropriate *brachot,* including the *Shehecheyanu.* Blessings often include a wish that the child will "grow to enjoy a life of *huppah,* Torah, and *ma'asim tovim* (good deeds)." The ceremony is often followed by a celebration that includes a festive meal and gifts for the newborn. Unlike a **brit milah,** there is no formally mandated time when the ceremony must occur.

Although it seems like a modern tradition, the celebration of the birth of a girl is mentioned in the Torah and **Midrash.** However, there is no formal liturgy. It is customary to announce for whom the baby is named. **Ashkenazic** Jews usually name a child in memory of a deceased relative; **Sephardic** Jews generally name a child after a living relative. Sometimes the child shares the same English name or the same Hebrew name as the deceased, other times it is simply the same initial letter or a name with similar meaning. Also called **brit chayim, brit bat,** and **simchat bat.**

Naphtali   The sixth son of **Jacob** and the second son of Bilhah, who was Jacob's concubine and **Rachel's** handmaid. Naphtali is also the name of one of the 12 **tribes of Israel,** whose members were said to be descended from him. The tribe settled northwest of the **Sea of Galilee.**

narrishkeit   n. Yiddish (NAH-rish-kite)   Foolishness; folly. "He buys a lottery ticket every week, thinking he'll hit the big one. What *narrishkeit!*"

National Council of Jewish Women (NCJW)   n. English   Committed to *tikun olam* (repairing the world), the organization works through research, education, advocacy, and community service programs to improve the quality of life for women, children, and families. Initiatives in the United States and the **State of Israel** include child care, gun control, reproductive rights, prevention of hate crimes, Social Security reform, and preventing discrimination in the workplace. It is the oldest national women's volunteer organization in America, with more than 90,000 members nationwide.

nebbish   n. Yiddish (NEB-bish)   A loser; an ineffectual, timid person. Used to describe someone you feel sorry for. "In that fancy restaurant, they gave him the table next to the bathroom and he didn't say anything. That nebbish!"

nefesh   n. Hebrew (NEH-fesh)   From the word meaning "breath." The soul; the aspect of a human being that is spiritual and immortal. Often used interchangeably with *neshamah.* However, in **kabbalistic** philosophy, the *nefesh* is the level of the soul that is connected with physical awareness, while *neshamah* is the part of the soul that resides in a person's character.

Negev   n. Hebrew (neh-GEV)   An arid region of southern **Israel,** portions of which are true desert. Bounded by the city of Beersheva on the north and **Eilat** on the southern tip, the Negev comprises 60 percent of the land area of Israel, yet it is the least populated because it has rocky, sandy soil and receives little natural rainfall. Through modern irrigation, the Negev is home to several agricultural **kibbutzim.** A variety of wildlife including ibex, desert foxes and lizards, as well as migrating birds, eagles and falcons, live here, too.

Neilah   n. Hebrew (neh-ee-LAH)   Literally, "shutting or locking." The final prayer service on **Yom Kippur.** Tradition says that this is the time when God is making the final decision about who has found forgiveness through repentance, charity, and prayer, and who has not. The shutting or locking refers to the image of the "gates of redemption and forgiveness," which are mentioned in the prayer. During the *Neilah* service, one is supposed to pray with particular attention and intensity *(kavanah),* in hope that prayers reach God before the gates are closed and Yom Kippur comes to an end.

ner tamid n. Hebrew (NEHR tah-MEED) Literally, "eternal light." The light fixture in front of the **ark** in every **synagogue** that is constantly lit. See **eternal light.**

nes gadol hayah sham Hebrew (NESS gah-DOLE hah-YAH SHAM) This phrase, which means "a great miracle happened there," is abbreviated on every dreidel by the letters *nun, gimel, hay,* and *shin.* The words recall the Maccabees' victory over the Syrians in 165 B.C.E. and the story of **Hanukkah,** when the oil in the rededicated **Temple** lasted for eight days instead of one. Dreidels made in Israel replace the letter *shin* (for the word "there"), with the letter *pay* for the Hebrew word *po,* meaning "here": a great miracle happened *here.*

neshamah n. Hebrew (neh-shah-MAH); Yiddish pronunciation (neh-SHAW-mah) From the Hebrew word *nasham,* "breathe." The soul; the aspect of a person that is spiritual and immortal. In the Book of **Genesis,** the Divine spark was "breathed" into Adam. In **kabbalistic** philosophy, there are three levels of the soul. The *neshamah* is the highest and resides in a person's character. The *ruach* is associated with emotional awareness, while the *nefesh* is the level of the soul connected with physical awareness.

neshamah yeterah n. Hebrew (neh-SHOW-muh yeh-ter-AH) Literally "heightened soul." The additional soul, or extra measure of soul, that God gives man on the eve of **Shabbat** to enhance his spirituality. According to the **Zohar,** the spices used during the **Havdalah** service revive the original soul after the *neshamah yeterah* departs at the end of Shabbat.

netzach n. Hebrew (net-ZACH) Literally "victory." The seventh of the 10 *sefirot,* or aspects of God's creative nature. According to **kabbalistic** teachings, *netzach* represents ambition and fortitude and the **Ein Sof's** active grace in the world. It is one of three *sefirot,* along with *hod* and *yesod,* in the category of nature or the functional world. Each *sefirah* is associated with a part of the body; *netzach* corresponds to the right leg.

Nevi'im n. Hebrew (nih-vee-EEM) The second of the three books that comprise the **TANAKH,** along with **Torah** and **Kethuvim.** The English name of Nevi'im is **Prophets.** The Nevi'im includes historical narratives (Joshua, Judges, Samuel 1 and 2, and Kings 1 and 2); writings of the three "major" prophets (Isaiah, Jeremiah, and Ezekiel); and writings of the 12 "minor" prophets (Hosea, Joel, Amos, Obadiah, Jonah, Micah, Nahum, Habakkuk, Zephaniah, Haggai, Zechariah, and Malachi). These 21 sections trace Jewish history from the time of **Moses'** death until the destruction of the **First Temple** in **Jerusalem** and the exile of the Jews to Babylonia. They contain detailed history and commentary on ancient Jewish civilizations. Nevi'im also has lengthy writings about monotheism, evil, and the wages of sin, much of which are written in a poetic form. The weekly **haftarah** readings are taken from the various books in Nevi'im.

New Year   See **Rosh Hashanah.**

next year in Jerusalem   English   The traditional phrase said at the end of the **Pesach seder.** In Hebrew, it is *"le-shanah ha-ba'ah be-Yerushalayim."* The most traditional interpretation is that by next Passover the **Mashiach** will come, gathering all Jews to Jerusalem. More commonly, it expresses the wish that all Jews will one day have the opportunity to visit or make *aliyah* to Israel.

nichum   aveilim   n. Hebrew (nee-KHOOM   ah-vay-LEEM)   Literally, "comforting mourners." Fulfilling this important obligation involves such actions as offering words of sympathy and friendship to mourners, making a **shivah** call, taking part in a **minyan** at the mourners' home, and sharing fond memories of the deceased.

niddah   n. Hebrew (KNEE-dah)   The laws relating to menstruation and marital relations. See *taharat ha-mishpachah.*

nigun   n. Hebrew (knee-GOON); pl. **nigunim** (knee-goo-NEEM)   A wordless melody; a tune. The term is most often used when talking about a prayer melody or a new tune for an existing prayer. **Hasidim** use *nigunim* as a method of focusing and creating *kavanah.*

Nisan   n. Hebrew (KNEE-san)   The first month in the **Jewish calendar.** Nisan falls in March or April.

nissuin   n. Hebrew (nih-soo-EEN)   Literally, "elevation." The second half of the Jewish wedding ceremony, representing the marriage itself. Considered the spiritual part of the service, the *nissuin* connects a husband and wife with God. It includes the **Sheva Brachot** and the **yichud.** It was traditionally separated from the **erusin,** the legal part of the proceedings, by the reading of the **ketubbah.** Today, these ceremonies have been combined into one, all conducted under the **huppah.**

Noahide Laws   pl. n. English   The seven ancient laws that Judaism considers relevant to all people. These laws were initially given to Noah. The first six prohibit idolatry, blasphemy, murder, adultery, robbery, and the eating of flesh cut from a living animal. The seventh commandment is an injunction to establish courts of justice. While Jews are expected to keep all the laws of the **Torah,** non-Jews are expected to keep only these seven laws. A non-Jew who keeps these laws is one of the *hasidei ummot ha-olam* (the righteous of the nations of the world) and therefore guaranteed a place in the world to come. See also **Righteous Gentiles.**

nosh   v. Yiddish (NOSH)   **1.** To have a little snack between meals, or to eat a little something before a meal is ready. "Dinner won't be ready for an hour. Nosh on the cheese and crackers." **2.** n. A snack, a small portion. "She always packs a nosh for the car ride."

nosher   n. Yiddish (NOH-sher)   Someone who eats between meals; a person with a sweet tooth.

nosherei   pl. n. Yiddish (NOH-sheh-rye)   Food for snacking. Often refers to the free samples on a deli or bakery counter.

Nova   n. English   An abbreviation for Nova Scotia smoked salmon that is prepared by brinecuring and cold smoking. It is less salty than **lox;** and often sugar is used in the brine. It is sliced thin and usually eaten with cream cheese on a bagel. Today few salmon are caught off Nova Scotia, but the name sticks.

nu   int. Yiddish (NOO)   A popular interjection with numerous shades of meaning; similar to a grunt or a sigh. An expression of uncertainty or questioning that requires a response, similar to "So?" "Well? or "Come on, tell me." "Didn't you have a blind date last night? Was it fabulous? *Nu?*"

nudnik   n. Yiddish (NOOD-nik)   Someone who persistently annoys or pesters another person. "He kept asking me questions during the movie. What a nudnik."

Numbers   n. English   The fourth book of the **Torah,** known in Hebrew as **Be-midbar.** Numbers includes the first description of the land of **Canaan,** the future home of the **Israelites** after leaving Egypt, as a "land of milk and honey."

nusach   n. Hebrew (nuh-SOCK)   **1.** The melody used for chanting a prayer. *Nusach* is not recorded as musical notation; it is handed down from generation to generation. The specific tune depends on the holiday, the time or day, and the congregation. **2.** A term that is sometimes used in the title of a **siddur,** such as *Nusach Ashkenaz* or *Nusach Sefarad.*

occupied territories pl. n. English The term used by some political groups to describe land captured by the **State of Israel** during wars. Because different ethnic groups and political entities lay claim to various areas of Israel, Jordan, and Syria, the term can be a loaded one, depending on which area is referred to as "occupied territories." Generally it is used to describe areas of the **West Bank,** where a mostly **Palestinian** Arab population lives under Israeli law. Some sections of the occupied territories are administered by the Palestinian Authority.

olam ha-ba   n. Hebrew (oh-LAHM hah-BAH) Literally, the "world to come." The term for the afterlife, which includes *Geihinnom* and *Gan Eden.* In one Jewish view, God uses the afterlife to provide ultimate justice based on one's behavior during one's lifetime. Judaism doesn't believe that Jews automatically go to heaven. The souls of the righteous are rewarded by spending eternity in *Gan Eden;* the souls of the wicked are punished in *Geihinnom.* Those who are somewhere in between spend time in *Geihinnom* before ascending to *Gan Eden.* Jews try to make the most of *olam ha-zeh* (this world) so as to be ready for *olam ha-ba.*

Old Testament   n. English   The name for the first of the two main divisions of the Christian Bible. The second is the New Testament, which details the life of Jesus and his disciples. Jews don't use the name Old Testament because they don't have a New Testament. They simply call it the **Bible** or the **TANAKH.**

olim   pl. n. Hebrew (oh-LEEM) sing. n. masc. **oleh;** fem. **olah** (oh-LEH) Literally, "ones who ascend." Immigrants to **Israel;** persons who make *aliyah.* Since 1948, nearly 3 million Jews have made *aliyah.* While some *olim* come to Israel to fulfill their **Zionist** dreams, others come to escape persecution, such as the thousands of Ethiopian **Falashas.**

Omer   n. Hebrew (OH-mare)   Literally, "sheaf." In ancient times, grain offerings (Omer)—specifically, about two quarts of barley—were made at the **Temple** in **Jerusalem** on the second day of **Pesach,** signaling the start of the harvest season, which culminated at **Shavuot.** The Omer was counted on each of the 49 days between Pesach and Shavuot in a tradition known as counting the

Omer. Today, the counting begins on the second night of **Pesach** at the **seder.** In Hebrew, counting the Omer is known as *sefirat ha-Omer.*

Oneg Shabbat   n. Hebrew (oh–NEG shah–BAHT)   Literally, "Sabbath delight." The informal reception held in **synagogue** after Friday night **Shabbat** services or on Saturday after morning services. It often includes wine and soft drinks and light snacks, such as cookies, **challah,** and sometimes herring. The phrase is often abbreviated in conversation to just the word *Oneg,* as in "Do you think they'll have chocolate chip cookies at the *Oneg* again this week?" Also called *Kiddush.*

ongeblozzen   adj. Yiddish (un–geh–BLUH–zin)   Sulky, pouty. A sourpuss. "We're not going out for pizza tonight. Stop acting so *ongeblozzen.*" Old-fashioned usage.

ongepotchket   adj. Yiddish (un–geh–POTCH–kit)   Thrown together, not matching. Also, disorganized and cluttered, in reference to a room. "She went right to school in the clothes she slept in, all *ongepotchket.*" Old-fashioned usage.

Oral Law   n. English   The body of commentaries, expositions, and rabbinic explanations of points of **Torah** that were passed down from generation to generation in ancient times, starting with **Moses.** In addition to the Torah—the **Written Law**—Judaism has a long tradition of Oral Law. For example, the Torah does not specify what is necessary for a Jewish marriage ceremony. Those specifics are part of the Oral Law. Around 200 C.E., the Oral Law was written down and codified in a text called the **Mishnah.** The Mishnah and the **Gemara** together comprise the **Talmud.**

ORT   n. English   An international technical and vocational training organization. With operations in more than 50 countries, ORT builds schools and trains students in a variety of skills. The organization pays special attention to immigrants who need to learn both language and retraining skills when they immigrate to the **State of Israel** or the United States. Founded in Czarist Russia in 1880 to provide skills in trades and agriculture, ORT was the acronym for the organization's Russian name. An English name—the Organization for Rehabilitation and Training—has been bestowed retroactively. Its official title is the World ORT Union. In the United States, fund-raising is done by chapters of Women's American ORT.

Orthodox movement   n. English   One of the four movements with which North American Jews identify themselves, the Orthodox movement is the most traditional in the practice of Judaism. The name was coined in 1795 to differentiate traditional from liberal Jews. Unlike the **Reform, Reconstructionist,**

and **Conservative movements,** it is not a unified movement with a single governing body but has many different sects, all adhering to the central belief that the **Torah** is the exact word of God without any human influence.

Orthodox sects differ in their views toward modern life, levels of observance, and the **State of Israel.** Orthodoxy requires a literal observance of **Torah, Talmud,** and *halakhah.* Orthodox Jews strictly adhere to the laws governing every aspect of daily life. For example, all the rules and regulations of **Shabbat** are observed in the exact manner set forth in the **Talmud.** Services are conducted predominantly in Hebrew, and men and women sit divided by a *mechitzah.* Women are not ordained as **rabbis,** counted toward a **minyan,** or permitted to lead worship services. The Orthodox consider theirs the only legitimate approach to Judaism. For example, if someone converted to Judaism under rulings of the Reform movement, an Orthodox rabbi would not consider him or her Jewish.

The Orthodox can be subdivided into several groups. The **ultra-Orthodox** are extremely conservative Jews who separate themselves from the secular world by their 18th-century modest dress and shunning of modern life. (See **Hasidism** and **Lubavitch movement.**) The **modern Orthodox** remain true to the principles of *halakhah* while accommodating some aspects of modern life. Yeshiva University is the rabbinical school for the modern Orthodox, and the rabbinical arm is the **Rabbinical Council of America.** There are hundreds of smaller Orthodox **yeshivot,** many of which grant their own rabbinical ordination.

oy int. Yiddish (OY)   Perhaps the most popular **Yiddish** expression, *oy* conveys dozens of emotions, from surprise, joy, and relief to pain, fear, and grief. Sometimes used as *oy oy oy.* Also common are *oy vay* (short for *oy vay iz mir*), meaning "Oh, woe is me," and *oy gevalt,* a cry of desperate protest.

oysgemutshe adj. Yiddish (OIS-guh-MOO-cheh)   Tired out, exhausted; worked to death. "I'm *oysgemutchet* when I run around all day doing errands."

Palestine   n. from *Palestina*, the name of a Roman province   **1.** The ancient land on the east coast of the Mediterranean Sea, also known in ancient times as **Canaan.** Palestine has been inhabited and conquered by many nations since biblical times. The Philistines, Israelites, Babylonians, Romans, Crusaders, Muslims, and British all conquered ancient Palestine and laid claim to the region. **2.** The British Mandate of Palestine. After World War I, Britain administered the area. On May 14, 1948, British rule over Palestine ended and the region was divided among Jordan, Egypt, and the newly established **State of Israel. 3.** The name used by some Arabs currently living in Israel, Jordan, Syria, and other countries to define their homeland. They hope to establish an independent state of Palestine within the borders of the **occupied territories** and partially within the borders of Israel.

Palestinian   n.   A person born or living in the area that was trans-Jordan and the British-ruled mandate of **Palestine.** The term is a politically charged one, mainly used by the Arabs who are advocating for an autonomous Palestinian Arab state. By contrast, there are Jews born in Tel Aviv in 1927 who could accurately describe themselves as Palestinians, but today they most certainly would call themselves Israelis. There are also large populations of Palestinians living in Jordan and Lebanon.

parashah   n. Hebrew (pah-rah-SHAH); pl. **parshiyot**   (par-shee-OTE) The weekly **Torah** portion. The Torah is divided into 54 sections (one for each week of a leap year on the Hebrew lunar calendar), and a specific portion, or parashah, is read each week during **synagogue** services. Each portion has a Hebrew name. On years with fewer weeks, some of the shorter portions are combined, and a double parashah is read. "The parashah for her **Bat Mitzvah** is Yitro." Also called *sidrah.*

parashat ha-shavua   n. Hebrew (pah-rah-SHAHT hah-shah-VOO-ah) Literally, "portion of the week." See **parashah.**

PARDES   n. Hebrew (par-DES)   An acronym for the four levels of understanding possible when reading a sacred text like the **Torah.** These are *peshat,* the literal, obvious meaning of the text; *remez,* the meaning that is only hinted at; *derash*, the symbolic, interpretive meaning of the text; and *sod*, the secret, hidden, or mystical meaning of the passage.

pareve   adj. Yiddish (PAR-ehve)   Literally, "neutral." The general term for food products that contain neither milk **(milchig)** nor meat **(fleishig),** according to the Jewish dietary laws of **kashrut.** Foods that are pareve include grains, all fruits and vegetables, fish, and eggs. These "neutral" foods can be combined with milk or meat in both cooking or eating. So, for example, an egg can be mixed with cheese for an omelet (making it milchig), or it can be added to the breading of a chicken cutlet (making it fleishig). A pareve dessert, such as fresh fruit or pecan pie made with vegetable oil or nondairy margarine, can be served with a meat or dairy dinner.

parochet   n. Hebrew (pah-ROE-khet)   The curtain that covers the *sifrei Torah* inside the **ark** in a **synagogue.** The ark has a solid door made of wood or another material. When that door is open, the *parochet* further shields the **Torah** scrolls. It is considered an honor to be asked to open the curtain during a service, an act called *petichah.*

Passover   n. English   The English name for the holiday of **Pesach.**

patriarchs   pl. n. English from Greek   The "founding fathers" of Judaism: **Abraham, Isaac,** and **Jacob;** the husbands of the four **matriarchs.** The names of the patriarchs are recited in many prayers, including the *Amidah,* which reads in part, "Blessed are You, God of our fathers, God of Abraham, Isaac, and Jacob." Their names are also included in a blessing for male children, a wish that they "grow up to be like Abraham, Isaac, and Jacob." On **Sukkot,** the names of the patriarchs and matriarchs are invoked in the custom of *ushpizin.* Today, they remain some of the most popular names given to Jewish children.

payot   pl. n. Hebrew (pay-OTE)   Long curls of hair that hang in front of the ears on **ultra-Orthodox** men and boys, who grow *payot* in keeping with the **Torah**'s prohibition against shaving the "corners" of the head. **Hasidim** wait until their sons are three years old before giving them their first haircut, at which time the hair is cut short but the *payot* left long. Also spelled *peyos* (PAY-iss), the Yiddish version of the word. See *upfsherin.*

Pentateuch   n. English   From the Greek word for "five." Another name for the **Torah.** This is also the name given to the actual book used in **synagogue,** which contains the Torah and commentaries on it. See *Humash.*

Pesach   n. Hebrew (PAY-sakh)   The Hebrew name for the holiday of **Passover.** Beginning on the 15th of **Nisan,** which corresponds to late March or early April, Pesach is a joyous holiday. It is celebrated for eight days among **Orthodox** and **Conservative** Jews, and for seven days among liberal American Jews and in the **State of Israel.** Along with **Sukkot** and **Shavuot,** Pesach is one of the three **Pilgrimage Festivals,** when the ancient **Israelites** traveled to the **Temple** in **Jerusalem** with gifts of the first fruit and offerings for God. It marks the ancient **Exodus** of the Israelites from generations of slavery in Egypt to freedom in the **Promised Land** of **Israel.**

The story of Passover begins when the Israelites were slaves of Pharoah in Egypt. They labored under harsh conditions for generations, making bricks and building pyramids and cities. When Pharoah ordered all Jewish baby boys killed, **Moses'** mother, Yocheved, and sister, **Miriam,** floated him down the Nile in a basket to save his life. He was rescued by Pharaoh's daughter and raised in Pharoah's house. When he was a grown man, Moses saw the Burning Bush and was led by God to return to Egypt to tell Pharaoh to let the Israelites go free. When Pharaoh refused, God unleashed **Ten Plagues** on the people of Egypt. Before the final plague, death of the Egyptians' firstborn sons, God told Moses to mark the doorways of the Israelites' homes so that the Angel of Death would "pass over" their families. This is one explanation for the name of the holiday.

Pharoah allowed the Israelites, led by Moses, to flee. They left Egypt in such haste that they did not even have time for their bread to rise. They had to eat unleavened bread, or **matzah.** This is the basis for one of the most important traditions of Pesach: eating only matzah, not bread or leavened products. During the week of Pesach, special cookies and cakes made with **matzah meal** and other *pesachdik* ingredients are eaten.

Before Pesach begins, a Jewish family cleans the entire home—especially the kitchen—to remove all crumbs and traces of regular bread and bakery products, called *hametz*. Many families even change their dishes and silverware, using special sets reserved for Pesach.

Pesach begins with a long, carefully ordered meal and service called a **seder.** On the table is a **seder plate** with symbolic foods: *beitzah, maror, haroset, zeroa,* and *karpas,* whose meanings are explained in the course of the seder. Other special items, such as matzah, **Elijah's Cup,** and sometimes **Miriam's Cup,** are also on the table. Participants use a prayer book called a **haggadah,** which includes the story of the holiday, the **Four Questions,** and traditional songs.

While Pesach is observed primarily at home, there are **synagogue** festival services on the first and last days. Biblical readings are from **The Song of Songs,** one of the five *megillot.* A *Yizkor* service is held on one of the last days.

pesachdik   adj. Yiddish (PAY-sah-dick)   Acceptable to be eaten on **Pesach;** a term used to describe foods that are not *hametzdik* and do not contain bread or any leavened products. "Are you sure those cookies are *pesachdik?* They look too good to be made with matzah meal."

peshat n. Hebrew (puh-SHAT) The literal, obvious meaning scholars give to a Jewish text. It can also refer to the simple interpretation of any issue or question. *Peshat* is in contrast to *derash,* the symbolic, more complicated interpretation of a text.

Pesukei de-Zimra n. Hebrew (puh-ZOO-key de-zim-RAH) Literally, "verses of songs." The collection of psalms and biblical passages that are part of the introductory prayers of the morning service *(Shacharit).* These verses, which praise God, prepare worshippers to recite the *Shema* and the *Amidah.*

petichah v. Hebrew (peh-tee-KHAH) The act of opening the doors or curtain *(parochet)* on the *Aron Kodesh* just before the **Torah** is taken out of the **ark** to be read. It is considered an honor, an *aliyah,* to be asked to open the ark.

peyos See *payot.*

Pharisee n. (FAR-uh-see) From the Aramaic word "*parash,*" meaning "separate." A member of an ancient sect of **Jews** in the time of the **Second Temple** (538 B.C.E.–70 C.E.) that emphasized the ongoing interpretation of the **Written Law,** rather than the strict adherence to it, as was customary among the **Sadducees.** The Oral Law that the Pharisees followed became the basis of the **Talmud**. The Pharisees believed in the coming of a **Messianic Age** and an afterlife where God would reward the just and punish the wicked. The Pharisees disagreed with the Sadducees on many other issues, including the importance of the **Temple,** the Hellenization of Jews, and how to apply laws to daily life. They disapproved of the **Essenes'** withdrawal from the community. Because the Sadducees and Essenes died out, the Pharisees are considered the ancestors of all modern Jews. **2. pharisee** A self-righteous or hypocritical person. This pejorative term comes from the New Testament, which characterized the Pharisees as the ideological enemies of Jesus.

phylacteries See **tefillin.**

pidyon ha-ben n. Hebrew (pid-YONE hah-BEN) Literally, "redemption of the firstborn." The ceremony of buying back a firstborn son from service to God. In ancient times, according to the Book of **Exodus,** a firstborn son was supposed to dedicate his life to the service of God. On the thirty-first day after the child's birth, the father could pay a priest five silver **shekels** to have his child released from this obligation.

Today, in a symbolic representation of this ancient pact, the ritual of *pidyon ha-ben* is acted out one month after the birth of a firstborn son. A **Kohen,** usually a friend of the family, holds the baby for a moment. Then he accepts five silver coins from the baby's father to symbolically redeem the child. The coins are often donated to *tzedakah*. Along with special prayers for the baby's long and healthy life, a *pidyon ha-ben* is a happy, joyous occasion celebrating the birth of a son. It is usually followed by a celebration for family and friends, including food and gifts for the baby.

pikuach   nefesh   n. Hebrew (pee-COO-akh NEH-fesh)   Literally, the "preservation of life." The Jewish obligation to protect and save life at all costs. The code of *pikuach nefesh* demands the suspension of all other laws to save a life, with the exceptions of the prohibitions against murder, idolatry, and incest. For example, a sick person or a pregnant woman is obligated to eat on **Yom Kippur** when others fast because of *pikuach nefesh*. An **Orthodox** Jew might drive his car on **Shabbat** if he needs to get his sick child to the hospital.

Pilgrimage Festivals   n. English   The festivals of **Shavuot, Pesach,** and **Sukkot.** In ancient times, on these holidays, **Israelites** would make a pilgrimage to the **Temple** in **Jerusalem** with gifts of the first fruit and offerings for God. The Hebrew term is *Shalosh Regalim.*

pilpul   n. Hebrew (pill-POOL)   Literally, "pepper." A method of interpreting the **Talmud** through intense analysis and academic debate. It is thought that *pilpuls*, the many fine distinctions and divergent opinions, will produce an essential bit of truth.

Pirke Avot   n. Hebrew (peer-KAY ah-VOTE)   The Hebrew name for *Ethics of the Fathers,* a collection of maxims, quotes, and popular sayings from ancient Jewish sages and scholars.

pisher   n. Yiddish (PISH-er)   A bed wetter, but more commonly used to describe a young, inexperienced person, similar to a "young squirt." Old-fashioned usage.

pisk   n. Yiddish (PISK)   Mouth. The word is often used insultingly to describe a bigmouth or a loudmouth.

piyyut   n. Hebrew (pee-YOOT); pl. **piyyutim**   (pee-yoo-TEEM)   A religious poem distinguished by its form: the rhyme, rhythm, and sometimes acrostic lettering (each phrase or sentence begins with the next letter of the **Hebrew** alphabet). Medieval poets wrote these long, carefully crafted verses for festivals and special occasions; a number of them are now prayers that are included in the **Shabbat** and festival prayer books and in **High Holy Day** *machzorim.*

plagues   See **Ten Plagues.**

plotz v. Yiddish (PLOTZ)   Literally, "to burst." To explode or collapse from excitement, suprise, or pleasure. "I won a prize in the raffle. That never happened before! I could *plotz.*"

pogrom n. Yiddish/Russian (puh-GRUM)   A massacre of Jews, referring usually to the organized, unprovoked attacks against Jews in Russia and Poland in the late 19th and early 20th centuries. The czar's Cossacks would ride into the **shtetl** to murder Jews, rape the women, and pillage and burn the homes and shops. Pogroms were often incited by government officials and church leaders, who made Jews the scapegoats for the hunger and poverty in the country. **Kristallnacht,** the start of the Nazi reign of terror, is perhaps the most famous pogrom in recent history.

potch v. Yiddish (POTCH)   To playfully smack or spank. Frequently used in the expression *potch in tuchis* (to slap on the bottom).

potchkee v. Yiddish (POTCH-key)   To fool around or mess around with something, without showing any expertise or making any progress. "He *potchkees* around with the piano, but he can't play."

Priestly Benediction   See *Birkat ha-Kohanim.*

Progressive Judaism n. English   An umbrella term for the liberal branches of Judaism, which see *halakhah* as continually evolving and dynamic rather than binding. In North America, the term generally refers to the **Reform** and **Reconstructionist movements**. In other countries, Progressive Judaism is a synonym for Reform Judaism. The World Union for Progressive Judaism, founded in 1926, supports congregations in nearly 40 countries.

prokas pl. n. Yiddish (PROCK-iss)   An Eastern European entree of stuffed cabbage leaves. *Prokas* are usually filled with ground beef, minced onion, and rice, and then sweetened with raisins or prunes, and served in a tomato sauce. Also called stuffed cabbage and holishkes.

Promised Land n. English   The land promised to the **patriarch Abraham** as an "everlasting inheritance" in **Genesis** 12:7. The Promised Land, also known as **Canaan,** is the portion of ancient **Palestine** between the Jordan River and the Mediterranean Sea. Today, this land is called the **State of Israel,** and this promise is used to support Jews' claim to the land.

Prophets n. English   The second of the three books that comprise the **TANAKH,** along with the **Torah** and **Kethuvim.** Known by the Hebrew name **Nevi'im.**

Protocols of the Elders of Zion   A booklet, contrived by Czarist officials in Russia at the beginning of the 20th century, which describes the alleged secret plans of Jewish leaders to take over the world. This falsehood has been widely used to incite **anti–Semitism** and is still in circulation today. In 2003, it appeared as a dramatic series on Arab TV.

pseudepigrapha   n. English, from the Greek for "false inscriptions."   A term for religious texts and writings dating from the time of the Second Temple., whose authors were ascribed to certain prophets and kings to enhance their authenticity. An example is King Solomon's **Song of Songs,** which most scholars believe is probably not entirely his work. Pseudepigrapha are distinct from **Apocrypha,** but both were referred to as *"sefarim hizonim"* (extraneous books) by ancient rabbis.

pulkes   pl. n. Yiddish (PULL-keys)   Thighs. It usually refers to chubby, cute baby thighs, but can also refer to those of a chicken. "Don't waste that big slice of white meat on me. I'll eat the *pulkes.*" Old-fashioned usage.

punim   See *shayna punim.*

pupik   n. Yiddish (PUH-pik)   Belly button, navel. Used in the Yiddish curse *"Zoll vaksen tsibiliss in zein pupik!* (Onions should grow in his navel!) Old-fashioned usage.

Purim   n. Hebrew (POOR-um)   Celebrated on the 14th of **Adar,** which corresponds to late February or mid–March, Purim is one of the most fun and relaxed holidays. It celebrates yet another rescue of the Jewish people in ancient times.

    Esther, a Jewish girl raised by her cousin **Mordecai,** became the second wife of **King Ahasuerus** of ancient Persia. Tradition says that Mordecai, an adviser to the king, refused to bow down to **Haman,** another of the king's advisers. In anger, Haman hatched a plot to kill the Jews of Shushan and built a gallow on which to hang Mordecai. Haman drew numbers (lots) to decide on what day the Jews would die. The word "purim" means "lots"; hence the holiday's name. Mordecai discovered the plot and asked Esther to intervene with the king to save her people. Haman was hanged instead. Purim is also known as the Feast of Esther and the Feast of Lots.

    It is considered a **mitzvah** to listen as the Purim story is read aloud from the **Megillah,** the **Scroll of Esther,** in **synagogue.** It is also traditional to come to synagogue dressed as the characters in the Purim story and to make noise— stomp feet and shake *gragers*—each time Haman's name is mentioned during the reading. The idea is to drown out his evil name so that it is never heard again. Triangular-shaped cookies, called **hamantashen,** are a Purim treat. One of the more unusual customs of Purim is for Jews to drink liquor until they can't "distinguish between Haman and Mordecai." Shots of whiskey are sometimes offered in synagogue to fulfill this injunction! As part of the hilarity of the holiday, people often dress up and put on short humorous skits called *Purim-spiels.* It is also customary to deliver **shalach manot**—gifts of fruit, hamantashen, and candy—to friends and neighbors. Synagogues often sponsor Purim carnivals, with games, prizes, and entertainment for children. In the **State of Israel,** children in costumes go from house to house, delivering *shalach manot* and collecting treats for themselves in return.

The day before Purim is known as the **Fast of Esther** (Ta'anit Esther), commemorating the three days that the Jews of ancient Shushan fasted and prayed before Esther pled her case before the king. Today, the Fast of Esther is not widely observed. The day after Purim, the 15th of Adar, is called **Shushan Purim.** Purim is celebrated on this day in walled cities, such as **Jerusalem.**

Purim-spiel n. Hebrew (POOR-um-SHPEEL) A humorous skit or show performed on **Purim,** usually in **synagogue** or **Hebrew school.** It is traditional for the costumed players to put funny new words to old Purim songs, spoof the Purim characters, or act out the holiday story with the addition of crazy characters. *Purim-spiels* are entertaining and lighthearted, in keeping with the spirit of the holiday.

pushke n. Yiddish (PUSH-kuh) A small container with a coin slot used to collect money for a charitable organization. In days past homemakers would usually put *pushkes* on the kitchen windowsill and add coins each week before the start of **Shabbat.** Perhaps the most famous *pushke* belongs to the **Jewish National Fund;** its tin "blue box" is still used to collect coins to purchase trees in the **State of Israel.** Old-fashioned usage. The term *pushke* has been replaced by *"tzedakah box."*

putz n. Yiddish (PUHTS) Vulgar slang for a penis. The term is most often used as an insult for someone who is not worthy of respect; worse than a jerk. "He dropped out of college and never finished, but his resume says he graduated in 1981. What a putz!"

Qumran   n. Arabic (KOOM-ran)   A rocky desert area on the northwestern shore of the **Dead Sea** in **Israel;** the **Dead Sea Scrolls** were discovered in a cave here. Today, the area contains a small museum and an archaeological dig that reveals the remains of an **Essene** settlement.

rabbi n. Hebrew (RAB-eye) Literally, "my teacher." **1.** The title given to the spiritual leader of a Jewish congregation. A rabbi leads services, gives sermons, educates children, and counsels the congregants in a **synagogue.** Not all rabbis lead congregations; they are trained for religious leadership and may work in other roles, including teacher, scholar, counselor, *mohel,* or *mashgiach.* The various movements of Judaism each have their own seminaries, which offer training and rabbinical ordination *(semikhah).* For example, the Reconstructionist Rabbinical College is the **Reconstructionist movement**'s seminary. The **Conservative, Reform,** and Reconstructionist movements all ordain women as rabbis. **2.** The word "rabbi" is sometimes used as a sign of respect when addressing a teacher.

Rabbinical Assembly, The n. English The international association of Conservative and **Masorti** rabbis, founded in 1901. The Assembly publishes prayerbooks and *Etz Hayim,* a Torah commentary. Its Committee on Jewish Law and Standards, the central authority on *halakhah* in the **Conservative movement,** shapes rabbinical practice on such issues as intermarriage and conversion.

Rabbinical Council of America (RCA) n. English The official rabbinical organization of the **Orthodox movement.** Established in 1935, it is the rabbinical authority of the **Union of Orthodox Jewish Congregations of America.** The RCA issues policies and position statements, publishes English and Hebrew journals, and is affiliated with two **yeshivot** in Israel.

rachamim n. Hebrew (rakh-ah-MEEM) Literally, "compassion." The Hebrew form of the word is often used in prayers to describe a compassionate and merciful God. The concept of *rachamim*—treating others with compassion, understanding, and empathy—is considered an important Jewish value. See *rachmones* and *El Male Rachamim.*

Rachel One of the four **matriarchs** of the Jewish people; the second wife of **Jacob,** one of the three **patriarchs.** Rachel was the woman whom Jacob truly loved and whom he married after his father-in-law tricked him into first marrying her older sister, **Leah.** The wedding custom of *bedeken* is said to be inspired by this story. After struggling to conceive, Rachel gave birth to **Joseph**

and **Benjamin.** She died giving birth to Benjamin, and today Orthodox Jewish women sometimes journey to Rachel's tomb to pray for fertility.

rachmones n. Yiddish (rakh-MUN-iss) Pity or empathy, but with a sympathetic rather than scornful tone. "He's been looking for a job for six months now. Have a little *rachmones* and see if you can get him an interview." See *rachamim.*

Rambam Another name for **Maimonides.** Rambam is an acronym for Rabbi Moses ben Maimon.

Rashi (1040–1105) Another name for Rabbi Shlomo ben Isaac, a French Hebrew scholar who is regarded as one of Judaism's greatest commentators. Rashi is perhaps best known for his concise, direct commentaries on the **Talmud.** His writings are still considered the definitive work in this area. Today, many of those studying the Talmud are taught to read Rashi's commentary, which is printed right alongside the actual text in Rashi script, before trying to figure out a meaning of their own. His commentary guides students through difficult **Aramaic, Hebrew,** and Greek passages and the twists and turns of logic, with attention given to the most direct, literal meaning of the text *(peshat)* as well as to interpretation *(derash).*

Rashi script n. English The semicursive **Hebrew** type that is used for **Rashi**'s commentaries on the **Bible** and **Talmud.** It was created by a printer in order to distinguish Rashi's commentaries from the Bible itself; it caught on and was used for other commentaries as well. (Rashi himself did not use the script.) Rashi script is one of two traditional Hebrew fonts used today; the other is block letters, also known as Assyrian script.

rav n. Hebrew (RAHV) Literally, "great" and "teacher." The word used by **Orthodox** and other traditional congregations to refer to their **rabbi.**

rebbe n. Yiddish (REH-bee) **1.** The name for the charismatic **rabbi**-leader of a **Hasidic** sect, thought to possess mediatory powers with the Divine. Also known as a **tzadik. 2.** The name used for a teacher in a traditional Jewish school.

rebbetzin n. Yiddish (REH-bit-sin) The term used for the wife of a **rabbi.** The role of a *rebbetzin* varies tremendously depending on which movement of Judaism she's connected with and the traditions of her husband's congregation.

Rebecca One of the four **matriarchs** of the Jewish people; wife of **Isaac,** one of the three **patriarchs.** Rebecca, known for her beauty and kindness, was the mother of the twins **Esau** and **Jacob,** who struggled with each other even in the womb. While Esau was Isaac's favorite, Rebecca favored Jacob and helped him trick Isaac and get a blessing that had been meant for Esau.

Reconstructionist movement   n. English   One of the four movements with which most North American Jews identify themselves, the Reconstructionist movement is the youngest and smallest Jewish denomination. It was founded by Rabbi **Mordecai M. Kaplan** in 1935. He taught that Judaism is more than a religion; it is an evolving religious civilization that reinterprets traditions in response to modern times. Reconstructionists are committed to protecting tradition while preserving contemporary meaning; they emphasize individual responsibility over commandments. Reconstructionist theology holds that the Torah was not revealed by God at **Mount Sinai;** but rather it and other sacred texts are the creation of the Jewish people over time. God is not a supernatural being who knows the mind of each individual, but the source of high ideals and virtues inside each human being.

The Reconstructionist prayer book has no references to Jews as the **Chosen People** and avoids all notions of a personal **Messiah;** it speaks instead of a **Messianic Age** that man can help bring about. Men and women participate equally during services, in education, and in Jewish rituals; Reconstructionists developed the **Bat Mitzvah** ceremony. Their services are similar to **Conservative** ones, with the addition of some creative readings. The movement is committed to support the **State of Israel** and Jews around the world, and members participate in social action and in interreligious programs in their local communities. The Reconstructionist Rabbinical College is its rabbinical school; Reconstructionist congregations generally belong to the **Jewish Reconstructionist Federation.**

Reconstructionist Rabbinical Association (RRA)   n. English   The professional association of **Reconstructionist** rabbis established in 1974. The RRA establishes egalitarian rituals, liturgy, and policies for life cycle events, including marriage and divorce. It also publishes a quarterly journal and issues policy statements on social issues such as stem cell research and same-sex marriage.

Reform movement   n. English   One of the four movements with which most North American Jews identify themselves, the Reform movement offers the most liberal approach to Judaism. It was introduced to the United States in 1854 by Rabbi Isaac Mayer Wise, a German-speaking immigrant, in a radical form—requiring no head covering during prayer and abolishing the dietary laws. Reform Judaism is far less radical today, and includes the practice of many traditional Jewish rituals, while at the same time stating that every Jew has a role in reinterpreting Jewish law to accommodate contemporary life. Main principles include the belief in God as defined in the *Shema* and the belief that the

Torah was written by human hands, in the language of its time, and with Divine inspiration.

The movement introduced changes to worship, including shorter services, more prayers in English than in Hebrew, a late Friday evening **Shabbat** service, and the use of musical instruments during Shabbat. It also ordained the first woman rabbi in the United States in 1972. Holidays may be celebrated with a minimum of observance in terms of length and regulations. Men and women participate equally during services, in education, and Jewish rituals. The movement is committed to supporting the **State of Israel** and Jews around the world, as well as involvement in social action and interreligious programs in their local communities. Its rabbinical school is Hebrew Union College–Jewish Institute of Religion; the Central Conference of American Rabbis is its official rabbinical body. Reform congregations generally belong to the **Union for Reform Judaism.**

refusenik   n. Russian/English (re-FUSE-nik)   A word coined in the 1970s to describe Russian Jews who were denied permission to emigrate from the Soviet Union. After protests, publicity, and visits to Russia by concerned Jews worldwide, many refuseniks were granted exit visas. Perhaps the most famous refusenik is Natan Sharansky, who spent nine years in Russian prisons before being allowed to immigrate to the **State of Israel,** where he has since served in the **Knesset.**

responsa   pl. n. from Latin (reh-SPON-sah)   The body of literature consisting of authoritative answers to questions of *halakhah* posed to **rabbis** and other religious authorities. In existence since ancient times, responsa literature continues to accumulate today. Scholars from all major branches of Judaism produce responsa rulings to guide their followers. Topics range from criminal behavior to modern ethical issues and women's roles in Judaism. For example, a 1983 responsa from the Jewish Theological Seminary's faculty permitted women to be ordained as rabbis within the **Conservative movement. Orthodox** rabbis have recently issued responsa dealing with the use of computers during **Shabbat.** The singular form is responsum.

retzuot   pl. n. Hebrew (ret-soo-OTE)   The leather straps, about two or three feet in length, that are attached to **tefillin.** There are two boxes of tefillin; one rests on the hand, the other on the forehead. The strap for the hand is wound seven times around the arm and then three times around the hand and three times around the ring and middle fingers, forming the Hebrew word *Shaddai,* one of the names of God. The strap for the forehead is tied in a knot and then left to hang loose.

Reuben   Firstborn son of **Jacob** and **Leah.**   He interceded for his brother **Joseph**'s life and guaranteed the safe return from Egypt of another brother,

Benjamin. Reuben is also the name of one of the 12 **tribes of Israel,** whose members were said to be descended from him. His tribe occupied the mountainous region northeast of the Dead Sea.

Righteous Gentiles   pl. n. English   The term that has been used since World War II for non-Jews who risked their lives to save Jews from the Nazis. Their heroism included hiding Jews in their homes, smuggling food to them, forging passports, and helping in other ways. The Hebrew term is *hasidei ummot ha-olam* (among the righteous of the nations of the world) and dates back to the **Talmud.** The term was used to describe Noah, a righteous man whom God chose to build an ark and save humanity. Perhaps the most famous Righteous Gentile in modern times is Raoul Wallenberg, a Swedish diplomat who worked in Budapest in 1944. He saved tens of thousands of Hungarian Jews by granting them Swedish citizenship; he was arrested and sent to a Siberian prison, and never seen again. The heroism of another Righteous Gentile, Oskar Schindler, is dramatized in Steven Spielberg's film *Schindler's List.* Denmark is considered a nation of Righteous Gentiles for its largely successful efforts to save the country's Jews during World War II. At the **Yad Vashem** memorial in **Jerusalem,** there is a special grove of trees in tribute to Righteous Gentiles. See also **Noahide Laws.**

rimonim   pl. n. Hebrew (rih-moe-NEEM)   Literally, "pomegranates." **1.** The name for the two small, decorative silver crowns placed on the *atzei chayim,* the wooden or ivory poles to which the **Torah** scrolls are attached. **2.** The **Sephardic** term for the finials on these poles. Originally the finials were carved like pomegranates.

rishonim   pl. n. Hebrew (rih-show-NEEM)   From the Hebrew word for "first." Earlier rabbis and scholars, who lived from around the 11th to the mid-15th century C.E., before the **Shulchan Arukh,** the compilation of Jewish law, was written. **Maimonides** is one of these well-known *rishonim.* See *acharonim* and *gaon.*

Rosh Hashanah   n. Hebrew (ROESH hah-SHAH-nah)   Literally, "head of the year." The Jewish New Year, which falls on the first of **Tishrei,** the beginning of the year on the **Jewish calendar** (usually during the month of September). Rosh Hashanah begins the 10-day period of self-examination, repentance, and prayer known as the **Days of Awe (Yamim Noraim)** that concludes with **Yom Kippur,** the Day of Atonement. Together, these two holidays are called the High Holy Days, or High Holidays. They provide an opportunity for renewal and a chance to make personal changes for the coming year.

Traditionally, it is believed that all people are judged on Rosh Hashanah. The **Talmud** explains that the **Book of Life** *(Sefer Chayim)* is opened for the righteous on Rosh Hashanah so that God can inscribe their names. The fate of all others is on hold until Yom Kippur. During this period, Jews have the opportunity to see where they "missed the mark," falling short of their ideals, so that they can make amends and get back on target. This return to righteousness and repentance is called **teshuvah.**

Jews spend much of Rosh Hashanah in **synagogue.** The specific prayers and songs for the holiday are contained in a special prayer book called a **machzor.** Services include the blowing of the **shofar** and the recitation of **Selichot,** or the penitential prayers. Even those Jews who don't attend synagogue year-round often come on Rosh Hashanah, and most synagogues offer tickets for seating because there are so many worshipers. Traditional Jews generally attend services for two days, liberal Jews for one. On the afternoon of the first day, **tashlikh** is performed. Congregants walk to a local stream and symbolically "cast away their sins" by throwing bread crumbs into the water.

Family and friends customarily gather on Rosh Hashanah eve for a festive meal that includes a special **Kiddush** and a round loaf of **challah,** symbolic of the cyclical nature of the years. Perhaps the most beloved tradition is that of eating apples dipped in honey to signify wishes for a sweet new year. Jews send New Year's cards to friends and family imprinted with the traditional holiday greeting: **le-shanah tovah tikatevu** (may you be inscribed [in the Book of Life] for a good year).

Rosh Hodesh n. Hebrew (ROESH HOE-desh) Literally, "head of the month." The celebration of the new moon. Rosh Hodesh falls on the first day of each month on the **Jewish calendar,** which is lunar-based. In **synagogue,** there are additional morning prayers and a **Torah** reading. At some synagogues, congregants gather outside after the **Ma'ariv** service that ends the **Shabbat** and recite the **Kiddush Le-vanah** (Sanctification of the Moon) prayer. Feminists have adopted Rosh Hodesh as their own and have developed rituals and readings for the holiday because, like menstruation, it follows a monthly cycle.

ruach n. Hebrew (ROO-ach) **1.** Spiritedness, morale. *Ruach* is the spirit that God breathed into the first human being. It is used now to convey the feeling of joy and connection at a celebration. This word is often used in Jewish youth groups and communal activities, such as Israeli dancing, to encourage the participants: "Have some *ruach!* Get things moving!" **2.** In **kabbalistic** philosophy, there are three levels of the soul. The *ruach,* or middle level, is associated with emotional awareness.

rugelach pl. n. Yiddish (ROO-geh-lakh) Bite-size crescent-shaped pastries, rolled around a variety of fillings, including chopped raisins and walnuts, apple, raspberry, or *mun,* and topped with a sprinkling of cinnamon and sugar.

Rugelach are usually made from a rich butter or cream cheese–based dough. A cousin of *shnecken.*

Ruth, Book of   n. English   One of the five books referred to as a scroll, or **megillah,** that are contained in **Kethuvim,** the third section of the **TANAKH**. The Book of Ruth is read in **synagogue** on **Shavuot** because it tells the story of a harvest. After the death of her husband, Ruth decides to convert to Judaism and accompanies her mother-in-law, Naomi, back to Bethlehem for the harvest. Ruth's famous declaration, "Where you go, I will go. Your God will be my God, and your people my people," is seen as an example of friendship and faith. Ruth is one of King **David**'s ancestors.

saba n. Hebrew (sah-BAH) Grandfather. In modern Israel, children use this word to address their grandfather. In America, the Yiddish word *zayde* is more common.

Sabbath See **Shabbat**.

sabbatical year See *shemitah*.

sabra n. Hebrew (SAH-bra) A person born in the **State of Israel.** The sabra is a cactus fruit native to Israel; it is tough and prickly on the outside, tender and sweet on the inside—a description that many say fits citizens of the Jewish state.

Sadducee n. Hebrew (SAJ-uh-see) A member of one of the Jewish sects in ancient Israel at the time of the **Second Temple** (538 B.C.E. to 70 C.E.). The Sadducees were generally the wealthier class; many were priests and their religious life was centered on the rituals and sacrifices at the Temple. The sect believed in the strict interpretation of the **Torah.** Unlike the **Pharisees,** the Sadducees did not believe in an afterlife. The Sadducees disappeared with the destruction of the Temple in 70 C.E.

safta n. Hebrew (sahf-TAH) Grandmother. In modern Israel, children use this word to address their grandmother. In America, the Yiddish word *bubbe* is more common.

sandek n. Hebrew masc. (SAN-deck); fem. **sandakit** (san-dah-KEET) The person given the honor of assisting the *mohel* at the *brit milah.* The *sandek* may hold the child on his lap during the **circumcision** or, as is common today, just hold the baby for a moment in a symbolic fashion. The honor is often given to one of the baby's grandfathers or to another relative or close friend.

Samaria See **Judea and Samaria.**

Samaritans n. (suh-MAR-ih-tins) A religious and ethnic group descended from the Jews of the northern kingdom of Israel; they claimed to be descendants of the tribes of **Ephraim** and **Menasseh.** Samaritans were believed to have intermarried with the Assyrians, who conquered Israel in 722 B.C.E. When Jews returned from the Babylonian exile, they rejected the Samaritans on religious grounds and would not let them worship at the **Temple** in Jerusalem. Today, a small community survives in Israel near the town of Nablus; Samaritans claim that they follow the true religion of the ancient Israelites.

Sanhedrin   n. Hebrew (san-HED-rin)   From the Greek word for "council." The Supreme Court of the Jews who lived in ancient **Israel.** Composed of 71 wise elders who dispensed legislation and judgment, it was the chief judicial and legislative body during the time of the **Second Temple** and for several hundred years after its destruction. The scholar **Hillel** served as its president at one time. It disbanded in 425 C.E.

Sarah   One of the four **matriarchs** of the Jewish people; wife of **Abraham,** one of the three **patriarchs.** Because Sarah could not bear children, Abraham had a child, **Ishmael,** with Hagar, Sarah's handmaiden. When Sarah was 90 years old, God told her that she would have a child. She laughed, but later gave birth to **Isaac.**

Saul   Chosen to be Israel's first king in the 11th century B.C.E., Saul successfully fought the Philistines, Moabites, and Amalekites. Ultimately, he lost favor with the Prophet Samuel, who chose young **David** to be the next king. In his last battle, when all was lost, Saul fell on his sword and killed himself.

schav   See *shav.*

Schechter, Solomon   (1847–1915)   Jewish educator, rabbi, and scholar. Born in Romania, Schechter moved to London where he became a professor of Hebrew at University College. He is known for his scholarly interpretations of the Cairo **Genizah,** a collection of rare medieval Jewish texts that had been hidden in Cairo and discovered during the late 1890s. In 1901, he moved to the United States and became president of the Jewish Theological Seminary. He was the founder and president of the organization that became the **United Synagogue of Conservative Judaism.** Today, many **Conservative day schools** in the United States are named in his honor.

schlemiel   See **shlemiel.**

schlep   See **shlep.**

schlimazel   See **shlimazel.**

schlock   See **shlock.**

schlub   See *shlub.*

schlump   See *shlump.*

schmaltz   See shmaltz.

schmatte   See *shmatte.*

schmeer   See shmeer.

schmeggegge   See *shmeggegge.*

schmendrick   See *shmendrick.*

schmo   See shmo.

schmooze   See shmooze.

schmuck   See shmuck.

schmutz   See *shmutz.*

schnapps   See shnapps.

schnecken   See *shnecken.*

Schneerson, Menachem Mendel (1902–1994)   The spiritual head and rabbi of the New York-based **Lubavitch** sect of **Hasidism** for more than 44 years. Born in Russia, the charismatic Schneerson was renowned for his meetings with the public, where he dispensed both wise advice and dollar bills. Under his leadership, the Lubavitch movement and its outreach efforts to the Jewish community grew. During his lifetime, many of his followers hailed Rebbe Schneerson as the long awaited *Mashiach* (Messiah) and his teachings, sayings, and writings are still revered. He died childless and no successor has been named.

schnook   See **shnook.**

schnorrer   See **shnorrer.**

schnoz   See *shnoz.*

schtick   See **shtick.**

scroll n. English A length of parchment or vellum on which the **Torah** and other holy books, such as *megillot,* are written. It is composed of strips that are sewn together to form a long roll. Each end is attached to a wooden pole. A scroll is written by a scribe *(sofer).* See *sefer Torah.*

Scroll of Esther See **Esther, Scroll of.**

Second Temple n. English The most holy place of worship and sacrifice in **Jerusalem** in ancient **Israel.** The Second Temple was built on the site of the **First Temple** 70 years after its destruction. Construction began in 538 B.C.E. and was finally completed in 516; the process is described in the Bible in the Book of Ezra. The Temple was refurbished and enlarged by King Herod during the 1st century B.C.E. and remained in use until it was destroyed by General Titus and the conquering Roman Empire in 70 C.E. Today in Jerusalem, the **Western Wall** and now the newly unearthed Southern Wall are revered because they are remnants of the outside walls of the mount, or base, of the Second Temple. See also **Holy of Holies.**

seder n. Hebrew (SAY-der); pl. **sedarim** (say-dah-REEM) Literally, "order." **1.** The traditional ceremonial dinner on **Pesach.** The seder includes prayers, songs and the ancient retelling of the **Exodus** of the Israelite slaves from bondage in Egypt. The centerpiece of the seder table is a **seder plate** that displays special foods symbolic of the holiday. The liturgy of the seder is contained in a small book called a **haggadah,** which details the order of the prayers, stories and songs, and the specific components of the meal. Sedarim sometimes last several hours. Some are traditional, with prayers and readings mostly in Hebrew and age-old stories and melodies that have remained the same for thousands of years. Other sedarim incorporate English explanations, newer songs brought home from religious school, and modern touches such as puppets to act out the story. In Israel, there is a seder on the first night only. In the **Diaspora,** traditional Jews have a seder on the first two nights of Passover; other Jews celebrate only the first night. Sedarim are most often held in the home with extended family and friends. It is traditional and a **mitzvah** for Jews to invite guests who have no seder of their own to join them in their home. There is a sentence in the haggadah that reads, "Let all who are hungry come and eat." Some synagogues sponsor community sedarim that are open to congregants and their friends; they might also sponsor a **women's seder** that celebrates women's roles in the Passover story and incorporates a **Miriam's Cup** in the ritual. **2.** A ceremonial meal, held with prayers, songs, and festive foods, for a holiday other than Pesach. For example, **Tu B'Shevat** is sometimes celebrated with a seder that includes fruits and nuts grown in Israel.

seder plate n. Hebrew/English (SAY-der plate) A special plate, placed on the dinner table at the **Pesach seder,** that contains foods symbolic of the holiday.

Maror, the bitter herb, usually horseradish, reminds us of the bitterness of slavery. *Zeroa,* a roasted shank bone, is symbolic of the offerings at the **Temple** in ancient times. *Beitzah,* a roasted egg, signifies rebirth, a new life in freedom for the **Israelites.** *Haroset,* often a mixture of apples, nuts, and wine, represents the mortar the Jewish slaves used to make bricks in Egypt. *Karpas,* celery or parsley, is a symbol of hope and the coming of spring. Most seder plates have a sixth place for an additional bitter vegetable *(hazeret).* In the course of the seder, each food is passed around the table and tasted as its meaning is explained. At some liberal or feminist sedarim, an orange is placed on the seder plate. This new tradition comes from a story in which a woman asked a rabbi about her role in the seder; his reply was that women are as necessary as an orange on the seder plate. A popular item of **Judaica,** some seder plates are ornate, handmade works of art; others are simple, with five or six small dishes for the ritual items.

sefer   n. Hebrew (SAY-fair)   Book.

Sefer   Chayim   n. Hebrew (SAY-fair khye-EEM)   Hebrew term for the **Book of Life.**

sefer Torah   n. Hebrew (SAY-fair toe-RAH); pl. **sifrei Torah**   (sif-RAY toe-RAH)   A **Torah** scroll; it always refers to the actual parchment scroll. Traditionally, a child reads in Hebrew from a *sefer Torah* as part of the ritual of becoming **Bar** or **Bat Mitzvah.**

Sefer Yetzirah   n. Hebrew   Literally, "Book of Creation." The first classic text of **Kabbalah.** It is considered to be an early Babylonian or Palestinian work dating from the 2nd century C.E. The *Sefer Yetzirah* theorizes that the 10 *sefirot* and the 22 letters of the Hebrew alphabet are the building blocks of creation and the channels through which Divine consciousness flows into creation.

sefirah   n. Hebrew (seh-fee-RAH); pl. **sefirot** (seh-fee-ROTE)   One of the 10 emanations, or varying aspects, of the Divine presence. This is one of the theories central to the Jewish mystical tradition, or **Kabbalah.** According to kabbalistic teaching, *sefirot* are the 10 attributes that *Ein Sof,* the infinite unknowable God, created and through which He can be known to man and the universe. *Sefirot,* sometimes called the building blocks of creation, are often depicted as spheres, pillars, or a **tree of life,** in which the roots are in heaven and the branches extend down toward earth. The *sefirot* are said to correspond with parts of the body. The 10 *sefirot* are *keter, hokhmah, binah, chesed, gevurah, tiferet, netzach, hod, yesod,* and *malchut. Da'at,* literally "knowledge," is sometimes used in place of *keter.*

sefirat ha-Omer   n. Hebrew (seh-fee-RAHT ha-OH-mair)   See **Omer.**

sekhel n. Hebrew (SAY-khel); Yiddish pronunciation (SEH-khul) Common sense; good judgment; using one's noodle. "Don't walk home in the dark at night in that neighborhood. Have a little *sekhel.*"

Selichot pl. n. Hebrew (slee-KHOTE) Literally, "forgiveness." **1.** The set of prayers for forgiveness recited several times during the **High Holy Days. 2.** The special service usually held on the Saturday night before **Rosh Hashanah.**

semikhah n. Hebrew (seh-MEE-khah) The term for rabbinical ordination. In ancient times, rabbinic ordination was granted in a ceremony in which the high priest placed his hands over the initiate's head, blessing him. This tradition comes from when **Moses** chose Joshua as his successor by placing his hands on Joshua's head; in the same fashion, Joshua chose the leader of the next generation of **Israelites,** and so on. Today, **rabbis** are ordained after graduating from a rabbinical seminary or **yeshivah.**

Semite n. Hebrew (SEM-ite) A member of any of the modern and ancient peoples that includes the Akkadians, Canaanites, Phoenicians, Hebrews, and Arabs. The word comes from the name Shem, the eldest son of Noah. Today, Semite often refers to persons of Jewish heritage and is used as part of the word "anti-Semite" to refer to someone prejudiced against Jews. See **anti-Semitism.**

Sephardim pl. n. Hebrew (seh-far-DEEM) The name given to those Jews who lived in Spain, Portugal, the Mediterranean Basin, North Africa, and the Middle East, and their descendants. *Sepharad* is the Hebrew name for Spain, where most of these Jews lived before their expulsion in 1492. Sephardim are distinct from—and smaller in number than—the **Ashkenazim,** the Jews of Central and Eastern Europe and their descendants. Most of the world's Jews can trace their ancestry to one of these two groups. While **Hebrew** or **Ladino** was their language of prayer, **Judeo-Spanish,** or **Judezmo,** (a mixture of Hebrew and Spanish) was their everyday language; the Ashkenazim spoke **Yiddish.** The holiday customs, liturgy, pronunciation of Hebrew, and cuisine distinguish Sephardim from the Ashkenazim. For example, Sephardim eat legumes and rice at **Pesach.** They call the raised platform in a synagogue a *tehbah* and they name their children in honor of a living relative, commonly a grandparent. Sephardim refer to the Sabbath as **Shabbat,** while the Ashkenazim have traditionally said *Shabbos,* the Yiddish pronunciation. The **State of Israel** has adopted the Sephardic pronunciation of Hebrew words, as have Jews in the United States. adj. **Sephardic.**

Septuagint n. English (SEP-too-uh-jint) From the Latin word for "seventy." A Greek translation of the **TANAKH,** produced from the 3rd to 1st centuries B.C.E. It is thought to have been translated by Jewish scholars at the request of Ptolemy II. It predates the **Masoretic text** by as much as 1,000 years.

seudah shelishit n. Hebrew (seh-oo-DAH shih-lee-SHEET) Literally, "third meal." **1.** The third and final meal of **Shabbat,** usually eaten late on Saturday afternoon after the *Mincha* service. **2.** The name given to the midday or afternoon meal served in **synagogue** on Shabbat. At some synagogues, it is common for a congregant to sponsor a *seudah shelishit* in honor of a pending marriage.

seudat hevrah n. Hebrew (seh-oo-DAHT hev-RAH) A meal of condolence; the first meal mourners eat after the funeral. Traditionally the meal was prepared by neighbors and friends, although these days it may be ordered from a deli or caterer. In either case, the point is that the mourners need not concern themselves with daily chores like cooking. This is also the reason friends sometimes bring cake or other food with them when they make a **shivah** call. The *seudat hevrah* sometimes includes hard-boiled eggs and bagels, symbolic of new life and the circle of life, respectively.

seudat mitzvah n. Hebrew (seh-oo-DAHT mits-VAH) The festive meal eaten after a joyous life-cycle event, such as a *brit milah,* **Bar** or **Bat Mitzvah,** or wedding. This Hebrew term is rarely used; in modern times the party and meal are referred to as a reception.

seven species pl. n. English Seven grains and fruits that grow in Israel and are mentioned in the **Bible**: wheat, barley, grapes (vines and wine), figs, pomegranates, olives, and honey from dates. All of these foods have been plentiful in Israel since ancient times. Today in downtown Jerusalem, huge fig trees drop ripe fruit on the sidewalks. Pomegranates can be found in almost every local garden, and date palms loaded with hanging fruit are common all over the country. In Hebrew, the seven species are *"shevat haminim"* (sheh-VAHT hah-mee-NEEM).

sha'atnez n. Hebrew (SHOT-nez) The mixture of wool and linen, prohibited according to Jewish law. This biblical injunction, one of the 613 **mitzvot,** is the only one related to clothing. Thus, a very traditional Jew would not wear a wool **tallit** with linen fringe or a wool jacket with linen thread around the buttonholes. Just as food can be certified **kosher,** clothing can be certified *sha'atnez.*

Shabbat n. Hebrew (shah-BAHT) pl. **Shabbatot** (shah-bah-TOT) The Jewish Sabbath; the day of rest. Shabbat begins at sunset on Friday night and ends Saturday evening when three stars are visible in the night sky. Shabbat is considered the most important day on the **Jewish calendar,** even more important than **Yom Kippur.** The three central rituals of Shabbat include saying the blessing when lighting candles, making *Kiddush,* and reciting *ha-Motzi* over **challah.** Strict observers of Shabbat follow the many laws of *melakhah,* spelled out in the **Torah** and **Talmud,** that dictate what activities are allowed and what are not. For example, traditional Jews do not work, spend money, drive, ignite a flame, or turn on electricity. The day is spent quietly praying, studying, reading, and eating.

Many Jewish families make Friday night Shabbat dinner a special time with a home-cooked meal. Children may wear *kippot,* use a special *Kiddush Cup* to drink grape juice, and cover the **challah** with a cloth they decorated in **Hebrew school.** Family members share highlights from the week and together sing special songs called *zemirot;* parents may say a blessing over their children.

Most **synagogues** hold special Friday night services that usher in Shabbat and include *Kabbalat Shabbat* and *Ma'ariv.* Saturday Shabbat services include *Shacharit, Musaf, Mincha,* and *Ma'ariv.* Often, a lunchtime meal or snack, called an *Oneg Shabbat,* is offered in synagogue. The Sabbath ends with the *Havdalah* observance on Saturday evening. **Bar** and **Bat Mitzvah** ceremonies typically take place during the Shabbat morning **Torah** service.

Shabbat candles pl. n. Hebrew/English (shah-BAHT CAN-dulz) The two or more candles that are lit on Friday evening to welcome the Sabbath. Families often have special Shabbat candlesticks. See **candlelighting.**

Shabbat ha-Gadol n. Hebrew (shah-BAHT hah-gah-DOLE) The name given to the **Shabbat** immediately before **Pesach** begins. Traditionally, parts of the **haggadah** are read, and the **rabbi** discusses the customs of **Pesach.** The service also includes readings from the Book of Malachi that mention the return of the Prophet **Elijah** and the coming of the *Mashiach.* Also called the Great Sabbath.

Shabbaton n. Hebrew/English (shah-bah-TONE) A special **Shabbat** program for learning and fellowship. These gatherings, often sponsored by a **synagogue,** usually have a social component, perhaps a meal, and some sort of educational aspect as well. "Will your family be joining us for the *Shabbaton* lunch-and-learn?"

Shabbat shalom n. Hebrew (shah-BAHT shah-LOME) Literally, "Sabbath of peace." **1.** The greeting exchanged on **Shabbat.** It is customary for Jews to say *"Shabbat shalom"* and kiss or shake hands with others sitting around them in **synagogue** at the end of services. **2.** The title of a popular children's song, sung in Hebrew, that celebrates the Sabbath.

Shabbat Shuvah n. Hebrew (shah-BAHT shoo-VAH) Literally, "Sabbath of Return." The name given to the **Shabbat** that falls between **Rosh Hashanah** and **Yom Kippur.** It takes its name from the **parashah** read that day, which talks about the **Israelites'** returning to the **Promised Land.** It is customary for the rabbi to discuss repentance in preparation for Yom Kippur.

Shabbos n. Yiddish (SHA-bis)   The Yiddish pronunciation of **Shabbat.**

Shabbos bride n. Yiddish/English (SHA-bis BRIDE)   A metaphor for **Shabbat.** Since the 3rd century C.E., Shabbat has often been personified with womanly characteristics, perhaps because this day of rest offers warmth, comfort, and respite, much as a mother provides to her family. The song **"Lekhah Dodi"** characterizes Shabbat as a bride with the words: "Come, my beloved, to meet the bride. Let us welcome the Sabbath."

Shabbos goy n. Yiddish (SHA-bis GOY)   A non-Jew who is hired to perform certain tasks for a strictly observant Jew, such as lighting a fire in the oven or fetching water, both of which are forbidden on **Shabbat.** This custom was common in the **shtetls** of Eastern Europe. Today, the term is almost never used because modern technology—like timers on lights and stoves and automatic elevators—has replaced the *Shabbos goy.*

Shacharit n. Hebrew (SHOKH-hah-reit)   Literally, "little morning." The traditional set of prayers said each morning at home or in **synagogue.** In many congregations, the **Torah** is read during *Shacharit* services on Mondays and Thursdays, as well as on **Shabbat.**

shadchen n. Hebrew (SHAHD-khan)   A professional matchmaker, prominent in Eastern European communities, who arranged Jewish marriages by matching up family backgrounds, qualities, and personalities. The *shadchen* received a percentage of the dowry for his or her services. These matchmakers, thought to be doing "God's work," held an honorable position in the community. Old-fashioned usage.

Shaddai n. Hebrew (shah-DYE)   Another name for God. The three letters that form the word *Shaddai—shin, dalet, yud—*are a synonym for God. The word *Shaddai* appears on the parchment that is placed inside a **mezuzah** case. Sometimes, mezuzot are designed with openings that allow the word to be visible. Other times, the letter *shin* appears on the outside of the case. When laying **tefillin,** the word *Shaddai* is formed by the *retzuot.*

shalach munis pl. n. Yiddish (shah-LAHKH MUN-iss)   Goodie bags or baskets containing **hamantashen,** candy, fruit and other treats that are given to family, friends, and the needy on **Purim;** they are sometimes delivered by children dressed in costume for the holiday. Also called *mishloach manot.*

shaliach n. Hebrew (shah-LEE-akh)   An Israeli citizen sent by the government to live in the United States for the express purpose of teaching Americans about Israeli life, encouraging support for the **State of Israel,** and facilitating immigration (making *aliyah*) to Israel. A *shaliach* serves for a few years and then returns home to Israel.

shaliach tzibbur   n. Hebrew (shah-LEE-akh tsee-BOOR)   Literally, "emissary of the congregation." Another name for a **cantor** or volunteer who chants the prayers and leads the songs for a congregation.

shalom   n. Hebrew (shah-LOME)   Literally, "peace." An ancient word used as a greeting; it can mean both "hello" and "good-bye" as well as "peace." The word has complex meanings; it comes from the Hebrew root word meaning "complete." Thus, when the word refers to "peace," it represents an ideal state of complete peace. When negotiating the peace treaty with Egypt, the **State of Israel** insisted on using the word "shalom" and its Arab equivalent, "salaam," to connote a full and lasting peace, rather than just an armistice. "Shalom" is often used along with another word, for example, *shalom bayit,* which means "peace in the home."

shalom aleikhem   int. Hebrew (shah-LOME ah-LAY-khem)   Literally, "peace unto you." **1.** A salutation used by traditional Jews as a greeting when seeing someone they haven't seen in a while. **2.** cap. The name of a song commonly sung on **Shabbat,** originally by the **kabbalists,** to welcome the angels who are thought to accompany people to and from the **synagogue.**

shalom bayit   n. Hebrew (shah-LOME BYE-eet)   Literally, "peace in the home." Contentment and harmony among family members. The Jewish tradition of *shalom bayit* requires, among other things, that family members not raise their voices to one another in anger, that a husband treat his wife as nicely as he would treat a neighbor, and that the commandment for children to treat parents with respect goes both ways.

shalom zachar   n. Hebrew (shah-LOME zah-KHAR)   Literally, "welcome to the male child." In the **Ashkenazic** tradition, this is a small gathering of family and friends on the first Friday night following a son's birth. Some **Sephardic** Jews celebrate it on the night before the *brit milah.* It is traditional to serve peas and beans to ward off evil spirits that might harm the child. The occasion, which has **kabbalistic** origins, is also called a *ben zachar.*

Shalosh Regalim   pl. n. Hebrew (shah-LOESH reh-gah-LEEM)   Hebrew term for the **Pilgrimage Festivals.**

shamash   n. Hebrew (shah-MAHSH); Yiddish pronunciation (SHAH-mish)   **1.** The ninth candle on the **menorah,** which is lit first and then used to kindle the other candles for **Hanukkah.** The *shamash,* which is often in the center of the menorah, is placed a bit higher than the other candles. **2.** An old-fashioned term for a **synagogue** caretaker. Today, most synagogues have a full staff of employees to oversee the daily operations of the synagogue.

shammes   See *shamash.*

shanah tovah   n. Hebrew (SHAH-nah TOE-vah)   Literally, "a good year." A shortened form of *le-shanah tovah tikatevu,* the New Year's greeting exchanged on **Rosh Hashanah.** "I saw them after synagogue and wished them *shanah tovah.*"

shanda   n. Yiddish (SHAN-deh)   Scandal, shame. "He has such a lovely wife and kids but everyone knows he had an affair. It's a *shanda* for the family."

shank bone   See *zeroa.*

SHAS   n. Hebrew (SHOS)   **1.** Another name for the **Talmud.** SHAS is an acronym for the term *shishah sedarim,* meaning "six orders." This refers to the fact that the Talmud is divided into six main sections. **2.** Shas. The name for the **Sephardic ultra-Orthodox** political party in the **State of Israel.**

shav   n. Yiddish (SHAV)   Cream of leek, sorrel, or spinach soup, usually served cold. This traditional Eastern European recipe was brought to America by Jewish immigrants. *Shav* is the green cousin of **borscht.**

Shavuot   n. Hebrew (shah-VOO-ote)   Literally, "weeks." Celebrated on the sixth of **Sivan,** which usually falls in May or June, Shavuot comes 50 days after **Pesach.** It marks the anniversary of **Moses'** receiving the **Ten Commandments** at **Mount Sinai** and the first harvest of the fruits of spring.

In ancient days, wheat would be planted after the first day of Pesach and harvested 49 days later. Each day was noted in a tradition called counting the **Omer.** Along with Pesach and **Sukkot,** Shavuot is one of the three **Pilgrimage Festivals,** when the ancient **Israelites** traveled to the **Temple** in **Jerusalem** with gifts of the first fruit and offerings for God. This gives Shavuot one of its other names, the Festival of the First Fruits (Hag ha-Bikurim). It is also known as the Harvest Festival and the Feast of Weeks.

Although Shavuot is not as widely celebrated as some other Jewish holidays, it is traditional to attend **synagogue.** The **Book of Ruth** and the Ten Commandments are read. Synagogues are often decorated with fresh fruit and flowers, recalling the harvest. People often eat dairy foods, such as **blintzes,** yogurt, and cheesecake, because in **The Song of Songs** the **Torah** is compared to milk.

At the end of the 19th century, the **Reform movement** introduced the **Confirmation** ceremony as part of Shavuot services. This ceremony has been widely adopted by the various branches of Judaism; it marks the occasion when Jewish teenagers (about age 16) complete their formal religious school education. The ceremony gets its name from the students' "confirming" their commitment to lead a Jewish life.

shaygetz n. Yiddish (SHAY-gits) A **gentile** boy or young man; male form of *shiksa*. A derogatory, old-fashioned term.

shayna punim n. Yiddish (SHAY-nah PUH-nim) Literally, "pretty face." An endearing expression often said by *bubbes* and *zaydes* as they pinch a grandchild's cheek.

shaytl See *sheitel*.

shechitah v. Hebrew (sheh-KHEE-tah) The ritual of **kosher** slaughtering, done by a *shochet,* that requires an animal be killed in a humane fashion. The *shochet* severs the jugular vein with one stroke so as not to cause unnecessary pain to the animal.

Shehecheyanu n. Hebrew (sheh-HEH-khee-YAH-noo) The blessing that thanks God for long life and for reaching a happy occasion. The *Shehecheyanu* translates as: "Blessed are You, *Adonai* our God, Ruler of the Universe who has given us life, sustained us, and brought us to this moment." This prayer is said aloud by family and friends to mark any joyous *simcha*—a wedding or any other life-cycle event. On holidays, it acknowledges another year of celebrating and a new time in the life of all gathered. Many people also say the *Shehecheyanu* to mark wonderful secular events, like a college graduation or a new job.

sheitel n. Yiddish (SHAY-tul) A wig worn by some **Orthodox** women after marriage, in keeping with the Jewish law that forbids a woman from leaving her hair uncovered in the sight of a man who is not her husband. It was traditionally worn by Orthodox **Ashkenazic** women in Eastern Europe. Today, many Orthodox women keep their hair covered with a hat or scarf instead.

shekel n. Hebrew (SHEH-kuhl) **1.** The silver coin, equal to about half an ounce, that was used by the Jews in biblical times. It is mentioned in **Genesis** as the coin used by **Abraham** and **Moses.** Today, it is the name for the monetary unit in the **State of Israel. 2.** Slang for cash or money. Old-fashioned usage.

sheket int. Hebrew (SHEH-ket) Literally, "be quiet." Often used with the Hebrew word for please, *bevakashah,* in **Hebrew school,** at children's religious services, and on other occasions as a call to order: *"Sheket bevakashah!"* (Quiet, please!)

Shekhinah   n. Hebrew (sheh-khee-NAH)   Literally, "dwelling." The ancient talmudic name for God's presence, which is commonly described as a light or radiance that illuminates the world. The *Shekhinah* is felt in certain places in the world, particularly at the **Western Wall** in **Jerusalem,** and at certain times. For instance, the **Talmud** teaches that the *Shekhinah* descends each Friday at sunset to transform Jewish homes during **Shabbat.** According to **kabbalistic** teachings, the *Shekhinah* represents the feminine presence of God, identified with the tenth *sefirah.*

sheloshim   n. Hebrew (sheh-loe-SHEEM)   The 30-day formal mourning period that follows the burial of a parent, child, spouse, or sibling. The first seven days of this period are called **shivah.** During the remaining days, the mourner begins to return to daily activities, including work, but traditionally does not participate in happy occasions, like parties. During this time, *Kaddish* is recited daily.

Shema   n. Hebrew (sheh-MAH)   The central prayer of Jewish liturgy, which comes from passages in **Deuteronomy** and **Numbers.** It expresses the concept of monotheism and declares one's faith in God: "*Shema Yisra'el Adonai Eloheinu Adonai Echad.* Hear, O Israel: *Adonai* is our God, *Adonai* is One." Further paragraphs of the *Shema* enumerate central commandments of Judaism, including hanging a **mezuzah,** laying **tefillin,** and teaching Jewish traditions to children. The *Shema* is supposed to be recited daily, in the morning and evening; it is also said as a bedtime prayer and sometimes before death.

Shemini Atzeret   n. Hebrew (sheh-MEE-nee ah-TSEH-reht)   Celebrated on the eighth day of **Sukkot,** this holiday marks the conclusion of the fall harvest festival. Special ancient prayers said on Shemini Atzeret thank God for the harvest and ask for winter rain to prepare the ground for spring planting. In the **State of Israel** and in some U.S. **synagogues,** Shemini Atzeret is combined with **Simchat Torah** observances.

shemitah   n. Hebrew (SHMEE-tah)   Literally, "release." The seventh, or sabbatical, year. According to **Leviticus,** all the land in the Land of **Israel** was to lie fallow every seventh year; plowing, planting, watering, and harvesting were forbidden. In addition, all debts were to be forgiven. Every 50th year was a **Jubilee** year; at this time, Jews were to free their slaves and return any land bought since the previous Jubilee. Later, more lenient interpretations of the *shemitah* allowed Jews to sell their land to Muslims for two years and then buy it back. **Hillel** introduced the *prosbul,* a legal formula for reclaiming debts after the sabbatical year; its purpose was to encourage wealthy people to continue to lend money during this period. These sabbatical year practices were largely abandoned by the Middle Ages.

Some of Israel's **Orthodox** rabbis have tried to reinstitute these *shemitah* observances. In the fall of 2000, which was the start of a *shemitah* year according to the **Jewish calendar,** they called on Israeli farmers to observe these biblical rulings. The rabbis asked farmers to let their land rest and fire their workers, and demanded that consumers boycott agricultural products grown in the **State of Israel.**

Shemoneh Esrei n. Hebrew (sheh-MOE-nah ESS-ray) Literally, "eighteen." Another name for the *Amidah,* a silent devotional prayer said while standing, that had 18 benedictions until an additional one was added.

Shemot n. Hebrew (sheh-MOTE) The second book of the **Torah,** known as **Exodus** in English.

shemurah matzah n. Hebrew (shih-MORE-ah MAH-tsah) Literally, "watched or guarded **matzah.**" *Shemurah matzah* is produced with wheat that has been watched from the time of harvest through the baking process to ensure that no water or heat will cause fermentation—or any other type of leavening—to take place. It is mixed, rolled, and baked by hand. This is in contrast to commercial matzah, which is machine-made. *Shemurah matzah* is popular on **Pesach** with traditional Jews who consider it "extra **kosher.**"

Sheol n. Hebrew (sheh-OHL) A word used in the **Torah** to describe the place the dead go for punishment and/or purification in the afterlife *(olam ha-ba).* See *Geihinnom.*

shep nachas v. Yiddish (SHEP KNOKH-iss) To reap joy and take pride, especially in the accomplishments or all-around greatness of one's children or grandchildren. "My parents will *shep nachas* when they come to the ballet recital and see their granddaughter perform."

Sheva Brachot pl. n. Hebrew (SHEH-vah bra-KHOAT) Literally, "seven blessings." **1.** The marriage blessings that are recited under the *huppah* during the wedding ceremony. They express how the universe rejoices when a bride and groom are wed, and thank God for creating "joy and gladness, bridegroom and bride, mirth and exultation, pleasure and delight, love, brotherhood, peace, and fellowship." They are usually recited by the **rabbi;** some couples honor special guests by asking them to recite some of the blessings. **2.** The week of festive meals after a wedding ceremony. In olden times, couples would spend the first week of marriage surrounded—and fed—by their family and friends. The *Sheva Brachot* would be recited during the Grace after Meals. Though most couples have abandoned this practice in favor of a honeymoon, it is still practiced in the **Hasidic** community and among some other traditional Jews. The Yiddish form is *Sheva Bruchas* (SHEH-vah BRAW-khus).

shevarim pl. n. Hebrew (shih-var-EEM)   One of the specific sounds, a series of notes, blown on the **shofar.** *Shevarim* is composed of three short notes blown together quickly. Before the shofar is blown, the **rabbi** or **cantor** will call out this word, signaling to the person blowing the shofar what sound to play—and to the congregants what sound they will hear. The shofar is sounded on **Rosh Hashanah** and **Yom Kippur.**

Shevat n. Hebrew (sheh-VAAT)   The eleventh month in the **Jewish calendar,** it falls in January or February.

shidduch n. Hebrew (SHIH-dukh)   An arranged marriage, traditionally planned by a *shadchen.* Today, the word is used as a more general term for a marriage, as in "Leslie and Mark are getting along so well. Maybe there'll be a *shidduch* soon."

shikker n. & adj. Yiddish (SHIH-ker)   Drunk. The word can be used as a noun to describe a habitual drinker or as an adjective to describe being a little tipsy. Jews are allowed to get *shikker* during the feast of **Purim** so that they can't recognize the difference between **Haman** and **Mordecai.** Old-fashioned usage.

shiksa n. Yiddish (SHICK-sah)   A **gentile** girl or woman. The word is a distortion of the Hebrew root *sheketz,* which refers to the flesh of a taboo animal in the **Torah.** Since intermarriage to non-Jews was taboo, this word was applied to them. This is a derogatory, old-fashioned term.

Shimon   A variation of the name **Simeon.**

Shir ha-Shirim n. Hebrew (SHEER hah-sheer-EEM)   The Hebrew name for **The Song of Songs,** the scroll, or **megillah,** that is read on **Pesach.**

shivah n. Hebrew (SHIH-vah)   Literally, "seven." The initial seven-day period of mourning that follows burial. During this time, members of the immediate family come together in one of their homes, where they can receive visitors, hold a **minyan** for prayer, share meals, and reminisce about the deceased. This time is called "sitting shivah," from the tradition of not sitting in a comfortable chair but on a low bench or box. A Jew is required to observe shivah for seven relatives: father, mother, sister, brother, son, daughter, or spouse. **Shabbat** is not observed as a day of mourning, although it does count toward the seven days. Some modern Jews observe shivah for only three days.

Strict observance of shivah means refraining from wearing leather shoes and cosmetics, shaving or cutting one's hair, going to work, bathing, having sex, or putting on fresh clothes. Often, mirrors in the house are covered because mourners should not be concerned with vanity.

During the week of shivah, prayers are said, both in **synagogue** and at the mourner's home. It is considered an obligation to pay a condolence call—"to make a shivah call"—during this first week. Friends and family will often come to the mourner's home at a specified time to ensure that there is a minyan so that prayers, including the *Mourner's Kaddish,* can be recited aloud.

Shivah traditions vary greatly. Some persons prefer a solemn atmosphere so they can mourn and pray in quiet reflection. Others prefer to discuss happy memories of the deceased, converse with relatives, and gain comfort from friends, family, and food. Visitors should take their cue from the mourners and the atmosphere of the home as to what is appropriate behavior. It is common to include children when making a shivah call; often, children who did not attend the funeral may spend time with the mourners at home. Food is usually a part of shivah; callers may bring food or sweets as a token of support or to fulfill the **mitzvah** of *seudat hevrah.*

Shivah Asar b'Tammuz   n. Hebrew (shee-VAH ah-SAR beh-tah-MOOZ) A minor **fast day,** celebrated on the 17th of **Tammuz.** It begins a three-week period of mourning that ends with **Tisha b'Av.** It is believed to commemorate five catastrophes that took place on that day, the most significant of which occurred when **Moses** returned from **Mount Sinai** with the **Ten Commandments** and found people worshiping the Golden Calf. On minor fast days, fasting begins at dawn and ends when stars appear in the sky.

shivah minyan   n. Hebrew (SHIH-vah MIN-yin)   A short prayer service, with at least 10 Jews, during which mourners say *Kaddish.* A shivah **minyan** often takes place in the home where a family is sitting **shivah;** friends coming to pay a condolence call might be asked to arrive at a particular time to ensure that with their participation there will be enough people on hand for the minyan. While liberal Jews include women in the minyan, traditional Jews count men only.

shlemiel   n. Yiddish (shlih-MEAL)   A loser, an incompetent. An awkward and unlucky person for whom things never turn out right; someone to be pitied. See **nebbish.** Old-fashioned usage.

shlep   v. Yiddish (SHLEP)   **1.** To carry, lug. "He shlepped the heavy carton home from the store." **2.** To drag someone someplace they don't want to go. "She shlepped me to the mall." **3.** To move slowly, to drag one's heels.

shlimazel   n. Yiddish (shlih-MAH-zull)   Someone born under an unlucky star; a born loser. An inept, bungling person who suffers from continual bad luck. The difference between a **shlimiel** and a shlimazel is commonly explained by the phrase "It's the shlemiel who spills soup on the shlimazel." Old-fashioned usage.

shlock   n. Yiddish (SHLOCK)   Worthless junk; something of cheap or inferior quality. "The toy he ordered online turned out to be shlock." adj. **shlocky.**

shlof   n. Yiddish (shluff)   Literally, "sleep." It is often used in the phrase *"gai shoflen"* (go to sleep) or more informally, *"gai shlofie."* "It's past 9:00 P.M.; let's give the kids a bath so they can *gai shlofie* already."

shlub   n. Yiddish (SHLUB)   A coarse, bad-mannered person; a clumsy oaf.

shluff   v. Yiddish (SHLUFF)   Literally, "sleep." Go to sleep. "It's past 9:00 P.M.; it's time for you kids to go *shluffy.*"

shlump   n. Yiddish (SHLUMP)   A dull, colorless person; a drip. Old-fashioned usage.

shmaltz   n. Yiddish (SHMALTZ)   Rendered chicken fat. In the days before cholesterol concerns and alternative products, most good Jewish cooks collected and saved their own poultry fat—shmaltz—to use as shortening in recipes and for frying food, because commercial lard is not **kosher.** Shmaltz is an old-fashioned Jewish delicacy. Some delis used to put a jar of shmaltz right on the table, like mustard, for customers to spread on rye bread and enjoy.

shmaltzy   adj. Yiddish (SHMALL-tsee).   Overly sentimental or romantic; gushingly sweet. Usually it refers to literature, art, or music, as opposed to food. "That old song is so shmaltzy. How can you like it?"

shmatte   n. Yiddish (SHMAH-tah)   Literally, "rag." An old, worn piece of clothing. "We're going out to dinner, so change out of that *shmatte.*"

shmeer   n. Yiddish (SHMEER)   **1.** A dab or spread, like of cream cheese on a **bagel. 2.** The whole package, the entire deal. "He went to get his son a new computer, and he came home with the whole shmeer—the scanner, a printer, everything." **3.** v. To spread or smear. "Shmeer some cream cheese on this for me, will you?" **4.** To bribe, as in "greasing the palm." "His father-in-law told him that he'd have to shmeer the maitre d' to get a good table in the restaurant."

shmeggegge   n. Yiddish (shmuh-GEH-gee)   An untalented loser; a whiner; a petty person. Old-fashioned usage.

shmendrick   n. Yiddish (SHMEN-drick)   Someone of no importance. A young man who is "wet behind the ears"; a pipsqueak. The opposite of **mensch.** Old-fashioned usage.

shmo   n. Yiddish (SHMOW)   A shorter, nicer way of saying **shmuck.** A jerk or fall guy. "I felt like a shmo waiting for you for so long."

shmooze   v. Yiddish (SHMOOZ)   To engage in friendly, heart-to-heart, gossipy conversation. "On the first day of school, all the moms stayed in the playground for a few minutes, just shmoozing."

shmuck   n. Yiddish (SHMUCK)   Vulgar term for penis. **1.** A derogatory term for an obnoxious or detestable person. Harsher and more insulting than **shmo** or **shnook. 2.** Someone who allows himself to be taken advantage of; similar to a "jerk" when used in a self-deprecating way. "I can't believe I waited for an hour at the restaurant for her and she never showed up. I'm such a shmuck; I never even mentioned it to her."

shmutz   n. Yiddish (SHMUTZ)   Dirt, stain, or filth. "Come here and let me wipe that *shmutz* off your face." adj. **shmutzig.**

shnapps   n. German (SHNOPS)   A strong, dry liquor, such as slivovitz or kirsch. In the early part of the 20th century, shnapps was a favorite drink of Jews who emigrated from Eastern Europe. It used to be served at a ***Kiddush*** along with **kichel.**

shnecken   n. Yiddish (SHNEH-ken)   Literally, "snail." A bite-sized pastry made by rolling a yeast dough filled with spices, sugar, nuts, and/or raisins. The individual pastries are then sliced from the roll and baked. Varieties of *shnecken* include cinnamon, chocolate, and fruit flavors. The recipe is thought to have come to America with German-Jewish immigrants.

shnook   n. Yiddish (SHNOOK)   An incompetent person who is deserving of pity but also likable. An affectionate, not derogatory, term. Old-fashioned usage.

shnorrer   n. Yiddish (SHNOR-er)   A moocher; someone who borrows with no intention of repaying. "I've invited them to dinner three times and they've never asked us back. What shnorrers!" Old-fashioned usage.

shnoz   n. Yiddish (SHNOZ)   A nose, especially a large, unattractive one. Old-fashioned usage.

Shoah   n. Hebrew (SHOW-ah)   Literally, "destruction." The Hebrew term for the Nazi **Holocaust,** the destruction of the European Jewish community between 1933 and 1945. See **Yom ha-Shoah.**

shochet   n. Hebrew (SHOW-khet)   A ritual slaughterer; a man who is specially trained in the rules of *shechitah* (**kosher** butchering). He must pass a difficult examination in Jewish law and animal anatomy and be an observant Jew. A *shochet* kills meat and fowl in a proscribed way to avoid inflicting pain on the animal, according to rules set forth in the **Shulchan Arukh.**

shofar   n. Hebrew (SHOW-far);   pl. **shofarot** (show-far-OTE)   A hollowed-out ram's horn that is blown like a trumpet. The shofar is an ancient musical instrument used for communication and celebration. Tradition says the shofar was sounded at **Mount Sinai** when the Jewish people promised to honor and obey God's commandments. Today, it is blown on **Rosh Hashanah** and at the end of **Yom Kippur** as part of the prayer services. Before the horn is blown, the **rabbi** or **cantor** will call out the name of the forthcoming blast, signaling to the shofar blower what sound to play and to the congregation what sound it will hear. The shofar makes several distinctive sounds, combinations of short and long blasts, that have special Hebrew names: *Tekiah* calls the congregation to attention. *Teruah* calls people together. *Shevarim* represents the hopes Jews have for a good new year, while *tekiah gedolah* welcomes the New Year. Some say the sound of the shofar serves as a reminder of the promise to obey the commandments.

shomer   n. Hebrew (sho-MAIR)   Literally, "guardian." One who watches. A person who sits at the side of the deceased from the time of death until burial, often reciting psalms. This is in accordance with Jewish law, which considers it disrespectful to leave the body alone. See *kavod ha-met.*

shomer Shabbat   adj. Hebrew (sho-MAIR shah-BAHT)   Literally, "Sabbath guardian." A descriptive term for a Jew who strictly observes the Sabbath according to *halakhah.* The phrase is also used to refer to someone who is religiously and *halakhically* observant in general. "He won't go swimming in a pool if women are there, too. He's *shomer Shabbat.*" The feminine form is *shomeret Shabbat.*

shoresh   n. Hebrew (shore-ESH)   Literally "root." The usually three-consonant root of a Hebrew word. Many Hebrew words can be boiled down to these few letters that give a clue to the word's meaning. Some roots are two or four consonants.

shpiel   See **spiel.**

shpilkes   n. Yiddish (SHPILL-kiss)   Literally "pins." Impatience, nervous energy, restlessness. Someone with *shpilkes* is fidgety and might be described as having "ants in the pants." "She had *shpilkes* while she was waiting to be called for her audition."

shtarker   n. Yiddish (SHTAR-ker)   A strong, brave person, a tough guy. Shtarker can refer to physical strength or mental endurance, such as someone with a lot of patience.

shtetl   n. Yiddish (SHTET-ull)   A little town or village, specifically the rural communities in Poland, Lithuania, and Russia where many Jews lived before World War II. **Yiddish** was the everyday language; these villages were the center of **Ashkenazic** culture until the **Holocaust** wiped them out. Jews in the shtetl were often poor; they were forbidden to own land and couldn't leave without permission of the police. Shtetl life has been immortalized in the paintings of Marc Chagall, the stories of **Sholom Aleichem,** and in the musical *Fiddler on the Roof.*

shtick   n. Yiddish (SHTIK)   Overused actions or behavior. Shtick has come to mean a contrived gesture or routine done by anyone, often an actor or comedian, designed to get a laugh.

shtreimel   n. Yiddish (SHTRAY-mel)   The black, broad-brimmed hat, sometimes trimmed with velvet or fur, that is commonly worn by **Hasidic** and **ultra-Orthodox** men, particularly for **Shabbat** and festivals.

shtup   v. Yiddish (SHTOOP)   Vulgar word for sexual intercourse. Immortalized in the mother's warning phrase: "No *huppah,* no *shtupah.*" Old-fashioned usage.

shuckle   v. Yiddish (SHUCK-uhl)   To sway back and forth during prayer or **Torah** study. Traditional Jews often *shuckle* while they *daven.* Some say the custom of *shuckling* symbolizes the soul as a flickering flame, moving and striving upward to God.

shul   n. Yiddish (SHOOL)   The most common **Ashkenazic** word for **synagogue.** From the German/Yiddish root word for "school," indicating that a synagogue is also a place of study. "Can we get together on Saturday? What time should I meet you after shul?"

Shulchan Arukh   n. Hebrew (shool-KHAN ah-ROOKH)   Literally, "the prepared table." This compilation of Jewish law *(halakhah)* was written by the **Sephardic** scholar Joseph Karo in 1565. The Shulchan Arukh summarizes the commandments governing traditional observance of **Shabbat** and daily practices, such as **kashrut,** prayer, and sexual relations. It is based on a careful reading of the **Talmud,** plus rabbinical opinions of the day. While the Shulchan Arukh is considered the most authoritative version of Jewish law, it was also written so that it could be used by everyone, not just scholars. See also **Mappah.**

Shushan Purim   n. Hebrew (SHOE-shan POOR-um)   The 15th of **Adar,** Shushan Purim marks the day on which the holiday of **Purim** is celebrated in walled cities, such as **Jerusalem** and Hebron. This unusual custom comes from a biblical ruling that Jews who live in walled cities celebrate Purim the day after, as the Jews of Shushan, Persia, did. If you are in the **State of Israel** during Adar, you can celebrate Purim twice, first on the 14th in **Tel Aviv** and then on the following day in Jerusalem.

shvartze   n. Yiddish (SHVART-sah)   Literally, "black." An African American. A derogatory term roughly equivalent to "colored." Old-fashioned usage.

shvitz   v. Yiddish (SHVITS)   **1.** To sweat heavily. "Turn the heat lower! I'm *shvitzing.*" **2.** n. steambath. Going to the *shvitz* was once a popular activity for Jewish men.

shwarma   n. Arabic (SHWAR-mah)   Spicy meat, usually poultry or lamb, roasted on a vertical spit, sliced off, and placed inside pita bread along with chopped cucumbers, eggplants, peppers, tomatoes, and other vegetables and condiments. In Israel, shwarma is a popular dish, served at both fine restaurants and roadside stands. Also spelled shawarma.

siddur   n. Hebrew (sih-DOOR); pl. **siddurim**   (sih-duh-REEM)   A book containing the set of prayers recited daily, on **Shabbat,** and for festivals. There are many versions of the siddur, containing distinct prayers, songs, and translations, that are used by the different movements of Judaism. For example, the **Reconstructionist** siddur, *Kol Haneshamah,* has gender-neutral English translations and newly created prayers.

sidrah   n. Aramaic (SIH-drah); pl. **sidrot** (sid-ROTE)   The weekly portion of the **Torah** that is read in **synagogue** on **Shabbat;** synonym for **parashah.**

siman tov   int. Hebrew (SIH-mahn TOV)   Literally, "good omen." An expression of congratulations used by the **Sephardim,** similar to the **Ashkenazic** *mazel tov. Siman tov* is often shouted at a bride and groom at the end of the wedding ceremony. A song entitled "Siman Tov and Mazel Tov," is sung by the guests at happy occasions.

simcha   n. Hebrew (sim-KHAH); pl. **simchot**   (sim-KHOTE); Yiddish pronunciation (SIM-khah)   Literally, "joy or happiness." A joyous occasion; a celebration. The term also refers to the party that traditionally follows the religious part of an event, such as a **brit milah,** a **Bar** or **Bat Mitzvah,** or a wedding ceremony. "Your son got engaged? *Mazel tov!* You better start planning the *simcha.*"

simchat bat   n. Hebrew (sim–KHAHT BAHT)   Literally, "daughter's joy." See **naming.**

Simchat Torah   n. Hebrew (sim–KHAHT toe–RAH)   Literally, "joy of the Torah." Celebrated on the 23rd of **Tishrei,** which corresponds to late September or early to mid–October, Simchat Torah is a joyous holiday that marks the completion of the reading of the **Torah.** It is observed chiefly in **synagogue** following the eight–day festival of **Sukkot.** The entire Torah is read over the course of a year; each week a particular portion **(parashah)** is chanted in synagogue. On Simchat Torah, the final verses of **Deuteronomy** are read, followed by the first verses of **Genesis.** Before the reading, congregants parade around the synagogue led by the **rabbi, cantor,** and members carrying several *sifrei Torah.* This circling parade, called a *hakafah,* is accompanied by singing and dancing. As the Torah passes by, Jews often "kiss" the scrolls by gently touching a prayer book or **tallit** to the Torah cover and then to their lips.

Congregants are often called up to the *bimah* in groups or individually for an *aliyah* so that everyone has a chance to celebrate the occasion. The **Consecration** ceremony, which marks the beginning of a child's formal Jewish education, is sometimes held at this time.

The eighth day of Sukkot is known as **Shemini Atzeret.** In the **State of Israel** and in some U.S. synagogues, Simchat Torah is combined with Shemini Atzeret observances.

Simeon   The second son of **Jacob** and **Leah.** Simeon is also the name of one of the 12 **tribes of Israel,** whose members were said to be descended from him. The tribe lived in the southernmost part of **Canaan.**

Sinai   n. Hebrew (SIGH–nigh)   The arid, mountainous peninsula bounded by the Mediterranean Sea on the north, **Israel** on the northeast, the Gulf of Aqaba on the southeast, the Red Sea on the south, the Gulf of Suez on the west, and Egypt on the northwest. Most of the Sinai is barren, rocky desert, but along the Gulf of Aqaba there are beautiful beaches and scuba diving among the coral reefs. The mountain where Moses saw the burning bush and received the **Ten Commandments** from God is somewhere in the Sinai. The Sinai Peninsula was captured by Israel from Egypt during the **Six–Day War.** It was returned to Egypt in 1979 as part of the Camp David Accords, the peace treaty between Israel and Egypt.

Singer, Isaac Bashevis (1902–1991)   Yiddish journalist, novelist, and author of hundreds of short stories. Born in Poland, the son of a long line of rabbis, Isaac Bashevis Singer fled Hitler's Germany and immigrated to the United States in 1935. He became a columnist for the *Jewish Daily Forward* and contributed to this legendary Yiddish newspaper for more than 40 years. His stories, which incorporate aspects of Jewish folklore, **Kabbalah,** mysticism, and sexual themes, are a look at Jewish **shtetl** life in pre-**Holocaust** Eastern Europe. Many of his stories examine the clash between traditional beliefs and the European way of life with the modern world. Singer chose to write most of his works in Yiddish because he believed that his native language best evoked this vanishing Jewish world and that his large audience still yearned to read Yiddish literature. As his novels became more widely known, he supervised their translation into English. In 1978, he won the Nobel Prize in Literature.

Sivan   n. Hebrew (SEE-von)   The third month on the **Jewish calendar,** it falls in May or June.

sivivon   n. Hebrew (sih-vee-VONE)   The Hebrew word for **dreidel.**

sisterhood   n. English   The women's auxiliary of a **synagogue.** Sisterhoods sponsor educational, community service, and social programs; their fund-raising efforts support various synagogue projects. Sisterhood initiatives might include providing the weekly **Oneg Shabbat,** sponsoring a **Hanukkah** gift bazaar, or making *shalach munis* for **Purim.** In many synagogues, Sisterhood members also run a gift shop that sells **Judaica.**

Six-Day War   n. English   The war between **Israel** and the Arab countries of Egypt, Jordan, and Syria, which lasted from June 5 to 10, 1967. In the weeks prior to the Six-Day War, Egypt, Syria, and Jordan announced a military alliance with the goal of destroying the State of Israel. Egypt's President Nassar closed the Suez Canal to all international ships bringing goods to Israel. The warring Arab states received aid from Iraq, Kuwait, Saudi Arabia, Sudan, and Algeria. When the fighting started, Israel destroyed the Egyptian Air Force in two days and captured the **Sinai** Peninsula. Israel's hardest battles and greatest losses were against Syria in the north, but Israel succeeded in capturing the **Golan Heights,** a strategic mountainous region from which Syria had previously been able to fire rockets literally downward onto Israeli towns and kibbutzim. Israel also captured East **Jerusalem,** including the Old City and the **Western Wall,** from Jordan uniting the Old City of Jerusalem for the first time since 1948.

siyag ha-Torah   n. Hebrew (see-YAG ha-toe-RAH).   See **fence around the Torah.**

siyum   n. Hebrew (see-YOOM)   A celebration or celebratory meal enjoyed when one has completed reading an entire text, such as a **tractate** of **Talmud,** or a program of study. Sometimes called *siyum ha-sefer.*

skakh   n. Hebrew (SKACKH)   The branches and leaves used to make the roof of a **sukkah.** Traditionally, evergreens are used because the leaves do not wither and dry, but any long branches, reeds, or plant material will do. *Skakh* should be plentiful enough to keep out the rain but sparse enough so that the sky and stars are still visible. See **Sukkot.**

skullcap   See *kippah.*

sofer   n. Hebrew (soe-FAIR)   Scribe; a specially trained scholar who carefully inscribes the Hebrew words on **Torah** scrolls and on the parchment inside **mezuzot** or **tefillin.** There are many laws governing the work of the *sofer.* The writing must be done by an observant Jew, using black ink and a quill from a **kosher** fowl (like a goose). The writing must be perfect, with no errors. A single mistake means the *sofer* has to start the page all over again.

Solomon   The son of King **David,** Solomon became king of **Israel** in the 10th century B.C.E. Regarded as a wise and great king, he was known for his brilliant and just decisions. Solomon was the last king to rule over the united kingdom of Judah and Israel. He was responsible for the building of the **First Temple** in **Jerusalem.** Jewish tradition says he was the author of three biblical books: **The Song of Songs, Ecclesiastes,** and Proverbs.

Song of Songs, The   n. English   One of the five books, referred to as a scroll, or **megillah,** that is contained in **Kethuvim,** the third section of the **TANAKH.** The Song of Songs is read in **synagogue** on **Pesach;** it is sometimes recited to usher in **Shabbat.** This biblical book is a series of love songs, thought to be composed by King **Solomon,** probably around 400 B.C.E. It is often described as an allegory of the love between God and the **Israelite** people. Called **Shir ha-Shirim** in Hebrew.

spice box   n. English   A small box with holes that is filled with cinnamon, cloves, or other fragrant spices *(besamim).* During the *Havdalah* ceremony that ends **Shabbat,** the spice box is passed around and sniffed while the appropriate blessing is said. Tradition says that during *Havdalah* one should worship God with all five senses. The spice box represents the sense of smell. The spices are also thought to cheer the soul, which is saddened by the departure of Shabbat. Spice boxes can be made of metal, olive wood, or other materials; they often are in the shape of a house or castle. Called *kusat besamim* in Hebrew.

spiel   n. Yiddish (SHPEEL)   A long, involved story or tale. Sometimes refers to a sales pitch or persuasive argument. "I made the mistake of telling him I was interested in buying a car. He gave me the whole spiel on why I should lease."

Spinoza, Baruch (1632–1677)   Dutch Jewish philosopher born in Amsterdam to **Sephardic** parents who had fled Portugal. He believed that **God** *was* nature, not its Creator. His philosophical system defined God as an impersonal diety and promoted rationalism and pantheism. He believed that everything happened as it must; therefore there was no free will. The Jewish community excommunicated him for his beliefs, which included the statement that God did not author the **Torah.** Under excommunication, no Jew was ever to speak with him again. One of his legacies is that rabbis decided excommunication was too harsh and humiliating a punishment and it is rarely issued today. Spinoza, whose greatest work was the *Ethics,* is considered one of the founders of modern biblical criticism. Also known as Benedictus de Spinoza.

Star of David   n. English   The six-pointed star that has been adopted as a symbol of Judaism. It was first used in the 7th century B.C.E. and became the official seal of Jews in the Middle Ages. It was later adopted by the First **Zionist** Congress as its symbol; the Nazis forced Jews to wear a yellow Star of David during the **Holocaust** years. In 1948 it became the centerpiece of the flag of the new **State of Israel.**

Because of the second of the **Ten Commandments,** which says "you shall not make a graven image . . . nor bow down to them," Jews do not use human figures as ornamentation. For example, you would never see a statue of King **David** or Queen **Esther** in a **synagogue.** So the Star of David is often used instead on synagogue windows and gates, tombstones, necklaces, and New Year's cards. Also called the **Magen David** and the **Jewish star.**

State of Israel   n. English   The modern country, founded in 1948 from the British mandate of **Palestine,** on the eastern shore of the Mediterranean Sea. **Israel** is bordered by Jordan on the east, Syria to the north, and Egypt to the south. In Hebrew, the modern nation is called Medinat Yisra'el, which is translated as "State of Israel." So the country is often referred to in English as the State of Israel.

streimel   n. Yiddish (STRIH-muhl)   A round, fur-trimmed hat worn by some **Hasidic** men on **Shabbat,** holidays, and other formal-dress occasions.

stuffed derma   See **kishka.**

sufganiyot   pl. n. Hebrew (SOOF-gah-nee-OTE)   Small jelly doughnuts fried in oil that are traditionally served at **Hanukkah** celebrations in the **State of Israel.** Because they are cooked in oil like **latkes,** *sufganiyot* are a reminder of the Hanukkah miracle of the oil that lasted for eight days. In the United States, *sufganiyot* are gaining in popularity. They are often served at **Hebrew school** and religious school parties, both to celebrate Hanukkah and to introduce American children to some of the traditions native to Israel.

sukkah n. Hebrew (SUH-kah) pl. **sukkot** (soo-COTE) The small hut built of branches and leaves that is constructed for the holiday of **Sukkot.** The sukkah's temporary nature is a reminder of the tents the **Israelites** lived in while wandering in the wilderness before they reached the **Promised Land.** They also are reminiscent of the structures Jewish farmers built thousands of years ago for sleeping in the fields while they brought in the harvest. *Minhag* calls for the construction of the sukkah on the night after **Yom Kippur.** A sukkah must have at least two walls and part of a third. Sometimes pieces of fabric or canvas are hung to make the walls. The sky and the stars must be visible through the branches *(skakh)* that make up the roof. Sukkahs are decorated with hanging fruits and vegetables, flowers and gourds, colorful decorations, and even children's artwork. Some families build their own sukkah in their backyard, while others decorate and visit the sukkah sponsored by their **synagogue.** During Sukkot it is traditional to eat meals in the sukkah, invite guests to visit it and share a meal, and enjoy its beauty. See *ushpizin.*

Sukkos n. Hebrew (SOOK-us) The Ashkenazic/Yiddish pronunciation of the holiday of Sukkot.

Sukkot n. Hebrew (soo-COTE) Literally, "booths." Beginning on the 15th of **Tishrei,** corresponding to late September or early to mid-October and observed for eight days, Sukkot is a joyous holiday. It celebrates the harvest of the Land of **Israel,** both in ancient times and today. Sukkot commemorates the **Israelites'** 40 years of wandering in the desert after the **Exodus** from Egypt. It is sometimes called the Festival of Booths or the Feast of Tabernacles. The last day of Sukkot is known as **Shemini Atzeret.**

Along with **Pesach** and **Shavuot,** Sukkot is one of the three **Pilgrimage Festivals,** when the ancient Israelites traveled to the **Temple** in **Jerusalem** with gifts of the **first fruits** and offerings for God. Today, Sukkot is similar to Thanksgiving, an annual festival thanking God for the blessings of the harvest and first fruits. **Synagogues** are often decorated with fresh flowers, pumpkins, and other fruits on Sukkot.

Traditionally, congregants construct a small hut—a **sukkah**—just outside the synagogue and decorate its roof with hanging fruits and vegetables. Many families also construct a sukkah in their backyard. Jews usually eat meals in the sukkah and invite guests to visit or dine with them as an expression of the **mitzvah** of *hakhnasat orchim.* Jewish biblical characters *(ushpizin)* are also welcomed to a sukkah. Other rituals of Sukkot include the waving and shaking of a *lulav* and *etrog,* symbols of the agricultural nature of the holiday, while reciting prayers of thanksgiving called *Hallel.* During synagogue services, congregants may parade around the sanctuary with their *lulav* and *etrog.* There are readings are from the Book of **Ecclesiastes,** one of the five *megillot.*

swastika   n. English from the Sanskrit meaning "good to be." The cross with arms of equal length, the ends of which are bent at right angles pointing in the same circular direction. Throughout history, the swastika has been used as a symbol by Celts, Hindus, and Buddhists, among others. In 1920, the Nazi Party co-opted the "hooked cross," and the swastika became a symbol of hate and Aryan supremacy. It is still in use by Neo-Nazi groups, although it can also be spotted as a design motif in current Hindu textiles, Native American artwork, and ancient Western architecture.

synagogue   n. English   From the Greek word for "house of assembly." The word most commonly used in the United States to refer to a Jewish house of worship. Since the destruction of the **Second Temple,** the synagogue has been the chief institution of Jewish life. It provides religious, educational, cultural, and social programs for its dues-paying members. Salaried officials include a **rabbi,** who serves as the congregation's religious leader, and a **cantor,** who leads the congregation in prayer. Synagogues generally are affiliated with a larger movement of Judaism: **Orthodox, Conservative, Reform,** or **Reconstructionist.** Today, most synagogues include a large central sanctuary for prayer, a rabbi's office, a kitchen, rooms for life-cycle celebrations, a library, and classrooms for children's religious instruction.

Szold, Henrietta (1860–1945)   Zionist, philanthropist, and founder of **Hadassah**, a women's charitable organization. Born in Baltimore and the daughter of a rabbi, Szold was a passionate scholar who fought for the right to study at the then men-only Jewish Theological Seminary. Szold made *aliyah* to **Palestine** in 1909 and then founded Hadassah. In the 1930s, Szold, with funding from Hadassah, formed a Youth *Aliyah* movement that rescued 22,000 Jewish children from certain death in Nazi Europe. Today, Hadassah Hospital in Jerusalem is the foremost hospital in the Middle East, providing top-notch care to Jews and Arabs alike.

ta'am n. Hebrew (TAH-ahm) **1.** Literally, "flavor." Usually used in conjunction with another word to convey the sense or flavor of an object, not necessarily food. For example, "Your daughter's essay about **Pesach** was wonderful. I really had a sense of the *ta'am* of your **seder**." Old-fashioned usage. **2.** The shortened form of the Hebrew phrase for **trope,** *ta'amei ha-mikra*.

Ta'anit Esther n. Hebrew (TAH-AH-neat ess-TER) See **Fast of Esther.**

Tabernacle n. English The portable sanctuary that the **Israelites** used in the wilderness after the **Exodus.** The Tabernacle was carried from place to place until the **Temple** in **Jerusalem** was built during King **Solomon**'s reign. The inner sanctum of the Tabernacle, called the **Holy of Holies,** contained the **Ark of the Covenant;** it was surrounded by curtains. Called *mishkan* in Hebrew.

Tachanun n. Aramaic (tah-khah-NOON) A penitential prayer recited by very traditional Jews each morning. The prayer is usually said with one's head resting on the arm.

tachlis n. Yiddish (TAKH-liss) Practical considerations, the bottom line. Used in the phrase "to talk *tachlis*," to get down to business. "Stop gossiping. Start this meeting and talk *tachlis*."

taharah n. Hebrew (tah-hah-RAH) Literally, "purification." The ritual cleansing of a dead body prior to burial. Today, the process is usually done at a funeral home; it includes washing the body with hot water, combing the hair, and dressing the body in a white linen shroud called a *takhrikhim*. A man is then customarily wrapped in his **tallit.** The person performing the preparations must treat the body with reverence, gentleness, and great respect *(kavod ha-met)*.

taharat ha-mishpachah n. Hebrew (tah-hah-RAHT hah-mish-pah-KHAH) Literally, "family purity." The Jewish laws concerning sexual relations, especially during a woman's menstrual period. While the **Torah** forbids intercourse only during the days of menstruation, levels of observance of *taharat ha-mishpachah* diverge. Some strictly traditional Jewish men do not kiss, hug, or even touch their wife during the forbidden days and for seven days after, until she has visited the **mikveh.** Some Orthodox males avoid even casual physical contact (like a handshake) at any time with a woman who is not their wife. Also called the laws of **niddah.**

tahini n. Arabic (tah–HEE–nee) A creamy paste made from ground sesame seeds. Tahini is often mixed with lemon juice, olive oil, chopped parsley, and spices and eaten as a dip, with pita bread and **hummus.** It's also used as a sauce on **falafel** and **shwarma.** Also called tahina.

takhrikhim n. Hebrew (takh–ree–KHEEM) The Jewish burial shroud, which is used for both men and women. It is traditionally made of simple in-expensive muslin, cotton, or linen. It has no pockets, symbolizing that man's pos-sessions cannot be taken with him after death. The shroud is white to represent the purity of the soul of the deceased. Jewish men and women may also be buried with the **tallit** or **kitel** they wore during their lifetime.

tallis n. Hebrew (TAH–liss) The Ashkenazic/Yiddish pronunciation of tallit.

tallit n. Hebrew (tah–LEET); pl. **tallitot** (tah–lee–TOTE) A scarflike rec-tangular prayer shawl with four fringes—**tzitzit**—one attached to each corner. A tallit may be embroidered or plain, colorful or white; the neck band, which should lay across the shoulders, is called an **atarah.** There are numerous laws and reasons for the wearing of a tallit. In the **Torah** it says, "That shall be your fringe; look at it and recall all the commandments of *Adonai* and observe them" (Numbers 15:39). Symbolically, putting on a tallit separates the wearer from daily concerns and provides a visual cue that it is time for prayer. Practically, a tallit serves as a cloth on which to hang the tzitzit.

A tallit is traditionally worn at all weekday morning **synagogue** services. Many people own a tallit and bring it with them to services in a small bag. There is usually a rack of *tallitot* in the entrance to the synagogue for those who wish to borrow one. A special blessing is recited before a tallit is put on.

Customs vary from synagogue to synagogue as to who is expected to wear a tallit. In many **Orthodox** synagogues, a tallit is traditionally worn only by married male worshipers, although all men may wear it when honored with an **aliyah.** In liberal congregations, it may be worn by all men and women after **Bar** or **Bat Mitzvah** age. In order for a tallit to be **kosher,** it cannot be a blend of linen and wool. If it is, it is considered *sha'atnez.* It's common for a tallit to be passed down from generation to generation. A tallit that has sentimental value may also be used as a *huppah.* This ritual garment is an appropriate gift for a Bar or Bat Mitzvah.

tallit katan n. Hebrew (tah–LEET kah–TAHN) Literally, "small tallit." A lightweight undergarment, usually made of linen or wool, that has **tzitzit** attached to its four corners. Many **Orthodox** males wear a *tallit katan* every day under their shirts as a symbol of religious piety. The strings of the tzitzit can be seen hanging out. Also called *arba kanfot.*

Talmud n. Hebrew (TAHL-muhd) The collection of ancient rabbinic laws, commentaries, and traditions related to the **Torah.** The Talmud is a compilation of two books: the **Mishnah,** or **Oral Law,** and the **Gemara,** which consists of commentaries on the Mishnah. Much of the Talmud follows a format in which a law from the Mishnah is cited, followed by rabbinic discussions and rulings on its meaning. The Talmud explains and elaborates on every aspect of Jewish life, including daily prayers, **mitzvot,** and holiday celebrations. The documents and commentaries—more than 2½ million words—that make up the Talmud were written, mostly in **Aramaic,** more than 1,500 years ago. Even today, many observant Jews spend years reading the tenets, commentaries, and variations of Talmud and looking for new interpretations. Talmudic scholars are regarded with respect and admiration; it is considered a noble and lifelong task to study the intricacies of Talmud. The word "Talmud" generally refers to two versions: the Jerusalem Talmud, compiled in the late 5th century C.E., and the more extensive Babylonian Talmud, compiled in the late 6th century C.E.

Talmud Torah n. Hebrew (TAHL-muhd TOE-rah) **1.** A traditional Jewish religious school where **Torah** and **Talmud** are studied. Students attend a Talmud Torah after elementary school *(heder),* in preparation for entering a **yeshivah.** These schools are popular in **Israel** and in **ultra-Orthodox** communities in the United States. **2.** The study of **Torah.**

Tammuz n. Hebrew (tah-MOOZ) The fourth month in the **Jewish calendar,** it falls in June or July.

TANAKH n. Hebrew (tah-NAHKH) An acronym for the three books that make up the cornerstone of Jewish beliefs: the **Torah, Nevi'im,** and **Kethuvim.** The Torah is the **Five Books of Moses: Genesis, Exodus, Leviticus, Numbers,** and **Deuteronomy.** Nevi'im contains the 21 books of **Prophets,** from which come the *haftarot.* **Kethuvim,** or **Writings,** includes Proverbs, Psalms, historical accounts, and the five scrolls, or *megillot.*

tannaim pl. n. Aramaic (tah-nah-EEM) Literally, "teachers." The ancient rabbis who are quoted in the **Mishnah.** The *tannaim* are contrasted with the *amoraim,* the rabbis whose commentaries are contained in the **Gemara.**

Tanya n. Aramaic (TAN-yah) Literally "it is stated in a *baraita.*" The first word and title of the fundamental text of **Hasidism,** written by Rabbi

Shneur Zalman, the founder of the **Lubavitch** sect. It was first printed in 1797. The *Tanya*, also known as the *Likkutei Amarim,* is considered to be a classic work of Jewish mysticism.

Targum n. Hebrew (tar-GOOM) Literally, "translation." Aramaic translations of the **TANAKH** believed to have been written during the **Second Temple** era. Each reflects the midrash of the rabbi who wrote it.

tas n. Hebrew (TAHSS) Literally, "plaque." A silver plaque that is inscribed with the name of a particular holiday or **Shabbat** service. It is placed in a window on a **Torah**'s breastplate *(hoshen),* indicating that the Torah has been rolled to the right place for the reading for the upcoming occasion. These nameplates are stored in a small box soldered to the *hoshen.*

tashlikh n. Hebrew (TASH-likh) Literally, "throw." A ceremony performed on the afternoon of the first day of **Rosh Hashanah,** the Jewish New Year. Jews gather at a stream, creek, or other flowing source of water and empty their pockets of crumbs (or bring along breadcrumbs to throw) into the water. *Tashlikh* symbolizes the casting away of sins and transgressions from the past year so that one may start the new year "empty," or with a clean slate. Prayers and appropriate verses for the holiday are recited during *tashlikh.* If Rosh Hashanah falls on **Shabbat,** the *tashlikh* ceremony is held on the second day.

tateleh n. Yiddish (TAH-teh-leh) "Little papa." A term of endearment for a little boy. Old-fashioned usage.

tayglach n. pl. Yiddish (tay-guh-LOCK) Sweet, sticky cookies made from small balls of dough that are shaped, boiled in a honey-sugar-ginger syrup, and often rolled in ground nuts. *Tayglach* are soft inside and crisp outside. An old Lithuanian sweet, *tayglach* is sometimes served for dessert at a Jewish holiday meal.

Tay-Sachs disease n. English (TAY-SACKS) A rare fatal genetic disease that affects newborns of **Ashkenazi** Jewish descent. Tay-Sachs, the most well-known Jewish genetic disease, is characterized by a red spot on the retina and progressive degeneration of the central nervous system, which includes blindness, mental retardation, and paralysis. There is no treatment and life expectancy is three to five years. Jewish couples planning to have children are advised to go for a blood-test screening to see if they carry the Tay-Sachs gene; about 1 in 30 Jews are carriers, compared with 1 in 300 of the non-Jewish population. Also, prenatal tests can diagnose Tay-Sachs before birth.

tchotchke n. Yiddish (CHACH-key) Literally, "doll" or "child's plaything." The meaning has been widened to refer to any cute but insignificant object,

such as a trinket, knickknack, or inexpensive souvenir. "I can't dust my book-
cases anymore. They're filled with so many *tchotchkes* from our trips."

tchotchkeleh n. Yiddish (CHACH-keh-leh)   Literally, "small doll" or "child's
plaything." The diminutive of *tchotchke.* It is often used to describe a sexy young
woman who is short on brains, similar to "dumb blonde." Old-fashioned usage.

teba n. Hebrew (tay-BAH)   Literally, "box." The word that **Sephardic** congregations use for the raised platform in a synagogue from which the entire
service is conducted, including the **Torah** reading. It is usually located in the
center of the sanctuary between the sections of seats. In **Ashkenazic** synagogues, the raised platform is called a *bimah.*

tefilah n. Hebrew (teh-fee-LAH); pl. **tefilot** (teh-fee-LOTE) **1.** Literally,
"prayer." Jewish prayers often praise God, express gratitude, and reflect on our
relationship with God and others, rather than petition God for something specific. The word is sometimes used in the phrase "to offer *tefilot.*" **2. Tefilah.** Another name for the *Amidah,* the "standing prayer" or "silent devotion."

tefillin n. Hebrew (teh-FILL-in)   The pair of small black leather boxes that
contain pieces of parchment on which passages from the **Torah** are inscribed.
Traditional, very religious Jewish men "lay tefillin" by wrapping the straps attached to the tefillin, called *retzuot,* to their arm and their forehead each morning while they recite prayers, except on **Shabbat** or holidays. Tefillin are a sign
of faith and devotion. The case that rests on the head represents intellectual loyalty; the case resting on the hand is a reminder to serve God with might and
strength. The meaning behind tefillin comes from the text of the *Shema,* which
reads in part, "You shall love *Adonai* your God with all your heart and with all
your soul and with all your might. Take to heart these instructions with which
I charge you this day. . . . Bind them as a sign on your hand and let them serve
as a symbol on your forehead" (Deuteronomy 6:4).

Tehillim n. Hebrew (teh-heel-LEEM)   The Hebrew name for the Book of
Psalms, which is included in **Kethuvim.**

tekiah n. Hebrew (teh-kee-AH)   One of the notes blown on a **shofar.**
Tekiah, one long blast, is the first note played when a shofar is sounded during
High Holy Day services. The sound of *tekiah* calls the congregation to attention. Before the shofar is blown, the **rabbi** or **cantor** will call out the name of
the note to be played.

tekiah gedolah n. Hebrew (teh-kee-AH geh-doe-LAH)   Literally, "great
tekiah." One of the notes blown on a **shofar.** It is a long, loud blast held for as long

as the person blowing the shofar can manage—often several minutes. It is the last note sounded when the shofar is blown, ending **Yom Kippur.** Before the shofar is blown, the **rabbi** or **cantor** will call out the name of the note to be played.

Tel Aviv   n. Hebrew (tell ah-VIVE)   Israel's largest city and commercial center, located on the Mediterranean Sea. While Jerusalem is known for its history and sacred sites, Tel Aviv is Israel's world-class secular city of skyscraper office buildings, restaurants, museums, expressways, and beachfront luxury hotels.

Temple   n. English, from the Latin for "house of God." **1.** The large, most holy place of Jewish worship and sacrifice in ancient **Israel.** The **First Temple** was built by King **Solomon** in the late 10th century B.C.E.; the **Second Temple** was built on its ruins and destroyed in 70 C.E. by the conquering Romans. The **Western Wall** in **Jerusalem** is all that remains of the outside retaining wall of the mount of the Second Temple. **2. temple**   In modern times, the word is used as a synonym for **synagogue** and it often appears in the name of the congregation, for example, Temple Beth Am.

tenaim   n. Hebrew (teh-nah-EEM)   Literally, "conditions." **1.** The original prenuptial contract, the *tenaim* dates from the 12th century. It detailed the dowry and other financial arrangements, the date of the wedding, and the penalty if anyone backed out. Some traditional and **Hasidic** Jews still prepare a *tenaim* and read it aloud at an engagement party or sign it before the wedding ceremony, at the same time the *ketubbah* is signed. **2.** A traditional name for an engagement party.

Ten Commandments   pl. n. English   The 10 laws on which Judaism is based. The Ten Commandments are: (1) I am the Lord your God; (2) You shall have no other Gods before me; (3) You shall not swear falsely nor take God's name in vain; (4) Remember the **Sabbath** and keep it holy; (5) Honor your father and mother; (6) Do not murder; (7) Do not commit adultery; (8) Do not steal; (9) Do not bear false witness against your neighbor; and (10) Do not covet anything that belongs to your neighbor.

   Jewish tradition says that the stone tablets containing the Ten Commandments were given to **Moses** by God at **Mount Sinai. Shavuot** celebrates this giving of the **Written Law.** The first five commandments describe the relationship of man to God; the next five describe the relationship of man to man. The motif of the stone tablets is a popular one in synagogues and religious decorative art, especially because Judaism forbids the making of images of God or the depiction of human figures in synagogues. Also known as the **Decalogue.**

Ten Plagues   pl. n. English   The punishments inflicted by God on the Egyptian people for enslaving the **Israelites** in ancient days. During the **Pesach**

seder, which tells the story of the **Exodus** from Egypt, the Ten Plagues are recited. They are blood *(dom)*, frogs *(tzefardayah)*, lice *(kinim)*, wild beasts *(arov)*, cattle disease *(dever)*, sores or boils *(shekhin)*, hail *(barad)*, locusts *(arbeh)*, darkness *(hoshekh)*, and killing of the firstborn Egyptian sons *(makat bekhorot)*. It is traditional to dip a finger into a wine glass and place a drop of wine on a napkin or plate as the name of each plague is recited. This is considered an expression of sorrow for the Egyptians, for the pain they suffered during the plagues. The English name of the holiday, Passover, comes from the fact that God "passed over" the houses of the Israelites and spared their sons when the last terrible plague came.

teruah n. Hebrew (teh-roo-AH) Literally, "alarm." One of the blasts of the **shofar.** The *teruah* glides from a low note to a higher note and is generally blown in groups of three in quick succession. Before the shofar is blown, the **rabbi** or **cantor** will call out the name of the note to be played.

terumah n. Hebrew (teh-ROO-mah) A gift or offering made to the high priests of the Temple in ancient times.

teshuvah n. Hebrew (teh-shoo-VAH) Repentance. In Judaism, repentance takes many forms and is the subject of many prayers, especially those associated with **Yom Kippur.** Jewish law says that in order to truly repent, a person must recognize his or her sin, feel remorse, undo any damage done, apologize, and vow never to do it again. As part of the soul searching and *teshuvah* of the **High Holy Days,** it is customary for Jews to ask their family and friends for forgiveness for any sins, insult, or slight they may have committed against one another over the course of the past year.

Tetragrammaton n. Greek (teh-trah-GRAM-uh-tohn) Literally, "four letters." The four Hebrew letters—*yud, hay, vav, hay*—that compose the inexpressible name of God. These letters are usually transliterated as YHVH. Today, because Jews believe that God's name is sacred, it is not spoken; instead the letters are usually read as ***Adonai*** or **ha-Shem.** Another common name in the Torah for God is ***Elohim.*** There are many other names of God, reflecting God's various roles. For example, in Exodus 3:14, God tells **Moses** that God's name is *Ehyeh-Asher-Ehyeh* (I Am That I Am).

Tevet n. Hebrew (teh-VET) The tenth month in the **Jewish calendar,** it falls in December or January.

tevilah n. Hebrew (teh-vee-LAH) Literally, "immersion." The process of submerging oneself for spiritual purification. This can take place in any natural body of water or in a specially constructed ritual bath known as a ***mikveh.*** The

Orthodox, Conservative, and **Reconstructionist** movements require *tevilah* for men and women who are converting to Judaism. Many traditional Jews immerse new dishes, utensils, and pots in a *mikveh* that is specifically reserved for this purpose to kasher them before their first use.

Thirteen Principles of Faith pl. n. English The basic doctrines of the Jewish faith according to **Moses Maimonides,** the great Jewish scholar and Talmudist, in his commentary on the **Mishnah.** They are: (1) **God** is the supreme Creator; (2) God is one being; (3) God is incorporeal, therefore, his powers are not physical; (4) God is eternal; (5) God alone is to be worshipped and obeyed; there is no intermediary; (6) the words of the prophets are true and direct communications from God; (7) **Moses** was the greatest prophet; (8) the **Torah** is the direct word of God; (9) the Torah is immutable, and man cannot change it; (10) God is omniscient and knows the actions of man; (11) God will reward those who follow His commandments and He will punish those who do not; (12) the Messiah will come; and (13) the dead will be resurrected.

tichl n. Yiddish (TIKH-ull) A large scarf worn as a head covering by married **ultra-Orthodox** women, in keeping with the custom of dressing modestly.

tiferet n. Hebrew (tih-fur-RET) Literally "beauty." The sixth of the 10 *sefirot,* or aspects of God's creative nature. According to **kabbalistic** teachings, *tiferet* represents the harmony and the balance between justice and kindness that the *Ein Sof* uses to rule the universe. It is one of three *sefirot*, along with *gevurah* and *chesed,* in the category of the heart or emotions. Each *sefirah* is associated with a part of the body; *tiferet* corresponds with the heart.

tik n. Hebrew (TEEK) Literally, "case." The cylindrical or octagonal case used to protect a **Torah** scroll in a **Sephardic** synagogue; it's usually made of wood or metal and ornately decorated. The *tik* is kept in a niche or on a table in the center of the sanctuary. A *tik* is hinged, and when opened the scroll can be read without removing it from the case. This enabled the Torah to be portable for use during the many times when Jews could not worship in synagogues. See **ark.**

tikun n. Hebrew (tee-KOON); pl. **tikunim** (tee-koo-NEEM) The special book in which **trope** marks for chanting the **Torah** are written. The pages of a *tikun* are set in two-column format; the trope and vowels are in the right column, and the text as it appears in the Torah, without vowels, is in the left column. There are *tikunim* for readers and *tikunim* for scribes. There may also be slight differences in trope marks from one *tikun* to another.

Tikun leil Shavuot n. Hebrew (tee-KOON LAYL shah-VOO-ote) Literally, "service on the night of **Shavuot.**" The custom of staying awake all night on the eve of Shavuot to study and pray. Jews sometimes gather in private homes or attend special **synagogue** study sessions. Often selections from the **Torah, Mishnah,** and **Zohar** are read.

tikun olam v. Hebrew (tee-KOON oh-LAHM)   Literally, "repairing the world." The Jewish ideal that each person, in partnership with God, is responsible for doing his or her share to make the world a better place. This concept was introduced by **kabbalist Isaac Luria.** *Tikun olam* is used as a call to action when asking for volunteers for social service projects, for example, tutoring immigrants in English. The concept is taught to children, along with **mitzvot,** to convey the importance of helping others and caring for the community. "For our *tikun olam* project in Hebrew school, we're going to pick up litter and paint the fence at the playground."

Tisha b'Av n. Hebrew (tih-SHAH beh-AV)   Literally, the "ninth day of **Av.**" A **fast day** observed on the 9th of Av. Tisha b'Av is a day of mourning, marking the dates of the destruction of both ancient holy **Temples** in **Jerusalem.** The **First Temple** was destroyed by the Babylonians on this date in 586 B.C.E. The rebuilt **Second Temple** was destroyed by the conquering Romans in 70 C.E. Legend says that throughout history, other terrible things occurred on this date as well, including a plague and the expulsion of the Jews from Spain. Tisha b'Av observances include fasting for 24 hours and not engaging in pleasurable activities. Today, many people feel that **Yom ha-Shoah,** Holocaust Remembrance Day, has more widespread relevance as a day of communal mourning.

Tishrei n. Hebrew (TISH-ray)   The seventh month on the **Jewish calendar,** it falls in September or October.

Torah n. Hebrew (toe-RAH)   **1.** The first five books of the Bible, also called the **Five Books of Moses** or the **Pentateuch.** The Torah is the most revered and sacred book of Judaism. It begins with **Genesis** and the creation of the world, and ends with **Deuteronomy** and the death of **Moses.** The Torah codifies the principles of the **Ten Commandments,** enumerates the **mitzvot,** and contains much of the ancient history and traditions of the Jewish people. The books of the Torah—the **Written Law**—are Genesis, **Exodus, Leviticus, Numbers,** and Deuteronomy. The Torah is the first of the three books that comprise the **TANAKH,** along with **Nevi'im** and **Kethuvim. 2.** An abbreviation for the phrase *sefer Torah,* which refers to a continuous parchment **scroll** on which a *sofer* has written the Hebrew words of the Five Books of Moses. A portion, or **parashah,** of Torah is read from a *sefer Torah* in **synagogue** every Monday and Thursday, on **Shabbat,** and on festivals and the **High Holy Days. 3.** A synonym for all Jewish law and learning. "Ask him your question about that holiday. He knows everything about Torah."

Torah mi-Sinai n. Hebrew (toe-RAH mee-see-NYE) Literally, "Torah from Sinai." The traditional belief that the **Torah** and all aspects of Jewish law are the direct word of God, given to **Moses** on **Mount Sinai.** If one believes in the concept of *Torah mi-Sinai,* it follows that there can be no deviation from—and no modern reinterpretation of—these laws because they are the literal and absolute word of God.

Tosefta n. Hebrew (toe-sef-TAH); pl. **Toseftot** (toe-sah-FOTE) Literally, "supplement." A compilation of *baraitot,* commentaries on the **Mishnah**.

tractate n. English One of the 63 sections of the **Mishnah.** The Mishnah commentaries are sometimes printed together with additional tractactes. In Hebrew, it's *massekhet.*

transliteration n. English The process of changing letters from one language into similar-sounding characters of another language. Prayers and other **Hebrew** words are often written in transliteration using English letters so that those who do not speak Hebrew can sound out the words and participate in the service. For example, the word for "peace," which is written in Hebrew with the letters *shin, lamed, vav,* and *mem,* is written in transliteration as **"shalom."**

Tree of Life n. English **1.** One of the two trees in the **Garden of Eden.** Fruit from the Tree of Life gave immortality to those who tasted it. **2.** An image, used in **Kabbalah,** to depict the *sefirot.* In this tree of life, the roots are in heaven and the branches extend toward earth. **3.** The wooden poles to which a **Torah** scroll is attached. This is a metaphor, in that the teachings and laws of the Torah are a "tree of life" to those who believe and follow them. In Hebrew they are called *atzei chayim.* **4.** A common artistic representation of a tree, used in synagogue art and **Judaica.** Because *halakhah* does not allow the use of human figures as ornamentation, trees of life, along with animals and fruit, are popular themes.

treif adj. Yiddish (TRAYF) Foods that are not allowed to be eaten under the Jewish dietary laws of **kashrut;** the opposite of **kosher.** Examples of *treif* foods include pork, shrimp, and shellfish, as well as combinations of dairy and meat. "He'll go with us for pizza as long as we don't order pepperoni. He won't eat anything *treif.*"

tribes of Israel pl. n. English The 12 clans into which the Israelites were divided in biblical times. Each tribe was descended from one of Jacob's 12 sons:

Reuben, Simeon, Levi, Judah, Dan, Naphtali, Gad, Asher, Issachar, Zebulon, Joseph, and **Benjamin.** When Joshua led the Israelites into **Canaan,** he gave each tribe a particular territory according to its size. Joseph was given a double portion of land, and later two of his sons, **Ephraim** and **Menasseh,** resided there, each of them gaining the status of a tribe. Levi did not take any land; his descendants scattered throughout the land and guarded and served the **Tabernacle.** After the death of King **Solomon** in 930 B.C.E., the Israelite kingdom was divided; 10 tribes occupied the northern kingdom of Israel and three tribes—Benjamin, Judah, and remnants of Simeon—occupied the southern kingdom and remained loyal to the Davidic monarchy. See **lost tribes of Israel.**

trope pl. n. Yiddish (TROPE)   The special musical notes—designated by a series of lines and dots—that indicate the tune for chanting prayers and readings from the **Torah** and **haftarah.** Trope symbols are not written on the *sefer Torah;* they are printed in a book called a *tikun.* There may be slight variations in trope marks from one edition to another. Trope may also be included in a *Humash.* To chant the Torah portion, the reader must memorize the trope along with the Hebrew words. Although the symbols are the same, the notes for Torah and haftarah trope are different; there are also special trope for the **High Holy Days** and for each of the five *megillot.* **Ashkenazim** and **Sephardim** have different melodies; there may also be variations from one individual community to another. These days, one can also learn trope online. The Hebrew term is *ta'amei ha-mikra.*

tsatske See *tchotchke.*

tsedrayte adj. Yiddish (tsuh-DRATE)   All mixed up, wacky, confused. "I had so much to do on Monday, I completely forgot about picking you up. I can't believe I was so *tsedrayte.*"

tsimmes See **tzimmes.**

tsuris n. Yiddish (TSORE-iss)   Troubles and worries; problems. "Her older son is so irresponsible, and her husband is having troubles at work. So much tsuris in that family."

Tu b'Av n. Hebrew (too beh-AV)   Literally, "the 15th of Av." A joyous and romantic day celebrated in **Israel,** similar to Valentine's Day. In ancient times, it marked the beginning of the wine harvest; dancing took place in the vineyards and offerings were brought to the **Temple.** It's considered an auspicious day to get married because, according to tradition, Jewish weddings are not permitted for several weeks preceding **Tisha b'Av** (the 9th of Av), making Tu b'Av the first day a wedding is allowed.

Tu b'Shevat n. Hebrew (TOO bih-she-VAHT) Literally, the "15th of **She-vat**." Celebrated in January or February, Tu b'Shevat is Israel's Arbor Day. It is a holiday on which to thank God for the beauty and bounty of trees and to celebrate the greening of the **State of Israel** through reforestation and planting. In the United States on Tu b'Shevat, people eat the fruits of trees native to Israel, such as figs, dates, oranges, almonds, and olives. In religious schools and preschools, children often make fruit salad. American Jews may donate money to the **Jewish National Fund** to plant trees in Israel, while Israeli families celebrate by planting trees.

tuchis n. Yiddish (TUH-khiss) Literally, "underneath." A vulgar term for the rear end or buttocks. Used in the phrase "*a potch in tuchis* (a slap on the behind)."

tushee n. Yiddish (TUSH-ee) A cleaned-up version of *tuchis,* this is a more acceptable euphemism for buttocks or rump. "Put your *tushee* in that chair and eat your lunch!"

twelve tribes of Israel See **tribes of Israel.**

tzadik n. Hebrew (tsah-DEEK) Literally, "righteous one." **1.** A wise or learned scholar; particularly one versed in Jewish law or thought. A tzadik was sometimes thought to be able to work miracles through prayer or religious thought. **2.** (TSAH-dick) The title **Hasidim** sometimes give to their religious leader, rather than **rebbe.**

TZAHAL n. Hebrew (TSAH-HAHL) An acronym of the Hebrew words for the **Israel Defense Forces,** the military units of the **State of Israel.**

tzedakah n. Hebrew (tsuh-DOCK-ah) Literally, "righteousness." Charitable giving; philanthropy. In Judaism, *tzedakah* means much more than charity; it embraces a larger principle of doing good to ensure that the needs of others are met. Since ancient times, giving *tzedakah* has been an obligation, a vital requirement of living a good Jewish life. In the 12th century, the famous scholar **Maimonides** wrote a "ladder of *tzedakah*" that listed the ways *tzedakah* could be given, from the worst way, grudgingly, to the most desirable way, which is giving anonymously so that the recipient can become self-sufficient. As preschoolers, Jewish children are taught to collect pennies, pass on toys, and "give *tzedakah*" as a **mitzvah.** Many Jewish homes have a *tzedakah box;* families commonly put in coins on Friday evening before **Shabbat** begins. Jews often make a donation to *tzedakah,* or do a *tzedakah* project, on the occasion of a *simcha,* such as a **Bar** or **Bat Mitzvah,** or in memory of a loved one.

tzedakah box n. Hebrew/English (tsuh-DOCK-ah BOX) A small container with a slot in the top, used to collect money for charity *(tzedakah)*. Sometimes it is an elaborate, handcrafted work of **Judaica,** often with the Hebrew word *tzedakah* inscribed somewhere on it. Others are made by children, for example, out of decorated paper milk cartons, cardboard boxes, or coffee cans. *Tzedakah box* is the term most often used today for the Yiddish term *"pushke."*

tzeniut n. Hebrew (tseh-nee-YOOT) The Jewish principle of modesty and decorum, which applies to more than outward dress and appearance. For many Jews, it also includes behaving appropriately. For example, a Jew might ask a friend not to tell an offensive ethnic joke. The **ultra-Orthodox** practice of dressing modestly (for example, women wear long sleeves and skirts, and cover their hair) comes from this principle.

tzimmes n. Yiddish (TSIM-ess) **1.** A sweet, baked dish of vegetables or fruit. Carrot tzimmes, a popular version, includes carrots, sweet potatoes, dried apricots, raisins, sugar, and cinnamon. **2.** To be in a tizzy over something minor. Because it takes time to cut up all the vegetables and assemble the ingredients for tzimmes, some say the second meaning came about because it put the cook in a tzimmes to make the dish.

tzitzit n. Hebrew (TSEET-tseet) The fringe affixed to the four corners of a **tallit.** Each tzitzit has 608 strands of thread and five knots, totaling 613, the number of commandments in the **Torah.** The reason behind tzitzit is this quote from the Torah: "That shall be your fringe; look at it and recall all the commandments of *Adonai* and observe them" (Numbers 15:39). Traditional Jews often wear their tzitzit all day long on an undergarment known as a *tallit katan.* If someone is buried in a tallit, one of the fringes will be cut off to show that the person is no longer obligated to observe Jewish law.

U

U   Symbol of **kosher** certification on manufactured or commercially prepared foods. The "U" is often enclosed in a circle; this is the *heksher* of the **Union of Orthodox Jewish Congregations of America.** The symbol **"K"** is also used to designate a kosher food.

ulpan   n. Hebrew (ULL-pon)   An intensive course to teach the **Hebrew** language to immigrants, tourists, college students, and others who need to learn language skills quickly. The concept originated in the **State of Israel.** The term is sometimes used today to describe adult education classes or other learning opportunities that give a quick but comprehensive introduction to a particular subject.

ultra-Orthodox   n. English   A term often used by other Jews to describe the most traditional members of the **Orthodox movement** and to distinguish them from the **modern Orthodox.** In general, the ultra-Orthodox separate themselves more from secular society and interpret *halakhah* more strictly than do the modern Orthodox. As with all branches of Judaism, even within the ultra-Orthodox communities there are varying views toward modern life and different levels of observance. In general, the ultra-Orthodox dress extremely modestly, but there are variations among sects. Some men trim their beards, others do not. Some women wear wigs, others simply cover their heads. The **Hasidim** are one of the most visible ultra-Orthodox sects because the men dress much as they did in the 19th century, with black hats and coats, untrimmed beards, and *payot.* The more extreme ultra-Orthodox groups do not support the **State of Israel.** They believe there can be no homeland for the Jews until the *Mashiach* makes it so. In Hebrew, the ultra-Orthodox are called *haredim,* meaning "fearful before God," a term they chose for themselves.

Union for Reform Judaism   n. English   The congregational arm of the **Reform movement** in North America. Founded in 1873 by Rabbi Isaac Mayer Wise, the organization now has more than 900 congregations and an estimated 1.5 million members. Its name was changed from the Union of American Hebrew Congregations in 2003. Under its umbrella are the North American Federation of Temple Youth (NFTY) for teens and KESHER, a college campus program.

Union of Orthodox Jewish Congregations of America (OU) n. English The central coordinating agency for **Orthodox** Jewish congregations in the United States and Canada. Also known as the Orthodox Union. Besides its outreach, educational, and social services, the organization is best known for its Joint Kashruth Certification Service, which places its trademark *heksher* (a U in a circle) on **kosher** products.

United Jewish Appeal (UJA) See **United Jewish Communities.**

United Jewish Communities (UJC) n. English The central fund-raising organization for Jewish communities in North America. The UJC supports a network of social, recreation, and humanitarian services in cities throughout the United States, Canada, **Israel** and worldwide. This organization was created in 1997 by the merger of the United Jewish Appeal, the Council of Jewish Federations, and the United Israel Appeal.

United Synagogue of Conservative Judaism (USCJ) n. English An association of more than 750 **Conservative** synagogues in North America, with over 1.5 million members. It was organized in 1913 by **Solomon Schechter.** Under the umbrella of the USCJ are the Solomon Schechter **day schools,** Kadima for middle school students, United Synagogue Youth (USY) for high school students, and KOACH, a college outreach program. Also affiliated are the Federation of Jewish **Men's Clubs,** the **Rabbinical Assembly,** and the Women's League for Conservative Judaism.

unveiling n. English A memorial service held at the cemetery to dedicate a headstone. A piece of cloth (the "veil") that has been draped over the stone is removed by a family member and the inscription on the tombstone is seen for the first time. An unveiling is a Jewish custom, not an obligation, and a **rabbi** is not always present. The ceremony, which may be held any time after the end of the formal 30-day mourning period *(sheloshim),* is usually scheduled 9 months to a year after the death. Visitors often leave small stones or rocks on the headstone as a marker to show that they were there.

upfsherin n. Yiddish (UP-sheer-in) Literally "cutting off." The traditional Jewish custom of cutting a boy's hair for the first time at age three. In **Hasidic** communities, a boy's hair is left unshorn until he reaches this age, at which time his hair is cut close while the long curls in front of his ears, the *payot,* are left long. Some boys may begin wearing a *kippah* and **tzitzit** at this time; others do so earlier. At an *upfsherin* celebration, guests are invited to snip a lock of the boy's hair and special blessings are recited. It's also common to give *tzedakah* in honor of this milestone.

ushpizin   n. Hebrew (oosh-pee-ZEEN)   Literally, "visitors." The ancestors who are summoned into the **sukkah** to "enjoy" a meal on **Sukkot**. This mystical custom, similar to reserving a cup for **Elijah** at **Pesach,** has roots in the **Zohar.** It is traditional to invite the three **patriarchs—Abraham, Isaac,** and **Jacob**—as well as **Joseph, Aaron, Moses,** and **David.** Some families include mention of the **matriarchs: Sarah, Rebecca, Rachel,** and **Leah.** It has also become customary to include mention of one's own ancestors—great-grandparents, grandparents, and others—who have contributed to one's Jewish heritage.

utz   v. Yiddish (UHTZ)   To goad, annoy, or bother.

va'ad ha-kashrut   n. Hebrew (VAH-ahd ha-kash-ROOT)   A local organization of **rabbis** and *mashgichim* that oversees standards of **kashrut** and bestows certificates of compliance.

Vashti   (VASH-tee)   In the story of **Purim,** Queen Vashti was the first wife of **King Ahasuerus** of Persia. Legend says that she displeased the king by refusing to show off her beauty at a banquet and was deposed and replaced by the heroine of the Purim story, Esther. Vashti is now thought to be the original feminist for standing up to the king and defending her rights as an independent woman.

Va-yikra   n. Hebrew (vah-YEEK-rah)   The Hebrew name for the Book of **Leviticus,** the third book of the **Torah.**

Ve-ahavta   n. Hebrew (veh-ah-HAV-tah)   The name given to the second paragraph of the *Shema,* the central prayer of Judaism. The *Ve-ahavta* is pivotal to every morning and evening service. This prayer begins with the words "You shall love the Lord your God, with all your heart, with all your soul, and with all your might." The customs of reciting morning and evening prayers, teaching Jewish traditions to one's children, wearing **tefillin,** and putting a **mezuzah** on a doorway come directly from the words of this prayer. The *Ve-ahavta* is written on the parchment found inside tefillin and mezuzot.

Ve-shamru   n. Hebrew (veh-SHAHM-roo)   The name, and first word, of a prayer sung during **Shabbat** evening services and often as part of the *Kiddush* before Shabbat lunch. The words, which come from **Exodus,** are a reminder that "the children of Israel shall keep the Sabbath and observe it through all generations as a sign of the covenant."

Vidui   n. Hebrew (veh-DOO-ee)   Literally, "confession." A special confessional prayer recited at **Yom Kippur** that is a long declaration of sins. The *Vidui* is also recited at the deathbed, by, or on behalf of, the one who is dying.

vilde chaya   n. Yiddish (VIL-dah KHI-yah)   A wild animal, or someone who behaves like one. "She shouldn't bring her daughter to the restaurant because the child runs around like a *vilde chaya.*"

Wailing Wall   n. English   An old-fashioned name for the **Western Wall,** the remaining outside retaining wall of the mount of the **Temple** in **Jerusalem.** This name is rarely used by Jews because of its negative connotations. The name comes from the "wailing" noise made when Jews chanted their prayers at the Wall.

War of Independence   n. English   The war fought by **Israel** against its Arab neighbors, from 1948 to 1949, during the period when the State of Israel was founded. In the years immediately after World War II, as British involvement in **Palestine** waned, violence between Jewish residents and Arabs steadily increased. Hundreds of Jewish settlers were killed by snipers, random bombings, and guerrilla attacks. The **Haganah** and Palmach, Jewish military groups, fought back. On November 29, 1947, the United Nations approved a plan to partition the British Mandate of Palestine into two states, one Jewish, one Arab. Immediately, Palestinian Arabs began increased hostilities against the Jewish population. They were joined by volunteers from surrounding Arab states and the violence and bombings increased. In May 1948, the British Mandate expired and Israel declared itself an independent country. That same day, thousands of soldiers from Jordan, Syria, Iraq, Egypt, and Lebanon attacked the new Jewish State. Despite being overwhelmingly outmanned, as new immigrants poured into Israel, the minimally equipped Israeli military forces grew. Some of the fiercest battles took place on the road that linked Tel Aviv with Jerusalem. Several truces were declared in the final months of 1948, but fighting continued to flare up for months as Israel sought to capture more territory to secure its borders. By July 1949, Israel had signed armistice agreements with Egypt, Lebanon, Jordan, and Syria; Iraq refused to negotiate with Israel. Also called the 1948 Arab-Israeli War.

Warsaw Ghetto   n. English   The walled Jewish quarter in Warsaw, Poland, established in 1940 by Nazi Germany. All Jews living in the city—nearly 500,000—were forced to move into the cramped and walled ghetto. They were forbidden to leave and many died from starvation and disease. On April 10, 1943, when the Nazis attempted to liquidate the ghetto and deport the remaining residents to **concentration camps,** they were shocked to meet organized resistance. Mordecai Anielewicz, a Polish Jew, led the various underground groups determined to fight the Nazis. The Jews held out for over a month before they were crushed by tanks and troops who burned the ghetto. The Warsaw Ghetto Uprising has become a symbol of Jewish resistance to the Nazis. **Yom ha-Shoah,** Holocaust Remembrance Day, is observed annually on the 27th of Nissan, corresponding to the date of the Warsaw Ghetto Uprising.

Weizmann, Chaim (1874–1952)   Zionist leader, Israeli statesman, and the first President of **Israel.** Born near Pinsk, Russia, and educated in Western Europe, Weizmann moved to England in 1905. He was a chemist at the University of Manchester and became friends with Arthur Balfour, who later became British Prime Minister. During World War I, Weizmann discovered how to produce acetone needed for explosives for the Allied war effort. In 1919, he represented the **Zionist** movement at the Paris Peace Conference and then became president of the World Zionist Organization. As efforts to establish the State of Israel heated up, he traveled to Washington many times on behalf of the Zionist cause. When the British government wanted to knight him for his scientific achievements, he asked them to instead support Zionist efforts to establish a Jewish homeland in Palestine. When **David Ben Gurion** became Prime Minister of the new State of Israel, Weizmann was asked to serve as President. He was active in the creation of a research institute that is now named in his honor: The Weizmann Institute of Science is Israel's leading scientific and medical research center.

West Bank   n. English   The bean-shaped section of land surrounding **Jerusalem** that lies to the west and southwest of the Jordan River. In ancient times, the area was known as **Judea and Samaria.** In 1948, Jordan annexed the area and began calling it the West Bank. Israel captured it from Jordan during the **Six-Day War** in 1967. Today, the West Bank includes several modern suburbs of Jerusalem, **Palestinian** shanty-towns, Jewish settlement towns such as Kiryat Arba, and Palestinian-controlled towns such as Hebron. Hebron is the site of the sacred, ancient Tomb of the Patriarchs (also called the Cave of Machpelah). Tradition says that Abraham purchased the cave 3,700 years ago as a burial place; he and Sarah, Isaac and Rebecca, Jacob and Leah are all buried there. Muslims have built a mosque on the site. Bethlehem, also part of the West Bank, is the site where Jesus was born and where the Church of the Nativity stands. See **occupied territories.**

Western Wall   n. English   The archaeological site in the Old City of **Jerusalem** believed to be the outside retaining wall of the mount of the **Second Temple.** It is joined to the Southern Wall, where recent excavations have exposed an ancient stone walkway and the remains of a Roman arcade. These walls are essentially all that remain of the Temple that was destroyed by the Romans in 70 C.E. Before 1967, the Old City section of Jerusalem was under Jordanian control and Jews were not allowed to visit the site. Israel's victory in the **Six-Day War** reunified the city and opened all of Jerusalem to all people. Today, an archaeological museum and extensive excavations near the Southern Wall make the area an impressive site. Above the Western Wall, on the Temple Mount, is the Islamic Dome of the Rock shrine and the El Aqsa mosque. In Hebrew, the Western Wall is called the **Kotel,** short for *Kotel ha-Ma'Arivi.* It is also known as "the Wall."

The Western Wall is revered by Jews who gather in the large plaza in front of it to pray, think, or just gaze at the massive stones. Many visitors to the Wall write their prayers or thoughts on small scraps of paper and then wedge them in cracks between the Kotel's gigantic stones. Some children hold their **Bar** or **Bat Mitzvah** service at the Wall. The plaza is divided into separate sections for men and women in deference to **Orthodox** demands. Sometimes the Wall becomes the center of protest, as Orthodox sects seek to limit women's access and participation in services at the Wall by violently attempting to disperse them.

wimpel   n. Yiddish (WIM-pull or vim-PULL)   The long band of material, usually two to three inches wide, that encircles and holds together the two rolls of a **Torah** scroll, like a belt. It is placed around the *sefer Torah* before the mantle, breastplate, and crown are put on, in a process known as "dressing the Torah." Sometimes, a blanket or cloth from a boy's *brit milah* is saved and remade into a decorative wimpel for the Torah that is read on the occasion of the youth's **Bar Mitzvah.** In recent years, many **synagogues** have revived the tradition of hand-crafting a wimpel—for daughters as well as sons—as a family project. Also called a *gartl.*

woman of valor   n. English   A tribute bestowed on a woman who exemplifies traditional Jewish values, such as keeping a Jewish home, raising children, doing **mitzvot,** etc. The phrase comes from a 3,000-year-old acrostic poem in Proverbs. The first line is the most often quoted portion; it reads: "A woman of valor, who can find? Her price is far beyond rubies." The phrase in Hebrew is *eshet chayil.* See **ORT.**

women's seder   n. English/Hebrew (SAY-der)   A **Pesach seder** specifically for women, often sponsored by a synagogue or a Jewish communal organization, which pays particular attention to women's roles and participation in the Passover story. A women's seder may use a **haggadah** with readings that emphasize the roles of **Miriam** and Yocheved (Moses' mother) in the Passover story. The seder includes ritual objects, such as a **Miriam's Cup.** Often mothers and daughters participate together.

Writings, The   n. English   The third of the three books that comprise the **TANAKH,** known by its Hebrew name, **Kethuvim.**

Written Law   n. English   The **Torah.** The term Written Law is used in contrast with **Oral Law,** which includes all the commentaries, expositions, and rabbinic explanations of points of Torah that were passed down from generation to generation since ancient times. Traditional Jews believe in the concept of *Torah mi–Sinai,* that the Torah and all aspects of Jewish law are the words of God, as given to **Moses** (and written down) at **Mount Sinai.**

yachne n. Yiddish (YOKH-neh) A gossip, a busybody. A coarse, loud-mouthed woman who carries tales. Old-fashioned usage.

yad n. Hebrew (YOD) Literally, "hand." A small pointer used when reading the **Torah.** Because a *sefer Torah* is fragile, handwritten, and easily damaged by dirt and oil from human hands, the *yad* is used to point to the words so the reader doesn't touch the **scroll.** A *yad* also allows the reader to follow the words without obscuring the view of others gathered around the podium for *aliyot.* A *yad* often is shaped like a human hand, with the index finger pointing outward. Usually made of wood or silver, the *yad* is attached to a chain or a string and hung from the Torah. A *yad* is sometimes presented as a gift to a **synagogue** in honor or memory of a loved one; it also makes an appropriate **Bar** or **Bat Mitzvah** gift.

Yad Vashem n. Hebrew (YAHD vah-SHEM) Literally, "a hand and a name." The museum and memorial in Jerusalem, dedicated to the Jewish victims of the Nazis, is the world's largest repository of information on the **Holocaust.** The main building contains an enormous archive of artifacts, maps, diaries, personal possessions, firsthand testimonies, and other information on World War II, displayed chronologically. Video monitors show survivors telling their miraculous stories. The Garden of the Righteous Among the Nations pays tribute to **Righteous Gentiles.** In an effort to find the "name and a face" of each of the six million Jews killed, of which 1.5 million were children, Yad Vashem maintains a vast repository of photos, testimonies, and a computer database about people who were killed in the *Shoah.* They are memorialized in the Hall of Names.

yahrzeit n. Yiddish (YAHR-tsite) Literally, "year's time." The anniversary of someone's death, which is marked in accordance with the **Jewish calendar.** The date is traditionally observed by lighting a yahrzeit candle, making a charitable contribution in memory of the deceased, and reciting *Kaddish* (generally at **Shabbat** services that week). In **synagogue,** it is customary for a **rabbi** to read the names of persons whose yahrzeits are being observed that week.

yahrzeit candle n. Hebrew/English (YAHR-tsite CAN-del) A special candle that is lit in memory of someone who has died. This small white or yellow candle comes in a glass so it can safely burn for at least 24 hours. Yahrzeit candles are lit on the anniversary of a person's death (the **yahrzeit**), on **Yom Kippur,** and on other remembrance days, such as **Yom ha-Shoah.**

Yahweh   See **Tetragrammaton.**

yamaka   See **yarmulke.**

Yamim Noraim   pl. n. Hebrew (yah-MEEM noe-rah-EEM)   Literally, "Days of Awe." The 10-day period of introspection and repentance beginning with **Rosh Hashanah** and ending with **Yom Kippur.**

yarmulke   n. Yiddish (YAH-mih-kah)   The small, round head covering worn by Jews as a symbol of respect and religious observance. This word is not used much anymore; it has been replaced by the Hebrew *kippah.*

yasher koach   int. Yiddish (YAH-share KO-akh)   Strength to you. The traditional exclamation of congratulations offered to someone who has completed an *aliyah* in synagogue, read from the **Torah,** or performed a good deed, a **mitzvah,** in the Jewish community. It is similar to the expression "May you go from strength to strength.""When Richard came down from the *bimah,* I shook his hand and told him, *'yasher koach!'*"

yenta   n. Yiddish (YEN-tah)   A gossipy woman; a blabbermouth. Someone who can't keep a secret. "I wonder what her husband does for a living. I'll have to ask Sylvia; she'll know, she's such a yenta."

Yerushalayim   n. Hebrew (yeh-ROO-shah-LYE-eem)   The Hebrew name for the city of **Jerusalem.**

yeshivah   n. Hebrew (yeh-SHEE-vah);   pl. **yeshivot** (yeh-shee-VOTE)   A Jewish school or seminary of higher learning, where students intensively study **Torah, Talmud,** and related texts. Because the traditional yeshivah is **Orthodox,** students are all male, generally in their late teens or early twenties, although today there are women's yeshivot as well. Students generally prepare for yeshivah by first attending a *heder* and **Talmud Torah.** Yeshivot have existed since ancient times because the study of sacred texts and interpretation of the laws have always been very important to Jews. Today, some modern yeshivot, like Yeshiva University in New York, combine religious training with a secular college education, but most yeshivot, especially those in **Israel,** focus only on Jewish subjects.

yeshivah bucher   n. Yiddish (yeh-SHEE-vah BOKH-er)   A young male **yeshivah** student; it can be slang for any young boy who is a good student of

Talmud or Jewish texts. "You did your **Hebrew school** homework before it was due? You're turning into a regular *yeshivah bucher.*"

yesod n. Hebrew (yeh-SOD)   Literally "foundation." The ninth of the 10 *sefirot,* or aspects of God's creative nature. According to **kabbalistic** teachings, *yesod* represents abundance and an all-engrossing creative state. It is one of three *sefirot,* along with **gevurah** and **chesed,** in the category of nature or the functional world. Each *sefirah* is associated with a part of the body; *yesod* corresponds to the reproductive organs.

yetzer ha-ra n. Hebrew (YET-zehr hah-RAH)   The inner impulse toward evil, similar to the notion of an inner voice or conscience that directs one's actions; the opposite of *yetzer ha-tov,* the impulse to do good. In rabbinic tradition, these two opposing forces exert their influence on everyone. Observant Jews sometimes use it to explain an urge, similar to the phrase "the devil made me do it." "The *yetzer ha-ra* made me skip services this morning."

yetzer ha-tov n. Hebrew (YET-zehr hah-TOV)   The inner impulse toward good; the opposite of **yetzer ha-ra.** In rabbinic tradition, these two opposing forces exert their influence on everyone. *Yetzer ha-tov* can be used as a compliment to describe someone very good or noble. It is used less frequently than the expression *yetzer ha-ra.*

yetzirah n. Hebrew (yet-zee-RAH)   The world of formation, the ideal version of our world and the spiritual origin of human emotion. According to **kabbalistic** theory, *yetzirah* is the third of the four worlds of existence, which emerge from the **Ein Sof's** infinite light and culminate in the physical universe. It exists just beyond **asiyah.**

YHVH   See **Tetragrammaton.**

yichud n. Hebrew (YIH-khood)   **1.** The short period of seclusion, immediately after the wedding ceremony, when the bride and groom are alone together for the first time as a married couple. This is a private time to bond and have a moment of peace before the celebration begins. Traditionally, couples who have fasted on their wedding day break the fast together during this time. Because of the custom of *yichud,* receiving lines are not a traditional part of a Jewish wedding; the bride and groom are not available to greet guests. **2.** Being alone with someone of the opposite sex. In keeping with the principles of **tzeniut, Orthodox** Jews avoid being "in *yichud*" with someone who is not their spouse.

yichus n. Yiddish (YICK-is)   Pedigree, lineage, family background. *Yichus* usually implies that someone comes from a distinguished family with status or prestige. *Yichus* comes with responsibility; you can't just depend on *yichus*; you must demonstrate virtue and do your part to live up to your lineage.

Yid   n. Yiddish (YID)   A Jewish man or woman. This old-fashioned term may be considered offensive.

Yiddish   n. Yiddish (YID-ish)   From the German *juedisch,* meaning Jewish. The everyday language of **Ashkenazic** Jews in the late 19th and early 20th centuries. It was distinct from **Hebrew,** which is the language of prayer. Yiddish is a version of High German, with words from Hebrew, Old French, Old Italian, and the Slavic languages sprinkled in. It is written with Hebrew characters. Yiddish was widely spoken by the Jews of Eastern and Central Europe, many of whom had emigrated from Germany and Bohemia. Yiddish is a colorful language, the vernacular of women and the home, often lovingly referred to as *mama loshen,* the mother tongue. It spawned a rich tradition of music **(klezmer)** and literature. With World War II and the destruction of Jewish communities in Eastern Europe, and the adoption of Hebrew as the official language of the **State of Israel,** Yiddish was considered a dying language. Today, however, it is enjoying a revival.

Yiddishkeit   adj. Yiddish (YID-ish-kite)   The group of qualities that define Jewishness; a feeling or flavor of Jewish traditions, culture, ethnicity, or manners. These qualities could refer to anything from the plays of Neil Simon to a deed like endowing a library in memory of a grandfather. If a person did something that reflected well on his Jewish heritage, it might be said that he acted with *Yiddishkeit.*

Yigdal   n. Hebrew (yig-DOLL)   A hymn based on **Maimonides' *Thirteen Principles of Faith.*** The verses of "Yigdal" affirm beliefs in one God, the Divine origin of the **Torah,** and the afterlife, among other things. "Yigdal" is sung at many **Shabbat** and holiday **synagogue** services, often as a closing song in place of **"Adon Olam."**

Yisra'el   n. Hebrew (yis-rah-ALE)   **1.** The Hebrew word for **Israel. 2.** A Jew who traces his lineage to the ancient **Israelites** rather than to a **Kohen** or a **Levite.** The majority of Jews fall in this category. A Yisra'el is traditionally the third person called for an *aliyah,* after a Kohen and a Levite.

Yizkor   n. Hebrew (YISS-ker)   Literally, "may He remember." A special memorial prayer recited for a deceased member of the immediate family. *Yizkor* is recited in **synagogue** on **Yom Kippur** and on the seventh days of **Passover, Shavuot,** and **Sukkot.** Unlike the *Kaddish,* it does not require a **minyan** to be recited. Today, many *Yizkor* services include mention of the six million Jews who died during the **Holocaust.** On Yom Kippur, synagogues may publish and distribute a small *Yizkor* booklet containing prayers and a list of the names of the decreased. Because of superstition, children with parents who are still living often leave the sanctuary when *Yizkor* prayers are recited, so as not to tempt the evil eye by participating in a memorial service.

Yom ha-Atzmaut   n. Hebrew (YOME hah-ats-mah-OOT)   Israel Independence Day. Celebrated on the fifth of **Iyar,** this joyous holiday commemorates the birthday of the modern **State of Israel** on May 14, 1948. In the United States, the day is often marked by parades featuring local religious schools and Jewish organizations, or by community gatherings, like a picnic, Jewish fair, or festival. In Israel, Yom ha-Atzmaut is also celebrated with parades and fireworks. Israelis observe the day before Yom Ha-Atzmaut as **Yom ha-Zikaron,** Remembrance Day.

Yom ha-Shoah   n. Hebrew (YOME hah-SHOW-ah)   **Holocaust** Remembrance Day. The 27th day of **Nisan,** the official day set aside by the Israeli **Knesset** for remembering the six million Jews murdered by the Nazis. The date corresponds to the start of the **Warsaw Ghetto** uprising, when on April 19, 1943, the Jews fought back, attempting to prevent the German soldiers from deporting them to concentration camps.

Because this is a relatively new holiday, there are no ancient traditions or formal rituals associated with it. In the United States, most **synagogues** and Jewish organizations hold special memorial services and programs open to the community. Often, *Kaddish* is recited or a **yahrzeit candle** lit to remember the victims of the Holocaust. Other ways of marking Yom ha-Shoah include holding public ceremonies at Holocaust monuments in various cities; often concentration camp survivors are invited to speak. In **Israel** on Yom ha-Shoah, a siren is sounded at 11 A.M.; for two minutes everything literally comes to a halt. Drivers pull their cars, buses, and trucks to the side of the road and get out of their vehicles to stand quietly. There are also ceremonies and remembrances at **Yad Vashem** and throughout the country.

Yom ha-Zikaron   n. Hebrew (YOME hah-zee-kah-RONE)   **1.** Remembrance Day. Celebrated on the fourth of **Iyar,** this solemn Israeli holiday honors the memory of the soldiers and others who have been killed defending the **State of Israel.** It is reminiscent of the United States's Veterans Day observance. When sirens are sounded, Israelis throughout the country stop their activities to remember those who lost their lives. This solemn occasion is followed the next day by **Yom ha-Atzmaut,** a joyous celebration of the birth of the **State of Israel. 2.** Another name for **Rosh Hashanah.**

Yom Kippur   n. Hebrew (YOME key-POOR)   Literally, "Day of Atonement." The most solemn day on the **Jewish calendar,** observed on the 10th of

Tishrei. Yom Kippur, a day of fasting and praying in **synagogue,** marks the culmination of the 10-day period of self-examination, repentance, and prayer (the **Days of Awe**) that begins with **Rosh Hashanah.**

Tradition says that Yom Kippur is the day on which God will seal the fate of every Jew. The **Talmud** explains that the **Book of Life** is opened for the righteous on Rosh Hashanah so that God can inscribe their names. The fate of all others is on hold until Yom Kippur.

Yom Kippur is a purely religious holiday, a day of fasting, meditation, and introspection, when Jews take stock of their lives. The fast, which includes abstinence from food and drink, lasts from sunset to sunset. All Jews of **Bar** or **Bat Mitzvah** age and up are supposed to fast, unless they are unable do so because of health reasons. Most Jews spend the majority of the day in synagogue. Those who take a break from services in the early afternoon often spend the remainder of the day quietly reading or talking, refraining from normal daily activities, such as working, shopping, and socializing. Even those Jews who don't attend synagogue year-round often come on Yom Kippur, and most synagogues offer tickets for seating because there are so many worshipers. The specific prayers and songs for the holiday are contained in a special prayer book called a *machzor.*

The holiday begins on the eve of Yom Kippur with the haunting melody of the *Kol Nidrei* prayer, in which Jews ask to be released from vows made but not kept during the past year and the year to come. Prayers focus on repentance and inner reflection and ask God's forgiveness for misdeeds of the past year. It is also customary for Jews to ask the forgiveness of other people—friends, colleagues, family—whom they may have offended or harmed, knowingly or unknowingly, during the previous year. Important prayers include *Al Het, Ashamnu, Avinu Malkeinu,* and *Vidui.* The *Yizkor* service takes place on Yom Kippur as well. Synagogue services end with the *Neilah* sevice, at which time God determines who will be written in the Book of Life. The conclusion of Yom Kippur is marked by a final blast of the **shofar.**

On Yom Kippur eve, families gather for a festive meal before the fast begins. They light **yahrzeit candles** in memory of their deceased loved ones as well as candles for the holiday. At sundown the next night, they assemble again to "break the fast." This lighter meal traditionally includes a fish platter with **lox** and **bagels.** Together, Rosh Hashanah and Yom Kippur are called the **High Holy Days** or **High Holidays.**

Yom Kippur War   n. Hebrew/English   The 1973 war that began when Egypt and Syria attacked **Israel** by surprise on **Yom Kippur,** the most solemn day of the year for Jews. The war began when Egypt invaded the **Sinai** Peninsula. Simultaneously, Syria attacked Israel in the north. After initially losing men and land, Israel gained the upper hand by the fifth day of the war. After two weeks of fighting, Israel had pushed Syria out of the **Golan** and captured significant territory in the north. In the south, the Israeli army had crossed the

Suez Canal and cut off several divisions of the Egyptian army. The war ended after 18 days when the United Nations declared a ceasefire. Also called the 1973 War or the October War.

yom tov n. Hebrew (YOME tove)   Literally, "good day." The Hebrew phrase for "holiday." This phrase is part of the **candlelighting** blessing recited on every Jewish holiday. However, it is not the phrase usually used to wish someone a "happy holiday." You would say "Good *Yontif*" or "*Hag Sameach*" rather than "Happy *Yom Tov*."

Yom Yerushalayim n. Hebrew (YOME yeh-ROO-shah-LYE-eem)   Literally, "Jerusalem Day." Observed on the 28th of **Iyar,** this Israeli holiday celebrates the reunification of the city of **Jerusalem** during Israel's victory in the 1967 **Six-Day War**. Before the war, parts of the Old City of Jerusalem were controlled by Jordan, and Jews were forbidden to enter. Today, Jerusalem is part of **Israel** and all people are free to visit any part of the sacred city, which contains buildings and relics important to Christians, Muslims, and Jews. The holiday is traditionally celebrated with festive services and a party. Along with **Yom ha-Atzmaut** and **Yom ha-Zikaron,** it is one of three Israeli holidays in the month of Iyar.

yontif n. Yiddish (YON-tiff)   A slur of *yom tov,* the Hebrew words for "holiday." "Passover is next week. Whose house are you going to for *yontif*?" *Yontif* is also used in the phrase "Good *Yontif,*" which is a greeting exchanged on Jewish holidays.

yordim pl. n. Hebrew (yore-DEEM)   Israelis who leave the **State of Israel** to live elsewhere. The verb form of this word translates literally as "to descend" or "to go down." By contrast, the word for immigration to Israel is *aliyah,* which literally means "going up." This choice of verbs reveals some of the contempt some Israelis have for those who leave Israel to live elsewhere.

zaddik   See **tzadik.**

zaftig   adj. Yiddish (ZOFF-tig)   Literally, "juicy." A full-bodied, voluptuous, well-rounded woman.

zayde   n. Yiddish (ZAY-duh)   A name given to a grandfather; the Yiddish version of Pop-Pop, Grandpa, or Grandpop. Also as an affectionate term for any grandfatherly older man.

Zebulon   Tenth son of **Jacob** and sixth son of **Leah.** Zebulon is also the name of one of the 12 **tribes of Israel,** whose members were said to be descended from him. The tribe inhabited the northern part of **Canaan.**

zemirah   n. Hebrew (zeh-meer-AH); pl. **zemirot**   (zeh-meer-OTE)   Literally, "song." A religious poem sung to different melodies. The **Ashkenazim** use the term for the songs sung during and after the **Shabbat** meal, while the **Sephardim** use *zemirot* to refer to the psalms recited before the main part of the morning service.

zeroa   n. Hebrew (zeh-ROE-ah)   The roasted shank bone placed on the **seder plate** on **Pesach.** The shank bone is a reminder of the paschal lamb that was sacrificed at Passover in ancient days in the **Temple** in **Jerusalem.** It is also a reminder of the lamb's blood used to mark the doorways of the **Israelites'** homes during the last of the **Ten Plagues.** As a practical matter, most cooks find it easier to use a chicken bone or any meat bone rather than a lamb shank bone as the symbol of the ancient sacrifice.

zetz   n. Yiddish (ZETZ)   A punch, a strong blow; a setback. "Breaking her hip was a *zetz* she didn't need." Old-fashioned usage.

Zevi, Shabbetai   (1626–1676)   A false **Messiah** and charismatic leader who many thought would liberate Palestine from Turkish rule and restore it as a homeland for Jews. Shabbetai Zevi was a **kabbalist** and mystic who used schemes, public displays, and forged ancient documents to advance his claim that he was the Messiah. His friend, Nathan of Gaza, claimed to be the "risen" Elijah, one of the antecedents of the coming of the Messiah. When Zevi went to the Sultan of Turkey, his native country, and demanded control of Palestine, the sultan ordered him to convert to Islam or be tortured to death. When Shabbati converted, followers of Sabbatianism were crushed and his career as the Messiah effectively ended.

zichrono livrachah int. Hebrew (ZIKH-roe-noe liv-rah-KHAH) Literally, "of blessed memory." The Hebrew equivalent of "rest in peace." This phrase of respect is often added after mentioning the name of a deceased man. When the person's name appears in print, the phrase is abbreviated and written as an acronym with the Hebrew characters *zayin* and *lamed*. The feminine form of the phrase is *zichronah livrachah*.

Zion n. Hebrew (ZYE-on) **1.** One of the biblical names for the ancient city of **Jerusalem.** Zion included the **Temple Mount** and the walled city. **2.** Another name for ancient **Israel.**

Zionism n. English A worldwide political movement that worked toward the establishment of a Jewish homeland. Its followers are called **Zionists.** The father of modern Zionism was **Theodor Herzl** (1860–1904), who sought the return of the Jewish people from the **Diaspora** to their ancient homeland in **Palestine.** He fought for the creation of a Jewish state as a response to worldwide **anti-Semitism.**

At that time, much of Palestine was owned by absentee Turkish landlords. Through the **Jewish National Fund,** Zionists began to raise money to purchase land in Palestine. Herzl convened several World Zionist Congresses and enlisted political support for his ideas. In 1917, in the **Balfour Declaration,** the British government acknowledged the right of the Jewish people to a homeland in Palestine. At the end of World War I, Palestine became a British mandate. In 1948, Great Britain relinquished control and the modern **State of Israel** was established. Herzl did not live to see his dream come true. He is buried on Mount Herzl outside **Jerusalem.** Today, the Zionist movement lives on, helping Israel develop and prosper.

Zionist Organization of America (ZOA) Founded in 1897, the ZOA is the oldest and largest pro-Israel organization in the United States. The ZOA was instrumental in mobilizing the support of the U.S. government and citizens for the creation of the **State of Israel.** Today, the ZOA works to strengthen U.S.-Israeli relationships through educational, cultural, and public affairs programs; supports pro-Israel legislation on Capitol Hill; and combats anti-Israel bias in the media, textbooks, and travel information.

zissen Pesach   int. Yiddish/Hebrew (ZEE-sin PAY-sakh)   Literally, "sweet Passover." Used in the expression, "Have a *zissen Pesach*," as a wish for a sweet, happy holiday.

zitzit   See **tzitzit.**

zocher ha-brit   n. Hebrew (zoe-KHAIR hah-BRIT)   Literally, "remembering the **covenant.**" Another name for *shalom zachar,* a seldom practiced ceremony held the night before a *brit milah* to protect the child from evil spirits.

Zohar   n. Hebrew (ZOE-har)   Literally, "radiance." A mystical book that is the core text of **Kabbalah**—one of only three canonized Jewish sacred texts (the other two are the **Torah** and the **Talmud**). The Zohar, written in **Aramaic,** includes interpretations and commentaries that explore the secrets and symbols in the Torah. The Zohar proposes a distinct theory of Creation in which emanations from *Ein Sof* created a secret spark of awareness, from which emerged and radiated all light. Levels of creation, *sefirot,* and the worlds above and below are discussed throughout the Zohar. The Zohar holds that **The Song of Songs,** with its allusions of love and eroticism, contains more secrets of the universe than any other Jewish text. The Zohar was introduced into Spain around 1290 by the mystic Moses de Leon, who claimed it was the mystical 2nd-century writings of talmudic sage Shimon bar Yochai. Most scholars believe that de Leon authored the text himself.

Bibliography

Berenbaum, Michael. *The World Must Know: The History of the Holocaust as Told in the United States Memorial Museum.* Boston: Little, Brown, 1993.

Blech, Benjamin. *The Complete Idiot's Guide to Jewish History and Culture.* New York: AlphaBooks, 1999.

———. *The Complete Idiot's Guide to Learning Yiddish.* New York: AlphaBooks, 2000.

Bluestein, Gene. *Anglish/Yinglish: Yiddish in American Life and Literature.* Lincoln: University of Nebraska Press, 1998.

Cohn-Sherbok, Lavinia, and Dan Cohn-Sherbok. *A Popular Dictionary of Judaism.* Chicago: NTC/Contemporary, 1997.

Cooper, David A. *God Is a Verb: Kabbalah and the Practice of Mystical Judaism.* New York: Riverhead Books, 1997.

Diamant, Anita. *The New Jewish Wedding.* New York: Fireside Books, 1985.

Diamant, Anita, and Howard Cooper. *Living a Jewish Life: Jewish Traditions, Customs and Values for Today's Families.* New York: Harper Perennial, 1991.

Eisenberg, Ronald L. *The JPS Guide to Jewish Traditions.* Philadelphia: Jewish Publication Society, 2004.

Einstein, Stephen J., and Lydia Kukoff. *Every Person's Guide to Judaism.* New York: UAHC Press, 1989.

Fisher, Adam. *My Jewish Year: Celebrating Our Holidays.* West Orange, N.J.: Behrman House, 1993.

Frankel, Ellen. *The Five Books of Miriam: A Woman's Commentary on the Torah.* San Francisco: HarperSanFrancisco, 1998.

Freedman, E. B., Jan Greenberg, and Karen A. Katz. *What Does Being Jewish Mean? Read-Aloud Responses to Questions Jewish Children Ask about History, Culture, and Religion.* New York: Fireside Books, 1991.

Glinert, Lewis. *The Joys of Hebrew.* New York: Oxford University Press, 1992.

Heilman, Samuel. *Defenders of the Faith: Inside Ultra-Orthodox Jewry.* New York: Schocken Books, 1992.

Kasdan, Sara. *Love and Knishes.* New York: Fawcett Crest, 1967.

Kogos, Fred. *1001 Yiddish Proverbs.* Edison, N.J.: Castle Books, 1970.

Kolatch, Alfred J. *The Jewish Book of Why.* Middle Village, N.Y.: Jonathan David, 1981.

———. *The Jewish Mourner's Book of Why.* Middle Village, N.Y.: Jonathan David, 1993.

Littell, Franklin H. *A Pilgrim's Guide to the Holy Land.* Jerusalem: Carta and the Jerusalem Post,1981.

Nathan, Joan. *Jewish Cooking in America.* New York: Knopf, 1994.

Olitzky, Kerry, and Ronald H. Isaacs. *The How To Handbook for Jewish Living.* Hoboken, N.J.: KTAV Publishing, 1993.

———. *The Second How To Handbook for Jewish Living.* Hoboken, N.J.: KTAV Publishing, 1996.

———. *A Glossary of Jewish Life.* Northvale, N.Y.: Jason Aronson, 1992.

Orenstein, Debra. *Jewish Women on Life Passages and Personal Milestones.* Woodstock, Vt.: Jewish Lights Publishing, 1994.

Rosten, Leo. *The Joys of Yiddish.* New York: Pocket Books, 1970.

Routtenberg, Lilly S., and Ruth R. Seldin. *The Jewish Wedding Book: A Practical Guide to the Traditions and Social Customs of the Jewish Wedding.* New York: Schocken Books, 1968.

Siegel, Richard, Michael Strassfeld, and Sharon Strassfeld, ed. *The First Jewish Catalog.* Philadelphia: Jewish Publication Society of America, 1973.

Silverman, Morris, ed. *Sabbath and Festival Prayer Book*. New York: Rabbinical Assembly of America and United Synagogue of America, 1973.

Stern, Chaim, ed. *Gates of Prayer: The New Union Prayerbook*. New York: Central Conference of American Rabbis, 1975.

Strassfeld, Michael, and Sharon Strassfeld, ed. *The Second Jewish Catalog*. Philadelphia: Jewish Publication Society of America, 1976.

————. *The Third Jewish Catalog*. Philadelphia: Jewish Publication Society of America, 1980.

TANAKH: The Holy Scriptures. Philadelphia: Jewish Publication Society, 1985.

Tarcov, Edith and Oscar. *Prayer Dictionary*. New York: KTAV, 1965.

Telushkin, Joseph. *Jewish Literacy: The Most Important Things to Know about the Jewish Religion, Its People, and Its History*. New York: William Morrow, 1991.

Trepp, Leo. *The Complete Book of Jewish Observance*. New York: Behrman House, 1980.

Category Lists

Bar and Bat Mitzvah

aliyah
Banot Mitzvah
B'nai Mitzvah
candlelighting
devar Torah
haftarah
hora
l'chaim
maftir
maftir aliyah
mazel tov
parashah
simcha
tallit
Torah

beliefs and concepts, Jewish

ahavat Yisra'el
Akedah
avodah
bikur holim
brit
chesbon ha-nefesh
covenant
derekh eretz
emet
emunah
fence around the Torah
gemilut hasadim
hakhnasat orchim
halakhah
hiddur mitzvah

hillul ha-Shem
Kabbalah
kavod
kavod ha-met
kibbutz galuyot
kiddush ha-Shem
lashon ha-ra
ma'asim tovim
Mashiach
Mattan Torah
menschlikhkeit
Messianic Era
minhag
mitzvah
nichum aveilim
olam ha-ba
pikuach nefesh
rachmones
ruach
shalom bayit
teshuvah
tikun olam
Torah mi-Sinai
tzedakah
tzeniut
yetzer ha-ra
yetzer ha-tov
Yiddishkeit

Bible—see texts, Jewish

birth

bris
brit bat

brit chayim
brit milah
circumcision
Elijah's Chair
kvater
kvaterin
mohel
naming
pidyon ha-ben
sandek
shalom zachar
simchat bat
zocher ha-brit

calendar, Jewish

B.C.E.
C.E.
erev
Jubilee
months
   Adar
   Adar II
   Av
   Elul
   Heshvan
   Iyar
   Kislev
   Nisan
   Shevat
   Sivan
   Tammuz
   Tevet
   Tishrei
shemitah

conversion

anusim
apostate
beit din
Converso
ger
hatafat dam brit
Jew by Choice
Marrano
mikveh
tevilah

death, afterlife

alav ha-shalom
burial
    hevrah kadishah
    kavod ha-met
    shomer
    taharah
    takhrikhim
Gan Eden
Gehenna
Geihinnom
gilgul
mourning, customs
    keriah
    minyan
    nichum aveilim
    seudat hevrah
mourning, periods
    aninut
    aveilut
    sheloshim
    shivah
nefesh
neshamah
olam ha-ba
prayers
    El Male Rachamim
    Kaddish
    Yizkor
ruach
Sheol

shivah minyan
unveiling
yahrzeit
yahrzeit candle
zichrono livrachah

divorce

agunah
get

Eastern European Jewry

Aleichem, Sholom
Ashkenazim
badchen
dybbuk
goldene medina
golem
heder
kehillah
klezmer
landsman
landsmanshaft
pogrom
shadchen
shtetl

ethnic groups

Ashkenazim
Falasha
Galitzianer
gentile
Litvak
Marrano
Semite
Sephardim

expressions

azoy
Baruch ha-Shem
b'tayvon
canary
farstay

genug
gevalt
gezuntheit
Gotenyu
halevai
hok a tchynick
kine-ahora
kol ha-kavod
kol tov
labreoot
l'chaim
lehitraot
le-shanah ha-ba'ah be-Yerushalayim
loch in kop
mazel tov
nu
oy
shayna punim
shep nachas
siman tov
zissen Pesach

family, names for

abba
bubbe
ema
kinder
machetayneste
machetunim
machuten
mishpachah
saba
safta
zayde

food

boreka
blintz
borsht
bread
    bagel
    bialy

challah
brisket
cholent
chopped liver
chremslach
dafina
desserts
   babka
   hamantashen
   kamishbread
   kichel
   lekakh
   macaroon
   mandelbread
   mun
   rugelach
   shnecken
   sufganiyot
   tayglach
falafel
farfel
flanken
fried matzah
gefilte fish
gribenes
haroset
helzel
hummus
kasha
kibbe
kishka
knaidel
knish
kreplach
khreyn
kugel
latke
lekvar
levivot
lokshen
lox
mandlen
matzah

matzah ball
matzah brei
matzah meal
Nova
prokas
shav
shmaltz
shnapps
shawarma or shwarma
tahini
tzimmes

God, names for

Adonai
Adoshem
Ein Sof
Elohim
G–d
ha-Kadosh Baruch Hu
ha-Shem
sefirot
Shaddai
Shekhinah
Tetragrammaton

greetings

chazak u baruch
gemar hatimah tovim
(good) *yom tov*
gut Shabbos
hag sameach
le-shanah tovah tikatevu
Shabbat shalom
shalom
shalom aleikhem
shanah tovah
yasher koach

Hanukkah

Antiochus IV, King
dreidel
Festival of Lights
gelt

Hanukkah
hanukkiah
Hasmoneans
latke
levivot
Maccabee, Judah
Maccabees
"Maoz Tzur"
menorah
nes gadol hayah sham
shamash
sivivon
sufganiyot

Hasidism

Baal Shem Tov
haredim
Hasidism
Lubavitch movement
rebbe
Schneerson,
  Menachem Mendel
tzadik
ultra-Orthodox

holidays, Jewish
(see also specific
listings)

Asarah b'Tevet
Fast of Esther
  (Ta'anit Esther)
Fast of Gedaliah
Hanukkah
Lag ba-Omer
Pesach
Purim
Rosh Hashanah
Rosh Hodesh
Shavuot
Shivah Asar
  be-Tammuz
Shushan Purim
Simchat Torah

Sukkot
Tisha b'Av
Tu b'Av
Tu b'Shevat
Yom ha-Atzmaut
Yom ha-Shoah
Yom ha-Zikaron
Yom Kippur
Yom Yerushalayim

Holocaust
"Ani Ma'amin"
anti-Semitism
concentration camp
Final Solution
ghetto
Holocaust
Kristallnacht
Righteous Gentiles
Shoah
swastika
Warsaw Ghetto
Yad Vashem
Yom ha-Shoah

Israel
aliyah
dati
geography
    Dead Sea
    Eilat
    Galilee, Sea of
    Gaza
    Golan/Golan
       Heights
    Haifa
    Jerusalem
    Judea
    Lake Kinneret
    Masada
    Negev
    occupied
       territories

Qumran
Samaria
Sea of Gallilee
Sinai
Tel Aviv
West Bank
Yerushalayim
"Hatikvah"
hiloni
Ivrit
kibbutz
Knesset
Kotel
Law of Return
Maccabiah Games
Masorti
mission to Israel
moshav
people
    Begin, Menachem
    Ben Gurion, David
    Ben-Yehuda,
       Eliezer
    Dayan, Moshe
    Eban, Abba
    Falasha
    kibbutznik
    Meir, Golda
    Palestinian
    olim
    sabra
    shaliach
    Weizmann, Chaim
    yordim
shekel
State of Israel
ulpan
wars, military
    intifada
    Israel Defense
       Forces
    Six-Day War
    TZAHAL

War of
   Independence
Yom Kippur War
Western Wall
Yad Vashem

Israel, names for
Canaan
Eretz Yisra'el
Palestine
Promised Land
State of Israel
Zion

**Jewish people,
   ancient sects**
Essenes
Hasmoneans
Karaite
Pharisee
Sadducee
Samaritans

**Jewish people,
   communities**
am Yisra'el
Chosen People
Diaspora
galut
Israelites
kehillah
klal Yisra'el
landsman
Semite

Judaica
dreidel
Elijah's Cup
hanukkiah
ketubbah
Kiddush Cup
kippah
menorah

mezuzah
Miriam's Cup
mizrach
seder plate
sivivon
spice box
tzedakah box
yad

Kabbalah
asiyah
atzilut
beriah
deveikut
dybbuk
Ein Sof
Gan Eden
Geihinnom
gematria
gilgul
Kabbalah
Luria, Isaac ben
  Solomon
nefesh
neshamah
neshamah yeterah
olam ha-ba
ruach
sefirot
  binah
  chesed
  gevurah
  hod
  hokhmah
  keter
  malchut
  netzach
  tiferet
  yesod
Shekhinah
Sheol
texts
  Sefer Yetzirah

Tanya
Zohar
tikun olam
yetzirah

kosher, keeping
blech
fleishig
glatt kosher
heksher
K
kasher
kashrut
kosher
kosher for Passover
kosher style
mashgiach
milchig
pareve
shechitah
shochet
treif
U
va'ad ha-kashrut

languages
Aramaic
Hebrew
Ivrit
Judeo-Spanish
Judezmo
Ladino
mama loshen
Yiddish

marriage
bashert
ceremony
  Birkat ha-Kohanim
  breaking the glass
  erusin
  huppah
  kiddushin

nissuin
Sheva Brachot
yichud
chossen
hatan
kallah
reception
  badchen
  crowning ceremony
  hora
  krenzel
  l'chaim
  mazel tov
  mezinke
rituals, before the
  wedding
  aufruf
  mikveh
  tenaim
rituals, on the wedding
  day
  bedeken
  chossen's tish
  hakhnasat kallah
  kabbalat panim
  ketubbah
  kinyan
shadchen
shidduch

**movements of
  Judaism**
Conservative
Hasidism
Humanistic Judaism
Jewish Renewal
Lubavitch
Orthodox
  modern Orthodox
  ultra-Orthodox
Progressive Judaism
Reconstructionist
Reform

organizations, Jewish

Aish HaTorah
American Israel Public Affairs Committee
American Jewish Committee
American Jewish Congress
American Jewish Joint Distribution Committee
Anti-Defamation League of B'nai B'rith
B'nai B'rith Organization
Central Conference of American Rabbis
Hadassah
HIAS
Hillel
Jewish Defense League
Jewish Federation
Jewish National Fund
Jewish Reconstructionist Federation
Kollel
landsmanshaft
National Council of Jewish Women
ORT
Rabbinical Assembly
Rabbinical Council of America
Reconstructionist Rabbinical Association
Union for Reform Judaism
Union of Orthodox Jewish Congregations
United Jewish Communities
United Synagogue of Conservative Judaism
Zionist Organization of America

people in the Bible

Aaron
Adam
Ahasuerus, King
Antiochus IV, King
David
Elijah
Esau
Esther
Eve
Hagar
Haman
Ishmael
Israel
lost tribes of Israel
Maccabee, Judah
Maccabees
matriarch
    Leah
    Rachel
    Rebecca
    Sarah
Miriam
Mordecai
Moses
patriarchs
    Abraham
    Isaac
    Jacob
Saul
Solomon
tribes of Israel
    Asher
    Benjamin
    Dan
    Ephraim
    Gad
    Issachar
    Joseph
    Judah
    Levi
    Menasseh
    Naphtali
    Reuben
    Simeon
    Zebulon
ushpizin
Vashti

Pesach (Passover)

bedikat hametz
food
    chremslach
    farfel
    macaroons
    matzah
    matzah ball
    matzah brei
    matzah meal
    shemurah matzah
hametz
hametzdik
hol ha-moed
kitniyot
kosher for Passover
leaven
maot hittim
Omer
Passover
Pesach
pesachdik
Pilgrimage Festivals
seder
    afikoman
    arba kosot
    Elijah
    Elijah's Cup
    Eretz Mitzrayim
    Exodus

four cups of wine
four sons
Four Questions
haggadah
Hillel sandwich
"Kaddesh Urechatz"
khreyn
le-shanah ha-ba'ah
* be-Yerushalayim*
"Mah Nishtanah"
Miriam
Miriam's Cup
Moses
Ten Plagues
seder plate
  beitzah
  bitter herbs
  haroset
  hazeret
  karpas
  maror
  shank bone
  zeroa
songs
  "Dayenu"
  "Eliyahu Hanavi"
  "Had Gadya"
Shabbat ha-Gadol
Shir ha-Shirim
The Song of Songs
women's seder

prayer books

bentscher
haggadah
machzor
siddur

prayer services

Havdalah
Kabbalat Shabbat
Kol Nidrei
Ma'ariv

Mincha
Musaf
Neilah
Selichot
Shacharit
tashlikh
Yizkor

Prayers

Ahavat Olam
"Akdamut"
Aleinu
Al Het
Amidah
An-im Zemirot
Ashamnu
Ashrei
Avinu Malkeinu
Avodah
Barchu
Baruch ata Adonai
Birkat ha-Kohanim
Birkat ha-Mazon
Birkat ha-Shachar
bracha
El Adon
El Male Rachamim
Hallel
ha-Motzi
hanukkat ha-bayit
Hineni
hoshanah
Kaddish
Kedushah
Kiddush
Kol Nidrei
Mi Khamokha
misheberakh
Modeh Ani
Pesukei de-Zimra
Shehecheyanu
Shema
Shemoneh Esrei

Tachanun
Ve-ahavta
Ve-shamru
Vidui

praying

aliyah
bentsch
bentsch licht
daven
deveikut
havurah
kavanah
keva
maftir aliyah
minyan
nusach
shuckle
trope

Purim

Ahasuerus, King
Esther
Fast of Esther
Feast of Esther
Feast of Lots
grager
Haman
hamantashen
lekvar
Megillah
misloach manot
Mordecai
mun
Purim
Purim-spiel
shalach munis
Shushan Purim
Vashti

religious garb

arba kanfot
atarah
gartl
kippah
kitel
retzuot
sheitel
streimel
tallis
tallit
tallit katan
tefillin
tzitzit
yarmulke

ritual objects—see Judaica

Rosh Hashanah

challah
Days of Awe
High Holidays
High Holy Days
le-shanah tova tikatevu
lekakh
machzor
Rosh Hashanah
Selichot
shanah tovah
shofar
tashlikh
Yamim Noraim

scholars, Jewish

acharonim
Akiva ben Joseph
Baal Shem Tov
Hillel
gaon (geonim)
Kaplan, Mordecai
Luria, Isaac ben
  Solomon

Maimonides, Moses
Nachmanides, Moses
Rambam
Rashi
rishonim
Schechter, Solomon
Spinoza, Baruch

schools, names for

beit midrash
beit sefer
day school
Hebrew school
heder
Talmud Torah
yeshivah

Shabbat

"Adon Olam"
candlelighting
challah
eruv
Havdalah
  besamim
    "Eliyahu Hanavi"
  spice box
Kabbalat Shabbat
Kiddush
Kiddush Cup
"Lekhah Dodi"
melakhah
melaveh malkah
muktzeh
neshamah yeterah
Oneg Shabbat
Sabbath
seudah shelishit
Shabbat
Shabbat candles
Shabbaton
Shabbos
Shabbos bride
Shabbos goy

shomer Shabbat
Ve-shamru
zemirah

Shavuot

"Akdamut"
blintz
Confirmation
Feast of Weeks
Festival of First Fruits
Harvest Festival
Omer
Pilgrimage Festivals
Ruth, Book of
Shavuot
Tikun leil Shavuot

shofar

baal tekiah
shevarim
shofar
tekiah
tekiah gedolah
teruah

Simchat Torah

Consecration
hakafah
Simchat Torah
Torah

songs, chanting, melodies

"Adon Olam"
"Ani Ma'amin"
"Dayenu"
"Ein Keloheinu"
"Eliyahu Hanavi"
"Had Gadya"
"Hatikvah"
"Havah Nagilah"
hora
Kabbalat Shabbat

"Kaddesh Urechatz"
klezmer
"Lekhah Dodi"
"Mah Nishtanah"
"Maoz Tzur"
mezinke
Mi Khamokha
nigun
nusach
piyyut
tikun
trope
"Yigdal"
zemirah

Sukkot

aravah
arba minim
Consecration
Ecclesiastes
etrog
Feast of Tabernacles
Festival of Booths
Four Species
hadas
hol ha-moed
hoshanah
Hoshanah Rabbah
lulav
Pilgrimage Festivals
skakh
sukkah
Sukkos
Sukkot
ushpizin

symbols, Jewish

chai
hamsa
Jewish star
Magen David
Star of David

synagogue, names for

beit knesset
shul
temple

synagogue, objects in

ark
Aron Kodesh
bimah
eternal light
genizah
Holy Ark
mappah
mechitzah
menorah
ner tamid
parochet
sefer Torah
siddur
teba
Torah scroll
　　atzei chayim
　　hoshen
　　klaf
　　rimonim
　　sofer
　　tas
　　tik
　　Torah
　　wimple

synagogue, people in

baal korei
baal tekiah
cantor
gabbai
hazzan
hakham
Kohen
Levi

men's club
rabbi
rav
rebbe
rebbetzin
shaliach tzibbur
sisterhood
tzadik
Yisrael

Temple, ancient

Ark of the Covenant
Birkat ha-Kohanim
dukhan
First Temple
Holy of Holies
Sanhedrin
Second Temple
Tabernacle
Ten Commandments
Western Wall

Ten Commandments

ark
Ark of the Covenant
Decalogue
Holy of Holies
Moses
Mount Sinai
Temple

texts, Jewish

Apocrypha
Dead Sea Scrolls
Ethics of the Fathers
Five Books of Moses
haftarah
Humash
Masoretic text
megillot
　　Ecclesiastes
　　　(Kohelet)
　　Esther

Lamentations
  (Eikhah)
Ruth, Book of
The Song of Songs
  (Shir ha-Shirim)
Mishneh Torah
Pentateuch
pseudepigrapha
Sefer Yetzirah
Septuagint
Shulchan Arukh
TANAKH
  Kethuvim (Writings,
    Hagiographa)
  Nevi'im (Prophets)
  Torah
  Deuteronomy
    (Devarim)
  Exodus (Shemot)
  Genesis (Bereshit)
  Leviticus (Va-yikra)
  Numbers
    (Be-midbar)
Tanya
Talmud (SHAS)
  Gemara
  Mishnah (Oral Law)
Targum
Tehillim
Thirteen Principles of
  Faith
Zohar

texts,
 words related to

aggadah
amoraim
baraita
derash
devar Torah
genizah
haftarah
haggadah

machzor
maftir
midrash
parashah
PARDES
peshat
pilpul
responsa
siddur
sidrah
tannaim

Torah,
 dressing the

gelilah
hagbah
petichah

traditional
 observance

baal teshuvah
beit din
blech
eruv
frum
halakhah
mechitzah
melakhah
melavah malkah
mikveh
muktzeh
niddah
payot
sha'atnez
sheitel
shomer Shabbat
shtreimel
tohorat ha-mishpachah
tevilah
tichl
Torah mi-Sinai
tzeniut
upfsherin

Yiddish words
adjectives
  chaloshes
  fapitzed
  farbissen
  farblondjet
  farchadat
  farkakteh
  farklempt
  farmisht
  geshmak
  goyish
  haimish
  ongeblozzen
  ongepotchket
  shmaltzy
  shpilkes
  tsedrayte
  zaftig
  zees
nouns
  bissel
  bubbe meise
  bubkes
  chazerai
  chutzpah
  dreck
  emes
  forshpeis
  gornisht
  gotkes
  keppe
  klop
  luftmensch
  mechayeh
  nosherei
  pisk
  pulkes
  pupik
  shanda
  shmatte
  shmutz
  shnoz

shtarker
shtick
spiel
tachlis
tchotchke
tsuris
tummel
tushee
vilda chaya
yichus
zetz
terms for people
  alter-kacker
  balabusta
  berrieh
  boychik
  bubbe
  bubbeleh
  bulvan
  chazer
  draykop
  gonif
  klutz
  k'nocker
  kuni lemel
  macher
  maideleh
  mameleh
  maven
  mensch
  nebbish
  nosher
  nudnik

pisher
putz
shlemiel
shlimazel
shlub
shlump
shmeggegge
shmendrick
shmo
shmuck
shnook
shnorrer
tateleh
tchotchkeleh
yachne
yenta
zayde
verbs
  burtshen
  fumfeh
  kibitz
  klop
  krechz
  kvell
  kvetch
  nosh
  nudzheh
  oysgemutshe
  plotz
  potch
  shlep
  shluff
  shmeer

shmooze
shvitz
utz

Yom Kippur
Al Het
Ashamnu
Avinu Malkeinu
Book of Life
Day of Atonement
Days of Awe
High Holidays
High Holy Days
kaparos
Kol Nidrei
machzor
Neilah
shofar
teshuvah
Vidui
Yamim Noraim
Yom Kippur

Zionism
Balfour Declaration
Haganah
halutz
Herzl, Theodor
Jewish National Fund
Palestine
Zionism
Zionist Organization
  of America